VYGOTSKY'S PSYCHOLOGY

D1419817

VYGOTSKY'S PSYCHOLOGY

A Biography of Ideas

Alex Kozulin

Harvard University Press
Cambridge, Massachusetts

First Harvard University Press paperback edition, 1999

Library of Congress Cataloging-in-Publication Data

Kozulin, Alex.
    Vygotsky's Psychology : a biography of ideas / Alex Kozulin.
      p. cm.
    Includes bibliographical references and index.
    ISBN 0-674-94365-1 (cloth)
    ISBN 0-674-94366-x (pbk.)
    1. Psychology—Soviet Union—History. 1. Vygotskii, L.S.
(Lev Semenovich), 1896–1934. II. Title.
BF109.V95K69   1990
150′.92—dc20   90-39118

Contents

Acknowledgments

THE CONTENTS of this book were discussed at a number of seminars, colloquia, and conferences at Boston University, Harvard University, University of New Hampshire, and at the First European Congress of Psychology in Amsterdam. Some excerpts from my article, "The concept of regression and Vygotskian developmental theory", published in *Developmental Review*, are used with the permission of Academic Press. A number of colleagues from Moscow shared with me their ideas and their knowledge of Vygotsky. Leon Chernyak, Peter Knapp, Karen Levin, Ivana Markova, Edward Mueller and Gün Semin read and commented on specific chapters of the book, while Linda Engelmann provided priceless advice regarding stylistic matters. Research for this book was supported in part by a NSF Scholars Award and a Harvard Russian Research Center fellowship.

Prologue

THIS BOOK is about Lev Vygotsky (1896–1934), his psychological theory, and the posthumous life of his ideas. At the same time it is also about cultural psychology, that is, psychological theory in which the human being is the subject of cultural, rather than natural, processes. Finally, this is a book about the crises and the vicissitudes of the development of psychology in the twentieth century.

To pursue all these themes—biographical, theoretical and historico-psychological—in one work becomes possible only because of what one may call "the phenomenon of Vygotsky". There is a remarkable and intriguing *literary* quality in Vygotsky's life, which often resembled the lives of the literary heroes of Thomas Mann, Hermann Hesse or Boris Pasternak. It is as if the invisible hand of a master had collected the central themes of intellectual life of the twentieth century and placed them in one biography, liberally adding elements of historical drama.

The beginning of this biography already reads as a familiar literary text: a precocious Jewish boy comes of age in a provincial city on the western outskirts of the Russian Empire. Next we see the hero as a young intellectual plunging into the cultural life of Moscow on the eve of the Russian Revolution. Names and terms later to become staples of intellectual history, such as

I

Russian Formalism, Stanislavsky, Freud and Marx, permeate his everyday life. In the next "chapter" the hero is caught in the middle of the merciless Civil War and famine, wondering whether there is any future for his literary and intellectual pursuits. Finally, he appears as a fresh and unexpected voice in the just-emerging field of Soviet psychology. At this moment the theme that becomes prominent is one of creative tension between a thinker and the new society that he is ready to serve, but whose practices do not square well with a thinker's ideas. Suffering from tuberculosis from an early age, Vygotsky works with hectic energy, almost single-handedly laying the foundation for the theory of psychological development based on the notion of the cultural, rather than natural, essence of human life. In the process the entire European intellectual tradition of thought, language and human development comes under review. In the last chapter of this remarkable "life as a novel", the hero dies at the age of thirty-seven, leaving a pile of unpublished manuscripts that would be banned in his own country for twenty years, and whose importance would not be recognized in the West until much later.

The life of Vygotsky's writings has been no less remarkable than that of their author. These writings reveal a free humanistic spirit for whom psychology was neither a mere occupation, nor a field of intellectual curiosity, but rather a medium for pondering the eternal questions of human existence. In this sense Vygotsky was primarily a thinker, psychology being just the most appropriate stage on which the drama of ideas could be played. The existence of this higher plane in Vygotsky's thought explains the dazzling versatility of his intellectual sources and areas of activity: from Humboldtean linguistics to Köhler's study of apes, and from the analysis of Shakespeare's tragedies to the rehabilitation of handicapped children. This humanistic encyclopedism caused Vygotsky to be misunderstood by his contemporaries, but at the same time it is responsible for the long posthumous life of his ideas.

Vygotsky's writings offer little in terms of ready-made answers to scientific puzzles. His skill was primarily that of turning what appeared to be answers to such puzzles into new and more profound questions. He could accomplish this only because for him any particular problem was always seen as just one of the many facets in the development of human scientific and humanistic thought taken in its totality. There is, of course, nothing specifically Vygotskian in this ability, which is the mark of any real thinker. Fortunately for psychology, Vygotsky was among those very few thinkers who made this field the arena of their activity.

The genre of this book can be defined as that of a commentary. Once a prominent, if not the only acceptable form of scholarly treatise, the genre of commentary in the last century fell into disrepute and was pushed aside by experimental monographs and systematic surveys of literature. There is a good reason for such a fate. To start with, a good commentary always takes as its subject a corpus of writings of a superior quality, and there are not many of those nowadays. Second, the very idea of commentary is incompatible with the popular view of human knowledge as a temporalized progression from inaccurate facts to accurate ones, and from immature generalizations to sophisticated ones. Commentary always aims at a *dialogue* with a superior text, the outcome of which is a new *reading* of this text and thus, by implication, a conception of the new one.

The choice of the phenomenon of Vygotsky as the subject of this commentary is not arbitrary. I am convinced, and will attempt to prove, that Vygotsky's *œuvre* has all the qualities of a superior text that is rich, dense and open enough to serve as a critical reflection of twentieth-century psychology, and to stimulate a fruitful interpretation. Moreover, Vygotsky's writings provide a special perspective—that of a "stranger" who, without belonging to the mainstream of Western psychology, was its astute observer and commentator. In a sense Vygotsky was even a double outsider; often misunderstood in his own country, he was for a long time also neglected by the West. A number of factors contributed to this fate. One of them was the unclear status of Vygotsky's scholarship. Although he earned degrees in humanities and law, he never received systematic psychological training. His PhD in psychology was granted for the book *The Psychology of Art*, which was neither typical psychology nor a PhD thesis in the ordinary sense. His interests ranged from the analysis of *Hamlet* to the rehabilitation of the deaf-mute—a dazzling range indeed in an age of growing specialization. Rather than picking a problem from within psychology

3

and elaborating on it, Vygotsky focused on the eternal problems of language, thought and development and attempted to find their projections on the plane of psychological inquiry. In addition, Vygotsky's reliance on Western intellectual sources set him apart from those of his contemporaries whose progression towards a radically new "Marxist psychology" included the denunciation of all things Western. No less important is the fact that for political reasons Vygotsky's writings were banned from the mid-1930s through the mid-1950s and, as a consequence, a whole generation of Soviet psychologists has been raised with very scant knowledge of his ideas.

Not fully understood in his own country, Vygotsky was even more a stranger in European and American psychology. Although some of his articles were published in English during his lifetime, his work had practically no impact on Western psychology prior to the 1960s. Characteristically, his major theoretical opponent, Jean Piaget, did not feel obliged to familiarize himself with Vygotsky's views until thirty years after Vygotsky's death. Thus, as far as Western psychologists were concerned, Vygotsky was not a party to the fundamental debates between behaviorists and cognitivists, defenders of psychoanalysis and their opponents, Piagetians and learning theorists, etc. And yet he did participate—invisible and unheard—in those important debates. To read his works today amounts to the sudden discovery of previously unknown testimony written by a witness to important intellectual events. Vygotsky serves as a mirror of twentieth-century psychology, providing an image only a stranger can give.

What then is at the center of Vygotsky's own understanding of psychology? His major objective was to identify specifically human aspects of behavior and cognition. The key words in his psychology are *consciousness* and *culture*. At first glance, there is nothing original in such an orientation, which looks more like an intellectual regression to the traditional subjects of early nineteenth-century psychology. The originality lies in the fact that Vygotsky returned to these themes in the post-classical period using nontraditional material. It is one thing to talk of consciousness within the framework of classical rationalism and empiricism, but it is entirely different to do so as a contemporary of Husserl and Freud. Similarly, it is one thing to accept culture

4

as the basis of discursive thought acquired through traditional European education (*Bildung*), and an entirely different thing to uncover the culturally specific mechanisms of cognition in a world that was no longer Europocentric and in which logic did not necessarily reign supreme.

Vygotsky revealed a remarkable intuition for the nascent ideas of twentieth-century psychology, the ideas recognized by his contemporaries only decades later. He sensed, for example, a profound difference between consciousness and intellect, and between ontological and epistemological positions. One may object by saying that these differences had been already elaborated by Husserl and Heidegger, but one should also admit that there were almost no psychologists at that time who considered these philosophical subtleties. For Vygotsky's contemporaries, language appeared as either a behavioral habit or an external envelope of otherwise nonverbal thought. Vygotsky, in contrast, revived the problems of Humboldtean linguistics with its emphasis on the process of thought becoming itself in the medium of language.

It took half a century for the majority of psychologists, particularly in the United States, to move away from the simplistic ideas of behaviorism, to accept the notion of information processing, and then to begin questioning the limits of the applicability of the information-processing model to human language and thinking. Vygotsky's thought seemed to sketch these transitions in just a couple of years, moving rapidly from the notion of artificial stimuli controlling individual behavior to the notion of semiotic mediation of human activity and further to the idea of *meanings* as constituent elements of human consciousness. This is not to imply that Vygotsky's foresight was merely a function of his extraordinary intelligence. His was a unique cultural position on the border between East and West, between tradition and modernity, and between science and the humanities. All the major ingredients of the future of psychology were already present in the 1920s, but it took the "estranged" cultural vision of Vygotsky to recognize what would become a figure and what background.

It is not surprising, therefore, that when Vygotsky's ideas began to percolate through to the West in the 1960s, only the most "compatible" were immediately accepted. Among these were notions of the unity of cognition and behavior, and the concept of the social origin of individual behavior. What for Vygotsky early on became a starting point for psychological inquiry, for his Western followers, like Jerome Bruner, was the result reached only after years of struggle with and within neobehaviorism. Next came the recognition of the importance of different modes of speech in child development. This time an appreciation of Vygotsky came on the wave of popularity for his former opponent, Jean Piaget. Later came a surge of interest in cross-cultural and literacy studies and once again Vygotsky's works proved to be relevant. Taking into account this step-by-step rediscovery of Vygotsky's works, it becomes clear that they should not be treated as an artifact of the past, but rather as still incompletely understood blueprints for the future of psychology. After all, a theory of cultural psychology was only sketched out by Vygotsky, and it is our task to develop it into a viable intellectual perspective.

In Chapter One I make a foray into the cultural milieu of the 1910s and the 1920s to explore the ideological background of the phenomenon of Vygotsky. This was a period of intense searches by the Russian intelligentsia for new modes of thinking and new forms of art. Many of the leading ideas of twentieth-century culture, such as structuralism in linguistics and poetics, abstractionism in painting, existentialism and hermeneutic ideas in philosophy, originated in that period. In particular, the influence of the school of literary Formalists is easily discernible in Vygotsky's first major project, *The Psychology of Art* (1925). In this work Vygotsky attempted to grasp the workings of the mind in its most revealing endeavor—the creation of a literary text. This concern with the highest forms of human mental activity became a trademark of Vygotsky's theory, which he called an "acme psychology", in counterdistinction to the "depth psychology" of psychoanalysis.

The subject of Chapter Two is Vygotsky's essay on *Hamlet*. Written when he was a twenty-year-old student, this essay will probably remain the best example of Vygotsky's humanistic prose. Neither a scholarly treatise nor literary journalism, the essay on *Hamlet* presents an existential self-analysis of his encounter with a text of superior quality and mythological dimensions. The most fundamental issues, such as the essential

6

tragedy of human existence, are pondered in this essay. The limits of the art form in rendering the enigma of life and death are discussed. *Hamlet* is interpreted as a mythological text and the melancholy prince as a cultural-historical hero called to establish the link between Being and Nothingness.

Chapter Three covers the beginning of Vygotsky's career as an academic psychologist. In a field dominated by reflexologists and "Marxist psychologists" he emerged as a defender of the category of consciousness and as a perceptive analyst of the crisis in contemporary psychology. In his analysis he foresaw the dramatic division of psychology into two opposing disciplines, one based on the methodology of the natural sciences and aimed at a materialistic *explanation* of all mental and behavioral acts, the other oriented toward the humanities and seeking to *understand* and comment on what is uniquely human and thus transnatural in psychological phenomena. Vygotsky also made far-reaching observations regarding the different forms of human practice that may require alternative definitions of the psychological subject and consequently different types of psychological inquiry.

Chapter Four provides a systematic overview of the cultural-historical theory developed by Vygotsky as an answer to the crisis in psychology. Psychological development can be seen as the transition from natural forms of behavior to higher mental functions that have a mediated structure. This structure is shaped by the use of signs, symbols and languages which serve as mediators of different degrees of complexity. The theory presupposes the existence of three planes of development: anthropogenesis, historical development and individual acquisition of higher mental functions. In each case the change in psychological processes is related to the change in sociocultural type of mediation. The cultural-historical approach also changes the nomenclature of psychological functions, with reading, writing and mathematical reasoning granted the status of functions on their own rather than being treated as derivatives of the presumably more fundamental faculties of intelligence, memory and imagination.

Chapter Five addresses Vygotsky's study of language in its capacity as a mediating mechanism for other psychological processes and as a mental function on its own. Vygotsky distinguished between preintellectual, purely communicative roots of speech, and the preverbal forms of intelligence. Human verbal thought comes into existence when these two lines merge. Thought and word, however, never coincide completely. For example, for Vygotsky—and here he disagreed with Piaget—egocentric speech is not a mere accompaniment to immature thought, but an important verbal form instrumental in cognitive development. Exploring various modes and genres of speech and different types of generalizations (from the syncretic agglomeration of images to "scientific" concepts), Vygotsky sought to unravel the mystery of thought realizing itself in word. He came to the conclusion that the central category of mental life is that of *sense* that becomes objectivized in words. The structure of human consciousness thus has a "semantic" layout. Vygotsky's cultural psychology, which started as an attempt to build an explanatory theory on a social-scientific basis, thus arrived at conclusions more resembling psychological hermeneutics.

Chapter Six examines the application of Vygotsky's theory to the problems of handicapped development and psychopathology. Not only a theorist but also a practitioner, he devoted considerable energy to the creation of programs for the rehabilitation of physically and mentally handicapped children. In the last years of his life he served as the scientific director of the Institute of Defectology, which remains the leading center for the study of the handicapped in the Soviet Union. Vygotsky's ideas continue to inform contemporary studies and occasionally stir controversy, as in the evaluation of the educational potential of the sign language of the deaf.

Psychopathology for Vygotsky was a key to understanding normal development, and vice versa. Using his insight in this field, it becomes possible for us to develop an alternative, non-psychoanalytic concept of psychological regression. In the process Vygotsky's work becomes theoretically connected to the ideas of Kurt Goldstein and Heinz Werner. Vygotsky's pioneering work on schizophrenic speech reminds us that the dissolution of mental functions occurs according to psychological laws even if the cause of dissolution in itself is not psychological.

Finally, in Chapter Seven, the posthumous development of Vygotsky's ideas is examined. Although his writings were banned from the mid-1930s through the mid-1950s, some of his ideas were fruitfully developed by his students: Alexei Leontiev in the theory of psychological activity and Alexander Luria in a series of neuropsychological studies. Now, when most of his works have been reprinted in the Soviet Union, they continue to generate intellectual debates. One of these debates focuses on the principles of the school curriculum and methods of instruction. The program of theoretical, as opposed to empirical, learning is based on Vygotskian premises but it also provides a constructive critique of his theory. The theme of the crisis of psychology also acquired a new meaning for a new generation of Soviet psychologists who used Vygotsky's work to chart paths toward the new humanistic psychology. Finally, Vygotskian ideas of the dialogical nature of human thought, together with those of his contemporary Mikhail Bakhtin, provide the foundation for a philosophical inquiry into the interaction of culturally diverse forms of thinking. A new type of logic is emerging which takes as a prototype the dialogic consciousness of the humanities, instead of the monologic thought of the natural sciences.

CHAPTER ONE

Toward the Psychology of Art

IT HAS BECOME common practice to dip into newspaper clippings of a period in order to secure a momentary "snapshot" of the world on the birthday of a great scientist. The only problem with this otherwise useful approach is that the future great scientists rarely confront the same world as existed on the date of their birth.

Born in 1896 to a middle-class Jewish family, Lev Vygotsky, as any other Jewish boy, had to pass through the ritual of bar mitzvah at the age of thirteen, a rite of passage to adulthood. This occasion allows us to select a meaningful date for the "portrait of the world" Vygotsky was about to confront as an adult. It was November 5, 1909.

Europe on that date was at peace. Newspapers anticipated neither wars nor revolutionary upheavals. The lack of internationally important events was so complete that the Moscow *Russkie Vedomosti*, the London *Times* and the *New York Times* were preoccupied exclusively with domestic problems. On the back pages one could find inch-long columns on the insurgency in Nicaragua, tensions between Greece and Turkey, and the presence of Russian troops in Iran. It was clear, however, that these were not the major preoccupations of either the East or the West.

Russia seemed to have one foot in the twentieth century, sharing its intellectual and some of its economic problems with Europe, but the other foot was still in earlier ages. The Russian Empire was still governed autocratically by Czar Nicholas II; it still lived by an antiquated calendar, so when it showed November 5, in Europe it was November 18; and the Russian alphabèt still retained the letters "i" and "ъ" which would disappear after the Revolution. At the same time the Russian people eagerly experimented with the recently established parliamentary body called the *Duma*. *Russkie Vedomosti* of November 5, 1909, devoted a good portion of its front page to an editorial about the political maneuverings of various *Duma* factions. The focus of debates in the *Duma* was on the proposed land reform, the future of district courts, and the illegal political activity of trade unions. As a curious reminder of the ambivalence of Russian "democracy" the same newspaper, several days earlier, published a report on illegal literature being sent to *Duma*'s library. The problem discussed was what to do with such literature. Suggested alternatives included (*a*) burn it, (*b*) lock it in a special collection, and (*c*) make it available for all members of the *Duma*. So, while censorship was very much in force, illegal books were published by commercial publishers and even, as a gesture of defiance, sent to the *Duma*.

The publication *Russian Calendar* for 1909 provides some useful statistics of the world in which Vygotsky was living. Vygotsky's home town, Gomel, some four hundred miles southwest of Moscow, together with surrounding settlements and villages, had a population of 40,000. A typical town belonging to the so-called "pale" of Jewish settlements where Jews were allowed to live and open businesses without restriction, Gomel's population was predominantly Jewish. The town had two secondary schools: one government-sponsored gymnasium and one private Jewish gymnasium. *Russian Calendar* provides candid information regarding the quotas for Jewish enrollment in institutions of higher learning. These quotas were: 3 per cent for St Petersburg, 5 per cent for all other universities outside the pale, and 10 per cent within the pale. There were just ten universities in the entire Russian Empire.

Newspapers paid little attention to international events, but monthly periodicals such as the liberal *Russian Thought* (*Rus-*

skaya Mysl'), which was probably read in Vygotsky's circle, revealed a keen interest in Western culture. The October 1909 issue featured lengthy articles on American pragmatist philosophy, the religious ideas of Ralph Waldo Emerson, cultural policies in Germany, and the French Socialist movement. Those interested in psychology could read *Problems of Philosophy and Psychology*, which reported on the Sixth International Congress of Psychology that convened in Geneva in September 1909. Among the speakers were those who ten years later would feature prominently in Vygotsky's reflections on the development of psychological scholarship. Oswald Kulpe represented German cognitive psychology; Edouard Claparede, the Swiss school of developmental psychology that would eventually become famous because of Piaget; Pierre Janet's report presented the views of the French psychopathological school, a forerunner-cum-opponent of psychoanalysis; American psychology was prominently represented by Robert Yerkes, a pioneer of animal learning theory; and Jacques Loeb discussed the then-popular theory of tropisms—simple, reflex-like movements thought to be a major mechanism of behavior. As a curious mark of the time, the report mentions the presence at the congress of a group of Esperanto specialists seeking to make this artificial language a medium of real international communication.

Vygotsky was the second of eight children. His father held a number of managerial positions at freight and insurance companies, and at one time he was head of a department in one of Gomel's banks.[1] The family appears to have been well respected in the town, being involved in some public endeavors such as the establishment of a library. Vygotsky's mother is remembered as a warm and intelligent person. She knew German well and her love of German poetry appears to have been shared by her children.

One political event put the town of Gomel temporarily into the spotlight and most certainly had an impact on Vygotsky as a child. In the fall of 1903 a trivial incident at the farmers' market in Gomel triggered a full-scale pogrom of the Jewish businesses and dwellings in the town. Unlike Jews in other places who failed to defend themselves, Gomel's Jews resisted and on some occasions defeated their attackers. As a result a large number of Jews were brought to trial for allegedly assaulting the Russians. The trial soon became the setting for a major confrontation between democratic forces demanding full rights for minorities and progovernment groups who were eager to place the blame on the Jews. Vygotsky's father, Simha (Semion in Russian) was called as a witness to testify about the general atmosphere in the town on the eve of the pogrom. Vygodsky Sr offered his opinion that after the famous Kishenev pogrom that had occurred earlier in 1903 it had become clear that the authorities would not defend the Jews and that pogroms would be perpetuated with impunity. He also elaborated on the psychological reasons for the heightened tension between Russians and Jews, suggesting that the growing awareness on the part of Jews of their human rights seemed to be offending some Russians: "As long as Jews did not talk about this, all was good, but when they started to consider themselves as people like others and talk about their human dignity, the attitude toward them has changed".[2]

These events could not but leave an impression on the eight-year-old Lev Vygotsky. And ten years later the anti-Semitic stand of the Russian government was to feature prominently once again in his life. In 1913 when he graduated from the gymnasium with honors and a gold medal, Vygotsky was naturally optimistic about his chances for admission to Moscow University. Of course he was aware of the quota for Jewish students, but his excellent grades should have been a guarantee for admission. The new executive order of the minister of education jeopardized these hopes, however, for while preserving the quota, it required Jewish applicants to be enrolled by casting lots. This deliberately discriminatory procedure made admission for Jews a matter of blind luck. Fortunately for Vygotsky he had good luck and was enrolled by the draw. One can imagine, however, the feeling of utter helplessness in front of a governmental machine that ignored all intellectual attainment and was only too eager to discriminate on the basis of race. One may well wonder whether Vygotsky, like many other young Jewish intellectuals, embraced the new Soviet regime primarily because it promised to end all forms of ethnic discrimination.

Vygotsky is remembered as an intellectually precocious child. His education was unconventional: he studied with private tutors for many years and entered the Jewish gymnasium only at high-school level. Vygotsky's tutor was Solomon Ashpiz, a mathematician by training, but who was able to teach all subjects. Ashpiz had spent some time in exile in Siberia for participating in revolutionary activity—an experience quite typical for Russian students of those days. Vygotsky's interests lay primarily in the domain of the humanities and social sciences. He is remembered as a connoisseur of Russian poetry, from the classics of Alexander Pushkin and Feodor Tyutchev to the modernist Alexander Blok and later Boris Pasternak. He was also particularly fond of the prose of Ivan Bunin, whose novella "The Gentle Breath" Vygotsky later used as an example of the master-crafted conflict between content and form. Among the Russian prose classics, Feodor Dostoevsky was a subject of his intensive reading and thought. While still at the gymnasium Vygotsky began working on his essay on *Hamlet* which was completed in 1916 but was not published until 1968.

The first indication of Vygotsky's interest in the social sciences is related to his activity at a discussion club organized by gymnasium students interested in Jewish history and culture. Although there is no written record of these meetings, one can easily surmise that they focused on such questions as "What does it mean to be Jewish?", "What distinguishes Jews from all other nations?" and "What is the historical destiny of Jews?" One should not forget that in the 1910s the western provinces of the Russian Empire were a hotbed of Zionist activism. Reaching beyond the mere historiography, Vygotsky tried to combine the issue of Jewish culture with a Hegelian understanding of the laws of history. According to one of Vygotsky's school friends, Hegel was probably one of the most important intellectual affections of the young Vygotsky, who was concerned with fundamental questions such as "What is history?" and "What is the role of the individual in history?" The Hegelian philosophical system offered intellectually attractive answers to these questions by unfolding a great dynamic picture of *Weltgeschichte*—universal history.[3]

Since the issue of development and its Hegelian underpinnings feature prominently in Vygotsky's later work, it is relevant here to recall some of the major points of the Hegelian system. The principle on which Hegel's philosophy of history rests is that Reason first manifests itself in nature but comes to its ultimate realization in man. The essence of history is the process of the self-expression of Mind. This process itself proceeds through stages which are identified in Hegel's philosophy of history and history of philosophy, and which correspond to the modern notion of different types of culture. Man in Hegel's theory is first and foremost a temporal, historical phenomenon. The universal law of history is a progression toward self-consciousness of freedom. The aspect of self-consciousness is extremely important here because historical laws are not deterministic, but originate and become actual only in man's conscious practice: "The transition that is involved in the actualization of Spirit is mediated by consciousness and will".[4] So if, for example, man fails to recognize and realize the movement toward a higher form of freedom, the law of progress ceases to operate.

Historical development is not a straight ascending line, but a complex trajectory replete with detours and reversals. The dialectic of historical change predicts that an advance to a higher plane first requires that the opposite forces inherent in the former state get the upper hand.

Another important aspect of the Hegelian system is the distinction between the natural world and the world of culture created by man. According to Hegel, in the course of universal history man creates a number of human worlds that are essentially different from the natural world. These social worlds ultimately become reflected in religious and philosophical ideologies. Being "the other" of man, nature is nevertheless a necessary precondition of conscious life. A purely cognitive, contemplative approach would not lead man to self-consciousness; what is needed in addition is motivation or desire. This desire is related to animal life (*Leben*) and thus to nature. The natural, animal component is necessary, but it is not sufficient. Biological desire is satisfied—with the help of biological action—with natural, biological content. The animal organism assimilates other substances, but it does not transcend itself as given, as a body. Animal existence coincides with its "being"; human existence is realized in "becoming". The animal has a feeling of itself, but it does not have a self-consciousness. Hegel related the attainment of self-consciousness to the functioning of desire in human society where the assimilation of things is mediated by their social meaning. It is no longer a simple, natural desire to consume, but an ideal desire to possess or dominate. Portraying the complex dialectic of the relationship between masters and workers, Hegel concluded that it is in work that man realizes his nonbiological activity. By working, man achieves satisfaction. Work therefore is a social, rather than a natural activity; it creates a non-natural, technical and at the same time humanized world. This world is adapted to human rather than biological desire.

Hegel further linked work with rationality. To be able to transform the naturally given in the act of work means to possess a technique. And the idea that engenders a technique is a scientific idea—a concept. To possess a system of scientific concepts is to be endowed with the faculty of abstract reasoning. Through work, man begins to perceive the world as a world of independent objects and acting subjects. And in this act of differentiation man achieves his self-consciousness, and this is revealed in language.

Finally, in any dynamic process Hegel distinguished two aspects: objectivation and disobjectivation.[5] Any process or activity is crystallized in certain structures or objects. These can be comprehended as something immediately and objectively present. But they can also be conceived of as *moments* of self-realization of the process. A mathematical formula, for example, can be handled as a concrete device for solving a limited number of problems, but the same formula is also a transit state, a moment in the development of mathematical knowledge as such.

It seems that all of Hegel's ideas outlined above left a lasting imprint on Vygotsky's approach to formulating scientific problems and attempting their resolution. First, let us consider the aspects of objectivation and disobjectivation. For Vygotsky the task of a scholar in general and a psychologist in particular was not only to apply a ready-made scientific formula to a particular situation, but first and foremost to formulating the subject matter and method of inquiry.[6] In a number of his works Vygotsky begins with some fact, like samples of child speech collected by Jean Piaget, and then proceeds toward the disobjectivation of this fact. This disobjectivation on the one hand reveals a "philosophy of fact" that stands behind any scientific data, and on the other it "returns" the fact—the egocentric speech of a child—back into its original, dynamic condition where it can be reinterpreted anew. The whole of *The Historical Meaning of the Crisis in Psychology*, which Vygotsky completed in 1927 (published in 1982), is devoted to the disobjectivation of psychological theory and to reaching for the unfinished forms of such psychological notions as consciousness, reflex and Gestalt.[7] This turning of psychology from a field of activity into a subject of inquiry placed Vygotsky in a category of his own, so that contemporary scholars do not tire of arguing whether Vygotsky's works should be considered a *philosophy* of psychology, or a psychology proper. I believe that for Vygotsky himself that was not a question: psychology as he saw it could not exist without the moment of disobjectivation and without self-reflection.

Further, Hegel's emphasis on the historical nature of the human being, reinforced by Marxist theory, significantly instructed Vygotsky's view on psychology as a science of an *historical*, rather than an abstractive universal man. Hegel's and Marx's discussions of the role of work in human history also found a receptive reader in Vygotsky. His notion of "psychological tools" has its roots in the Hegelian idea that work, together with the transformation of the world of things, brings about the transformation of human consciousness.[8]

Finally the Hegelian dialectic of Becoming informed Vygotsky's preference for the study of development and the formation of mental processes over the study of their performance. For him, to study any psychological function required knowledge of how it came about. Data collected during the "warm-up" stage of an experiment, for example, are commonly disregarded as observations of something that is not yet performance. Vygotsky believed that such data provide particularly important information because they reveal the *process* of habit, skill or concept formation. In performance, psychological functions are objectivized and their dynamic determinants concealed; conversely, during the process of formation these determinants are revealed. Similarly, Vygotsky's approach to education was influenced by the idea of the yet-unrealized potential of the child. The "performance" of a child, which becomes possible only in co-operation with an adult, rather than a well entrenched performance on a standardized individual test, was taken by Vygotsky to be the true measure of his or her development.

The other major intellectual influence on the young Vygotsky was his acquaintance with the book *Thought and Language* (*Mysl i Yazyk*) by the nineteenth-century Ukrainian linguist, Alexander Potebnya.[9] In the age of the growing influence of the positivist world-view, Potebnya brought the philological and humanistic ideas of the great German thinker Wilhelm von Humboldt to Russia.[10] It was in Potebnya's book that Vygotsky first confronted the mystery of the relationship between language and thought. Their relationship is traditionally conceived of in three alternatives: (*a*) thought coincides with language, (*b*) language serves as an external envelope of thought, and (*c*) thought achieves its becoming in language. Humboldt, and Potebnya after him, developed this latter alternative, and convincingly showed that nothing warrants the original identification of thought with language. Nonverbal thought is as real as a preintellectual speech. For example, there is a nonverbal, puzzle-solving type of intellect, and preintellectual, emotive speech. At the same time Humboldt and Potebnya refused to accept the idea of language's externality with respect to thought. Conceptual content is in no way independent of its linguistic form. To clarify this point Humboldt introduced a potent concept of the "inner form" of language. The existence of the inner form of a word is clearly felt by any translator struggling to render a certain concept in another language. To borrow Potebnya's example, the formal intellectual content of such words as the English *wages*, the Italian *pensio* and the Russian *zhalovanie* is similar, indicating monetary compensation for work done. But the inner form of these words leads our thought in different directions. Wages is derived from *gage*, which means pledge; *pensio* is related to the act of weighing certain amounts of something; and *zhalovanie* derives from the act of love.

The importance of the inner form of language for thought resulted in the different language-based world outlooks (*sprachliche Weltansicht*) of different peoples. Comparative linguistics is therefore not just a science of different linguistic structures, but also a science of how people refract reality through the prism of their language. According to Humboldt, language is a world of its own (*wahre Welt*) which mediates the world of objective phenomena and the inner world of man. This idea served as a guideline for Vygotsky's own inquiry into the dynamics of human comprehension of the world depending on changing systems of symbolic mediators.

Potebnya also pointed to the inherent ambivalence of language, which is objective as a common property of a given linguistic group and yet is subjective in the speech of each individual. This duality is apparent even in the inner speech of an individual who strives to clarify his innermost thoughts and feelings using a medium that is shared by others. Humboldt claimed that man understands himself only after he has tested his words on others. The same ambivalence reveals itself in the duality of expression versus comprehension. What is said never coincides with what is comprehended. There is an inescapable gap between the speaker and the listener. Humboldt believed that people understand each other not because they exchange the signs of objects and not because they evoke in the other's mind an exact copy of one's concept; people understand each other because they touch in the other the same link in a chain of images and primordial inner concepts, because they press the same key on the keyboard of their soul, and as a result a corresponding but not identical meaning "resonates" in the consciousness of the other.[11]

Finally, it is important to note that Humboldt defined language as *activity* (*Tätigkeit*), rather than as a finished structure. Language is not a finished thing, but a creative process; it is not "ergon" but "energeia".[12] Vygotsky's studies of child language also followed this line of reasoning in their attempts to show how linguistic and cognitive structures are engendered by verbal activity, and how a child engages in the creative work of building his or her own language.

Besides the great authors, Vygotsky had a more personal contact with the world of language and literature. His cousin David, several years older than himself, had been a promising young philologist and critic, well connected in the literary and academic circles of Moscow and St Petersburg. David was probably the first to direct Vygotsky's attention to the world of the new literary theory of the so-called Formalists. The key figures in this world were Victor Shklovsky, Boris Eichenbaum, Roman Jakobson, and others whose names were later to appear in Vygotsky's book *The Psychology of Art*. David also watched closely the development of new poetry in Hebrew and reviewed its progress. One may assume that David introduced Vygotsky to the editors of the journal of the Jewish intelligentsia, *The New*

Way (*Novy Put'*). Vygotsky's first essays, written in a romantic style and dedicated to the fundamental problems of Jewish culture, were published in this journal.[13]

Taking into account the range of Vygotsky's interests it seemed logical for him to enroll at the liberal arts program at one of the metropolitan universities. But if not Vygotsky himself, then his parents saw the choice of school in a more practical light. The only realistic job for a liberal arts graduate was that of a gymnasium teacher. But the majority of gymnasia in Russia were government-sponsored and did not allow Jews to hold teaching posts. So it seemed much more practical to study either law or medicine; a graduate of either discipline became a professional who could practice outside the pale of the Jewish settlements.

In Moscow Vygotsky registered first as a medical student, but quickly changed his mind, and ended up in a law school. He also enrolled at Shanyavsky Public University where he majored in philosophy and history. Shanyavsky emerged as an alternative to the government-controlled Moscow University which had recently carried out politically motivated student expulsions resulting in the mass resignation of the faculty in protest. Shanyavsky was unable to award degrees, but it had a strong and progressive faculty and it attracted gifted and independently minded students.

ARCHAISTS AND INNOVATORS

To understand Vygotsky's intellectual development one should be aware of the unique phenomenon of the Russian intelligentsia. As noted by many authors, the notion of an intelligentsia does not coincide with either the educated classes in general, nor with intellectuals in the narrow sense. The Russian intelligentsia is best characterized as a group united by common cultural values, a heightened sense of social justice, and a desire to work for the betterment of society as a whole. A particular feature of the Russian intelligentsia was the importance they attached to works of literature, which they saw not only as the ultimate embodiment of culture, but as the most concentrated form of life itself.

Literary characters were routinely judged by the Russian intelligentsia as real social and psychological types, while political and historical debates were commonly conducted in the form of literature and about literature. Within this framework of values, the innovation in the field of letters amounted to the discovery of a new historical path. An author was perceived simultaneously as a demiurge of national language, as a prophet, and as a social critic. No task seemed more important for a member of the Russian intelligentsia—whatever his or her occupation—than to define his or her own position regarding these processes reflected in the world of letters.

At the moment when Vygotsky entered into the cultural life of Moscow it seemed that the entire world was split between the "archaists" sticking to already established and recognized canons, and the "innovators" standing at the forefront of change. In Russia, the borderline between the old and the new, between the archaists and the innovators fell between the last nineteenth-century poetic school of the Symbolists and a new school of literary scholars later designated the Russian Formalists.[14] With the passage of time it became clear that what had appeared to be a fight between the Symbolists and Formalists was just one skirmish in the overall battle being waged not only in Moscow and St Petersburg, but also in Paris and Munich, Vienna and Rome; the battle that distinguished people as different as Picasso the painter, Schoenberg the composer, and Khlebnikov the poet. At the center of this battle was the problem of "liberation of form" in the arts, and, even deeper, the problem of the self-reflection of the arts and literature. At stake was the question of what makes a given thing a work of art.

This question is closely related to the even more fundamental philosophical issue of objectivation and disobjectivation, terms already introduced in conjunction with Vygotsky's interest in Hegelian philosophy. The fundamental philosophical question of the disobjectivation of *knowledge* has been with us for centuries, starting with Plato. Essentially, disobjectivation is the problem of grasping thought and life in their dynamic and "open" form before they are "finished", before they become *things*. The disobjectivation procedure applied to human thought lies at the heart of Socratic *dialectic*. In the Socratic dialogues dialectic appears as a device for turning commonsense statements into problems by revealing their self-contradictory nature. In Hegel's philosophy the dialectical method serves to point out how thought can become its opposite and then "return back" enriched. In the course of this estrangement and return the objectivations of thought become understood as *moments* of its self-development and self-negation.[15]

But what looks convincing as a grand philosophical design is not necessarily and immediately realized when applied to specific areas of human activity. Moreover, it would be utterly naive to think that human thought works systematically and unidirectionally from general philosophical design to specific applications. It was not until the beginning of the twentieth century, for example, that Hegel's ideas, absorbed by the so-called neo-Kantians, started to inform the history of the natural sciences. The future poet Boris Pasternak, then a philosophy student at Marburg University, described the situation as follows: "If current philosophy tells what this or that writer thinks, and current psychology, of how the average man thinks; if formal logic teaches how to think in a baker's so as to get the right change, then the Marburg School was interested in how science thinks in its twenty-five centuries of uninterrupted authorship . . .".[16]

Science thus appeared not as a cumulative account of incontrovertible facts but as a continuous logical effort to construct the object of inquiry. These early attempts at disobjectivation of the history of science are echoed in the more recent and more radical notions of scientific revolutions and the anarchistic theory of knowledge.[17]

But if it was difficult with the history of physics, it was no easier in the realm of literature and the arts. It is true that the German Romantics, the spiritual teachers of Hegel, caused the rationalist and empiricist theories of art to crack. The winds of Becoming swept the corridors of art theory. But it was not until the early twentieth century that the problem of art's self-reflection returned as the focus of discussion, posing in earnest the questions of what is art in its elementary form, and what is the elementary particle of artistic Being.

In Russia, literature's modernist self-reflection had already begun within the Symbolist school, particularly in the work of the poets Andrei Bely and Vyacheslav Ivanov. Although the

Symbolists, with their emphasis on figurative and symbolic images in poetry, were not well prepared to carry out the program of radical disobjectivation, they produced the remarkable phenomenon of the poet-theoretician. For those poet-scholars the assertion of the unique creative role of the imagination went hand-in-hand with the analytic task of dissecting the symbolic tissue of a particular verse and discovering its sound symbolism. Poet-theoreticians, for example, inquired into the process of automatization and disautomatization of poetic language—a topic that was to become the central issue for the Russian Formalists. From the Symbolist point of view gradual automatization of poetic language occurs when words lose their symbolic meanings and become simply abstract notions. It takes the creative genius of a true poet to introduce a new system of symbols and thus to rejuvenate poetic speech in general.

The next step in the direction of critical reflection upon the literary process was taken by the immediate successors-cum-opponents of the Symbolists, who called themselves the Acmeists, whose ranks included poets Nikolai Gumilev, Anna Akhmatova and Osip Mandelstam. The Acmeists' reflections upon the literary process followed their manifesto, which aimed at replacing the intangible intuitions of the Symbolists with a vision of poetry as craftsmanship. The Acmeists even called their organization the Guild of Poets to emphasize their appreciation of professionalism. A strong didactic element in the Acmeists' activities inevitably led to their posing the "last questions" of poetics. Later, when the guild itself disappeared, Mandelstam would restate these last questions of poetics in the context of the study of the specific nature of the poetic word, the problem of literary evolution, and the broader problem of the historical role of literature in different cultures. The sounds and images of Mandelstam's poetry found their way into the pages of Vygotsky's works, and the ideas expressed in Mandelstam's essay "On the nature of the word" became integral elements of Vygotsky's discussion of the relationship between thought and language.[18]

The most explicit confrontation between the archaists and the innovators occurred only when Cubist art reached Russia, the Futurist poetry of Khlebnikov and Mayakovsky became a scandal of the day, and a young literary scholar Viktor Shklovsky published his programmatic paper "The resurrection of the word". The Cubist influence is important because it was in Cubism that the notions of the "shifting image" and "difficult perception" appeared for the first time. Cubist artists such as Picasso were dissatisfied with "objective" art, which seemed to place the viewer into a passive position of someone who simply *recognizes* familiar things and human figures. Objects are "finished" in realistic art, argued the Cubists; there is no dynamic left, no freedom for seeing things in their Becoming. The technique of the shifting image, which presented one and the same object simultaneously from several points of view, is aimed precisely at allowing the spectator to become a co-author, to form the image instead of simply recognizing it. "Difficult perception" also helps to focus attention on the artistic form itself which, according to the Cubists, is a true subject of esthetic experience.

A similar argument against the notion of esthetic experience through a simple recognition of the finished literary expressions was advanced in the programmatic statement of the Russian Formalists:

> We do not experience the familiar, we do not see it, we recognize it. We do not see the walls of our rooms. We find it very difficult to catch mistakes when reading proofs (especially if it is in familiar language), the reason being that we cannot force ourselves to see, to read, and not just "recognize", a familiar word. Be this a definition of a "poetic" perception, or of an "artistic" perception in general in any case the definition is the following: "artistic" perception is a perception that entails awareness of form; perhaps not only form, but invariably form.[19]

A palpable poetic alternative to the poetry of "recognition" was offered by the Futurists, who focused on the inner capacities of the "word as such". The notions of the shifting image and difficult perception were almost literally adopted by the Futurists, who used cut-words, artificially difficult rhymes, neologisms and trans-rational texts. One alternative for the change in poetic language realized by the Futurists was the creation of neologisms based on the unrealized possibilities of Russian grammar. These neologisms, though "illegitimate" in a communicative sense, may have an esthetic value. Velemir Khlebnikov tried to convince his readers that, "By changing just one sound in the old word, we immediately create a pass from one valley of language to another; we create the means of transportation in the country of words crossing the mountain ridges of verbal silence".[20] Vygotsky recalled this "transportation" metaphor of Khlebnikov in his discussion of the impossibility of the immediate expression of thought in words: "Because a direct transition from thought to word is impossible, there have always been laments about the inexpressibility of thought . . . To overcome this problem, new paths from thought to word leading through new word meanings must be cut. Velemir Khlebnikov compared his Futuristic poetry with the construction of roads . . .".[21]

The Futurists viciously attacked nineteenth-century Russian literature, which in their view forgot the task of bringing a poetic message, and substituted it with moral, educational or propagandistic content. They disdainfully called it a Salvation Army literature. In their own theory of art, the Futurists focused on the inherent poetic value of the word itself. Their rejection of all nonpoetic aspects of literary work also led to depsychologization of the literary process. Not only was the psychological element in the objects of poetry considered irrelevant, but the "subjective poetry" (*Ich Dichtung*) as such was perceived as a fruitless archaism. Futurist poetry was supposed to be not only "objectless" but also "authorless"; the nature of language was proclaimed to be the only true author of this poetry. Mayakovsky likened his verses to the processes of nature, saying that since the genius who is the "author" of the earth is unknown, the same is true of the real author of Mayakovsky's poem "One Hundred and Fifty Million" (at that time, the total population of the Soviet Union).[22]

This attempt to dispense with the notion of the subjective creative process and to discover the objective processes that turn shapes and colors into a work of art, and vowels and consonants into poetry, was not confined to the Futurist school. In a way it was characteristic of the entire modernist movement. In the process, however, the notions of objectivity and subjectivity often changed places. This is how the fictional character of Thomas Mann's novel *Doctor Faustus*, Adrian Leverkuhn, describes the modernist revolution in music theory: "In art, at least, the subjective and the objective intertwine to the point of being indistinguishable, one proceeds from the other and takes the character of the other, the subjective precipitates as objective and by genius is again awaked to spontaneity, 'dynamyzed' as we say . . . . The form of variations, something archaic, a residuum, becomes a means by which to infuse new life into form". And then comes a strange, dialectical coincidence of absolute freedom with the absolute domination of the objective form: "In him music abstains from all conventional florishes, formulas, and residua and so to speak creates the unity of the work anew at every moment, out of freedom. But precisely on that account freedom becomes the principle of all-round economy that leaves in music nothing casual . . . . I mean the complete integration of all musical dimensions, their neutrality towards each other due to complete organization".

The fictional Leverkuhn proceeds to describe a very real theory of the twelve-tone music developed by Arnold Schoenberg. The description bears a striking resemblance to the Futurist concept of poetic language: "Words of twelve letters, certain combinations and interrelations of the twelve semitones, series of notes from which a piece and all the movements of the work must strictly derive". When his interlocutor interjects that such a style can be very impoverished, Leverkuhn answers with a purely Futuristic suggestion that "one must incorporate into the system all possible techniques of variation, including those decried as artificial."[23]

If the Futurists were shock troops who assaulted traditional poetry and published provocative manifestos, then the Formalists could be compared to an intelligence office of the general staff.[24] What the Futurists enacted in real life, Formalist critics analyzed on the theoretical plane. Moreover, while the Futurists often called for the replacement of traditional literature by the modernist, the Formalists were eager to show that the esthetic value of traditional literature itself derives not from its "realism", or its "social usefulness" but from the keen literary techniques employed by Gogol or Tolstoy.

One of the leaders of the Formalist movement, Boris Eichenbaum, succinctly defined his credo as follows: "In principle the question for the Formalist is not how to study literature, but what the subject matter of literary study actually is".[25] One may find this position congenial to that of Vygotsky who, instead of simply studying child behavior or adult cognition, attempted to define what it is that ought to become the subject matter of psychological research.

Another Formalist, Roman Jakobson, developed Eichenbaum's thesis contrasting the Formalist position with those of its predecessors and its opponents: "The object of literary scholarship is not literature, but literariness—that is, that which makes a given work a work of literature. Until now literary historians have preferred to act like the policeman who, intending to arrest a certain person, would, at any opportunity, seize all persons who chanced into the apartment, as well as those who passed along the street. The literary historians used everything—anthropology, psychology, politics, philosophy. Instead of a science of literature, they created a conglomerate of homespun disciplines".[26]

In search of this "literariness", the Formalists embarked upon a study of differences between "poetic" (that is, literary) language and everyday conversational speech. To understand this dichotomy it is useful to consult the schema of verbal acts developed by Jakobson.[27] According to this schema the Addresser sends a Message to the Addressee. This Message may have a number of functions. The most obvious is a referential or *communicative* function, when the Message refers to and carries information about a certain object or situation. "Four plus four equals eight" is an example of such an informative Message taken in its communicative function. The same simple Message can, however, acquire a new, emotive or *expressive* function if for example it is uttered in a self-mocking tone and accompanied by an expressive gesture indicating that the Addresser has no more than eight dollars in his pockets. The expressive attitude conveys the emotional status of the Addresser. Jakobson relates that one former actor of the Moscow Arts Theater was able to convey forty emotional situations by saying each time just one short phrase, "This evening". The whole dramatic system of the theater's famous director, Stanislavsky, was based on the emotive subtext each actor was supposed to convey by linguistic and paralinguistic means. Stanislavsky's system left a lasting impression on Vygotsky, who used Stanislavsky's notes for the actors to demonstrate the role of emotive subtext in the decoding of verbal messages.[28]

Message may also carry a *contact* function, which is directed at the Addressee and serves to initiate or prolong the, communication. For example, if a boy approaches a girl and after looking at the girl's math exercise book utters "Four plus four equals eight", this message carries no important information, but is used as an opening gambit in an attempt to engage the girl in conversation. Another function of the message is a *metalingual* one. This function is directed at that specific verbal *code* the Addresser is using. A child asking "What does equal mean?" requests a metalingual answer such as "Equal means quantitatively the same", which presents the information about the lexical code the Addresser is using. And finally there is a *poetic* function when the focus is on the *Message* for its own sake; not as a denotate of some object or event but as a self-sufficient Being.

On the phonetic level the poetic function is achieved by introducing a group of "difficult" sounds, or unusual combinations and rhymes that arrest the reader's attention and bring sounds into the "bright field of consciousness", to quote another Formalist, Lev Jakubinsky. The same is true for the higher-order verbal levels. Vygotsky understood the psychological importance of such "difficulties" and irregularities; in this connection he quoted Pushkin:

> As rose lips without a smile,
> Without error in the grammar
> I Russian language will despise . . .

and commented that these lines carry a much more serious message than is usually assumed.[29]

By focusing on the difference between poetic language and everyday speech the Formalists came up with the following schematic dichotomy. Everyday speech is automatic, predominantly referential, that is, oriented toward the material, and focused on a story (*fabula*). In literary language, lánguage is defamiliarized, estranged; it appears in its poetic function oriented toward the form, and the predominant element is the plot (*suzhet*). The phenomena of defamiliarization and the study of plots versus stories became the focal point of the Formalists' study of prose. "The technique of art", asserted Shklovsky, "is to make objects unfamiliar, to make forms difficult, to increase the difficulty and length of perception because the process of perception is an esthetic end in itself and must be prolonged.

Art is a way of experiencing the artfulness of an object; the object itself is not important".[30]

Sometimes the whole *attitude* of a work of art serves as an estrangement device. Shklovsky mentioned as one such example Tolstoy's story *Kholstomer* in which the narrator is a horse, rather than a human. Ordinary events that are hardly noticeable if presented from the human point of view acquire a fresh, unusual meaning and artistic value when refracted through the eyes of the horse.

As mentioned above, the difference between the story and its artistic presentation in the form of a plot lies at the heart of the Formalist theory of prose. The story is an aggregate of events taken in their causal and chronological order; the plot is a system of these same events but presented in the order chosen by the author. For example, the story may include the marriage and the death of a character, naturally, in this order; the plot, however, can start with the scene of the death and only later return to the issue of marriage. The esthetic function of the plot is precisely in weaving an intricate net of temporal and causal advances, returns and digressions, lending the work of art its own meaning irreducible to the real-life events used as material.

To underscore this theoretical point, Shklovsky undertook an analysis of the plot structure of Laurence Sterne's *Tristram Shandy*. The choice of Sterne's novel was not arbitrary, for Shklovsky contended that Sterne was a sort of eighteenth-century Futurist who not only readily employed innovative literary techniques but also purposively revealed them, laid them bare. The action in *Tristram Shandy* is continually interrupted with various digressions; the plot runs ahead of the story on one page only to return to earlier events on the next. Sterne does not pretend that he is unaware of this; indeed, he turns his awareness into a device as well:

> I will not finish that sentence till I have made an observation upon the strange state of affairs between the reader and myself . . . . I am this month one whole year older than I was this time twelve-month; and having got, as you perceive, almost into the middle of my fourth volume—and no farther than to my first day's life— 'tis demonstrative that I have three hundred and sixty-four days more life to write just now, than when I first set out; so that instead of advancing, as a common writer, in my work with what

I have been doing at it—on the contrary, I am just thrown so many volumes back.[31]

"If we visualize the digressions schematically", suggested Shklovsky, "they will appear as cones representing the event, with the apex representing the causes. In an ordinary novel such á cone is joined to the main storyline at its apex; in *Tristram Shandy* the base of the cone is joined to the main storyline, so that all at once we fall into a swarm of allusions".[32] Actually, the storyline does not advance much in the first two hundred pages, because the subject is still Tristram's birth, although the plot has already taken the reader through a number of digressions and digressions within digressions. Sterne not only digresses, but constantly reminds the reader that he is doing so.

The willingness of Sterne to lay bare his technique—and to make this revelation into a device of its own—goes as far as drawing the graphs of the plots in the five volumes of *Tristram Shandy*. "In the fifth volume I have been very good," winks Sterne to his reader, "the precise line I have described in it being this:"

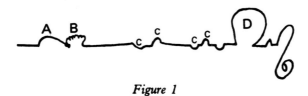

Figure 1

Sterne proceeds to explain his major digressions marked A, B and D and in the same ironic manner concludes that "as for *cccc* they are nothing but parentheses, and the common *ins* and *outs* incident to the lives of the greatest ministers of state; when compared with what men have done,—or with my own transgressions at the letters A, B, D—they vanish into nothing".[33]

Concluding his own analysis, Shklovsky repeated that the "contours" of a work of art derive from the immanent laws specific to the given art form, and not from the justification provided by their realism. By driving the formal devices of the novelistic genre to their extreme, Sterne created a "prototypical novel" rather than a deviant one.

Shklovsky successfully probed the "mechanics" of disautomatization as a literary device. Some questions remained unanswered, however, such as how different techniques interact with each other, and how changes of literary device occur. These questions were addressed by another Formalist, Yiri Tynyanov, in his essay "On literary evolution".[34] First, Tynyanov suggested that a study of literary change should be bifurcated depending on the locus of analysis. One may inquire into the *origins* of a specific literary phenomenon, but one may also focus on the *development* of a given literary form. Tynyanov argued that the term "development" does not coincide with a historical identification of superficially similar literary forms in the texts of different epochs. The "same" element plays one role in one literary system and an entirely different one in another. Rhythm as a device has one role in twentieth-century poetry and another role in eighteenth-century prose. The central problem is therefore the question of *systematic change* in literary history. A number of extraliterary impulses may contribute to the genesis of a literary phenomenon, but once it is incorporated into a literary series, its subsequent development depends on systemic changes. Thus it is not enough to study a particular literary technique because different techniques employed in a given genre—lyrical poetry, for example—are interacting with each other.

To study a literary element means therefore to study its *functional relations* within a system and between systems. Thus, for example, a lexicon of a given literary work must be compared with (*a*) other formal elements of this work, and (*b*) the lexicon of contemporary literature in general and with the lexicon of everyday speech. It is meaningless, therefore, to talk of a literary device *per se* because its functioning essentially depends on the system within which it is embedded. For example, one and the same archaic form provides a quality of a "high-flown" language to Lomonosov's poetry (eighteenth century), but the very same form is used as a technique of irony in the nineteenth-century poetry of Tyutchev. Tynyanov concluded that the existence of a literary form ultimately depends on its function as a systemic element related to other literary and extraliterary elements of speech.

It is clear that Tynyanov's approach owes much to the fundamental debate initiated by the Swiss linguist Ferdinand de Saussure on the synchronic and diachronic dimensions of language and the systemic character of linguistic change.[35] For the purpose of this analysis it is more important, however, that Tynyanov's elaboration of the notion of systemic and literary evolution had a direct bearing on Vygotsky's understanding of the concept of system as applied to psychological development. In his later works Vygotsky argued that psychological functions such as perception, memory or problem-solving do not develop as separate entities, but are engaged at any given moment in complex systemic relationships. They evolve as a system, and their relative contributions are determined by their positions in this functional system. In any given phase in the developmental process one function may assume a dominant position subordinating the others. In young children, for example, memory plays a dominant role in relation to problem solving, the latter being subordinated to the former. A young child thinks through remembering. In adults these functions are often reversed with recollections serving as a support for logical problem-solving mechanisms.

There is a substantial affinity between Vygotsky's systemic approach and the concept of literary dominants developed by Tynyanov. Tynyanov argued that the interaction of various elements within the literary system is not equipotential, but presupposes some dominants. The dominant element characterizes the whole literary work and predetermines its literary function. The dominant thus becomes a differentiating element of the literary system. For example, the genre-differentiating element in the modern novel is the nature of its plot. Plot is thus the genre-dominant of the novel. In a different historical period, however, the genre-differentiating function for the novel was carried by another element, namely the presence of romantic intrigue.

If in their early works the Formalists emphasized the difference between poetic language and everyday speech, then, with the idea of systemic organization supplanting the idea of a solitary artistic device, they came to a more comprehensive account of the continuum of verbal expressions. Any literary element could now be judged on the basis of its position on at least three different systemic levels: (*a*) the system of all elements in a given literary work; (*b*) the system of all literature in its totality, including such subsystems as styles and genre; and (*c*) the system of the culture including nonliterary elements. To use an already mentioned example, an archaism may have a specific role within a given literary work, but to assume this role it must be recognized *as an archaism*, this recognition being a function of its position in relation to other lexical elements of a given language. So at a certain moment such a *linguistic* fact as an archaism becomes a *literary* fact, a literary device. In place of an *a priori* dichotomy of literary verses nonliterary, of art versus life, comes a much more complex dialectic of literary forms that become automatized and are ultimately incorporated into everyday speech, while colloquial speech forms become recognized as new literary devices.

One step farther in this direction was made by Jakubinsky in his paper "On verbal dialogue".[36] For Jakubinsky the opposition of poetic versus everyday language was just one of many oppositions constituting the functional characteristics of language. He believed that forms of communication are of paramount importance: direct speech differs from indirect, and the language of dialogue is not that of monologue. Each of these forms of communication has its own particular linguistic, psychological and potentially artistic dimensions. For example, verbal activity such as letter writing is perceived as an element of everyday life in one epoch, only to become a popular literary genre in the other.

The major opposition Jakubinsky considered in detail was that of monologue versus dialogue. In his view an extreme case of dialogue would be a rapid *conversation* concerning some everyday matter. In such a dialogue each response is completely conditioned by the preceding utterance of the other side. Conversations of this type are rarely planned in advance, and they often lack intentionality. An extreme example of monologue could be a well thought out, rather long speech that is not intended to evoke an immediate response, and whose elements depend on the whole. Of course there are many mixed forms between these two extremes, such as a "written dialogue" when a listener in a lecture hall writes comments on what the speaker is saying.

Jakubinsky, following in this another Russian linguist, Lev

Scherba, considered dialogue to be a *natural* form of communication. One should be taught to listen without interrupting a speaker, but no one needs special training in how to produce an immediate verbal response. This observation of Jakubinsky had a lasting effect on Vygotsky's concept of natural versus artificial in language and other cognitive processes. In the dichotomy of monologue versus dialogue Vygotsky found one of the realizations of the fundamental dichotomy between "natural" and "cultural" processes. In a face-to-face dialogue language as a symbolic system is not independent; it is still part of a syncretic whole that includes such paralinguistic forms of communication as facial expression, gesticulation and also a shared environment. Moreover, the verbal message in a face-to-face communication is still very similar to a purely behavioral response, up to the possibility of mutual substitution. For example, instead of responding verbally, "I wouldn't be surprised", one may simply raise an eyebrow, and this "response" will be readily accepted as one of the turns in the continuing dialogue. Dialogue is also compositionally rather simple, because a good deal can be presumed to be already known to the interlocutor with whom the speaker has a shared apperception of characters, events and circumstances.

Monologue, on the other hand, is a purely verbal art form that is further removed from the natural form of response-like behavior. First, monologue presupposes a generalized other as a listener. In written speech monologue becomes in addition an indirect form of communication. Monologue is a conscious enterprise in which at least some planning is invested. Finally, in the monologue a linguistic form comes to the foreground because the speaker has more time to work not only on the content of the message but also on its artistic form.

The discoveries and the doubts of the Formalists were destined to become an intellectual greenhouse for Vygotsky. He did not became an apologist for the Formalist school, nor did he confine himself to the narrow issue of poetic discourse. What he found in the works of the Formalists was a broad theoretical quest for a study of human language as an instrument of human activities as diverse as the writing of a novel and an exchange of expletives between drunkards. Moreover, when Vygotsky approached problems that are fundamental to psychological theory, such as the problem of development and the problem of systemic organization, he certainly recognized that they held certain theoretical elements in common with already familiar issues of literary evolution and literary systems.

THE PSYCHOLOGY OF ART

The years Vygotsky spent studying at Moscow University were not only a time of enthusiastic learning of all that was new and challenging in the sciences, the humanities and the arts; during this time he also first published as an art reviewer and literary critic. He wrote of the problems of Jewish culture, about the "experimental" novel *Petersburg* by Andrei Bely, on the book of Symbolist poet-theoretician Vyacheslav Ivanov, and on new trends in the theater.[37] He also collected material for two longer studies: the monograph on *Hamlet* (to be discussed in Chapter Two), and *The Psychology of Art*, which he would later submit as a PhD thesis at the Moscow Institute of Psychology in 1925.[38]

With the benefit of hindsight one can now easily recognize in *The Psychology of Art* some of the magisterial ideas of Vygotsky's future psychological system. In that system Vygotsky suggested that one can distinguish between lower or natural mental functions and higher or cultural mental processes. Higher mental functions in their turn include both more primitive and more advanced processes depending on the form of mediation. The role of mediator of the higher psychological functions is played by semiotic systems that could be as simple as a gesture or as complex as a literary discourse. The development and composition of human higher mental processes depends on culturally and historically specific forms of semiotic mediation.

In light of this future context, *The Psychology of Art* looks like an overambitious first step in the implementation of this psychological program. Vygotsky posed a fundamental question: What is it that distinguishes human consciousness as an historically and culturally specific function? To answer this question he started from the very top, from the mediation of the human psyche by literary discourse: "Psychology in its attempt to explain the whole of [human] behavior cannot but be attracted by the difficult problems posed by esthetic reaction".[39] But what is this "esthetic reaction"?

Even in this early work Vygotsky showed a deep concern with the problem of subject matter and the method of psychological inquiry. He was not ready to accept the traditional approaches as scientific "givens". To paraphrase the Formalists, Vygotsky refused to be concerned with a psychological study until the subject matter of psychological inquiry had been discussed. The psychological approach itself should be disobjectivized first, that is, laid bare for what Vygotsky called a methodological analysis. (The word "method" stands here for a set of philosophical, ideological and cultural assumptions guiding a particular scholar or a particular field of knowledge in its inquiry.) With regard to the psychology of art Vygotsky concluded that: 'So far psychological studies of art have been carried out in one of two directions: either as a study of the author's psychology [understood] on the basis of what has been created, or as a study of the experience of the reader and spectator who is perceiving this creation".[40] Because both processes—the creation and the perception—if taken in the individual psychological plane are rooted in the unconscious of the author and the reader, the frontal attack, according to Vygotsky, will be fruitless. What was needed was an indirect method of reconstruction, perhaps resembling a criminal investigation of events that happened in the past, such as a murder. Such an investigation relies primarily on material evidence, on a number of contradictory statements of witnesses or people involved, and on other indirect or circumstantial evidence. Direct testimony is often impossible, or its veracity uncertain (its seems that his years at law school were not wasted).

Vygotsky argued that such an indirect method is common in the social and natural sciences. The geologist has no first-hand experience of the processes that happened a billion years ago, and so reconstructs them on the basis of theoretical hypotheses and indirect evidence such as fossils. Historical studies of the French Revolution are carried out by people who did not participate in the actual events, so they too rely on the system of indirect evidence such as personal letters, tax documents, etc. Similarly, Vygotsky concluded that any psychological inquiry into the arts must start with the art object, such as a work of literature, rather than with its author or its reader. There is nothing immediately psychological in this object, but the same is true of the material evidence of a crime and the clues used in probes made by geologists.

Once he decided to start with the text of a literary work, Vygotsky became solidly allied with the Formalists in their critique of the traditional interpretation of art as a system of images. Vygotsky argued that those who sought to explain poetry as a system of images missed the point, because they neglected the immanent form of poetry, which is its organization by rhyme, rhythm and meter. To make his point Vygotsky related a humorous apocryphal story about the masters who were ordered to cast a statue of Shulamite and decided to take literally a poetic description from the Song of Songs: "Thy hair is as a flock of goats / That lie along the side of mount Gilead / Thy teeth are like a flock of ewes that are newly shorn . . .". One can only imagine what kind of a statue they produced! Vygotsky also challenged the apologists for the theory of images to show how lines by Mandelstam such as "black ice burning on the lips" and "the memory of Stygian tolls" could be interpreted as a set of images.

The Formalists also helped to change the traditional understanding of the "form" and the "content" of a work of art. Everything that the artist finds as ready-made elements suitable for his or her craft, such as words, sounds, stereotypical images, verbal cliché, and even the ideas developed in a given work— all of them belong to the *material* of the art. The *arrangement* of this material in a given work is its *form*. Such an arrangement is called an artistic "device" or "technique". One of the most important devices in prose is the plot (*suzhet*) with respect to which the story (*fabula*) or "what happened' serves as the material: "Plot stands in the same relation to the story, as verse relates to the constituent words, and melody relates to the notes."[41]

The Formalists also revealed the illusory character of so-called realistic art, rejecting all attempts to "explain" the behavior of literary characters through an appeal to the reader's knowledge of individual psychology. Thus the lack of resolve in Prince Hamlet stems not from human psychological weakness, but from the structural laws inherent in Shakespeare's tragedy. But Vygotsky, although he acknowledged the importance of artistic technique as a first step in the analysis of a work of art, categorically refused to consider it the last step. "Art is a technique", the Formalists claimed, and this is true, but the statement begs the question: a technique of what? Technique for technique's sake is not an artistic device, but a simple trick. Each and every technique finds its own meaning only in the overall poetic system within which the technique is working.

But this overall system necessarily includes not only the formal elements but also the "material" of the given work, and this material is related, among other things, to extraliterary phenomena. This very conclusion was reached by some of the more farsighted of the Formalists, such as Jakobson and Tynyanov in their concept of the literary system.[42] The Formalists demonstrated that a work of art whose "form" is damaged loses its artistic function. Vygotsky argued that the same is true in the case of damage to or a misplacement of the material.

Here Vygotsky touched upon one of the crucial theoretical problems of any psychological inquiry, namely, the problem of formal versus essential identification of behavioral or cognitive phenomena. The starting point is that the discovery of the similarity between the formal, structural aspects of the two phenomena does not guarantee their essential similarity. For example, an apparent similarity in the behavior of chimpanzees and young children actually obscures the differences in their respective development of reasoning. On another occasion Vygotsky demonstrated how an apparent similarity in the concepts used by children and those used by adults masks a profound difference in the conceptual systems that alone lend a particular concept its specific value.[43] The problem of the relationship between the form and the material reaches to the very heart of the concept of the cultural development of the human mind. According to Vygotsky culture not only provides a structural framework for the organization of naturally inherited impulses, but it furnishes the very material of human behaviour.

Returning to the feasibility of the Formalist theory of art, Vygotsky believed that only through a study of the interaction between the form and the material could the inherent one-sidedness of Formalism be overcome. This interaction, according to Vygotsky, is best understood in terms of *catharsis*. Vygotsky used this term from Aristotle's *Poetics* to designate the discharge of emotions that build up in a spectator or a reader under the influence of a work of art. The cathartic "purification" not only discharges the tension but also transforms human feelings. In the study of catharsis, as elsewhere, Vygotsky suggested to start not with the experiencing individual, but with the objective property of the work of art that makes catharsis possible.

To get some idea of how the cathartic model works, consider the following analysis of Bunin's novella "The Gentle Breath". In approaching this text Vygotsky, following the Formalists, defines the material as those everyday events, human characters and circumstances that together provide the basic storyline (*fabula*) of the novella. Regarding the form, Vygotsky explains: "When we are talking about the order and the deployment of the elements of this material as they appear to the reader, i.e. *how* then story is told, then we [are talking] about the form".[44] This ordering and deployment of material constitutes the story's plot. Plot is a generative principle of a literary text, and the composition of elements here is no less important than is the order of sounds in a melody, or the order of words in a phrase. Moreover, a study of literary form must not stop at a simple cataloguing of technical devices. This will be only the "anatomy" of the text, which should be complemented by its "physiology", the teleological understanding of the respective roles of each device and each technique. Devices and techniques are not thrown into a text for their own sake—as some Formalists claimed—but are used with a functional goal in mind.

The storyline of Bunin's novella is roughly as follows: Olya Mescherskaya, a high-schoolgirl, lives a life that is no different from that of any other average, pretty and well-to-do girl from a provincial Russian town. Then something happens. She has a love affair with Malyutin, a landowner and friend of her father's who is much older than herself. Then she has a liaison with a Cossack officer whom she attracted and promised to wed. All this leads her astray. As a result the Cossack officer, betrayed yet still in love with Olya, shoots her in a crowded railway station. Olya's schoolmistress chooses the deceased as the subject of her passionate worship and frequently visits her grave.[45]

The story thus has two character lines, one of the schoolgirl and the other of the teacher. The girl's chronological axis has fourteen episodes, from *A* to *O*, and the teacher's has seven episodes from *a* to *g*.

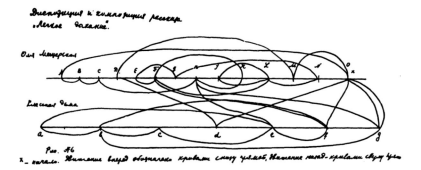

Figure 2

If, however, we connect these episodes in the sequence in which they become known to the reader, a much more complex structure emerges with some episodes running ahead of their chronological time (indicated by arches above the axes) and some returning to the time passed (indicated by arches below the axes). The straight line represents the chronologically arranged story, while the arches in their totality represent the plot of Bunin's novella. To comprehend the functional role of the plot, Vygotsky suggests starting at the opposite pole—with the life material reflected in the novella. This life material is "muddy". The story offers no bright or redeeming feature. The life depicted—and it is depicted with brutal objectivity—is rather dull and senseless from the beginning to the tragic end. There is nothing in the storyline that transcends the "muddy water of life", as Vygotsky calls it. Nevertheless, the general feeling evoked in the reader of this novella is quite the *opposite* of that conveyed by the material. This resultant feeling is one of liberation. It is this light, gentle breath of the title that is the real theme of the novella, rather than the muddled life of a flirtatious schoolgirl. The main trait of the novella as a whole is "that feeling of lightness, transparency and other-worldliness which in no way can be derived from the life events on which [the story] is based".[46]

If we take a chronologically related story to be a reality, then the intersecting arches of the plot are the *construction* of this reality, its "gentle breath". The material of the story is arranged in such a way that separate episodes lose their natural, real-life connections, and form a new melody. As in the evangelical miracle the plot turns the simple water of life into a pure wine of art. Step by step Vygotsky analyzes the text of the novella and shows how Bunin deliberately severs all natural connections between events and extinguishes all natural causes of interest. The murder of the schoolgirl is not only known from the beginning of the novella; the key word "shot" is buried in the middle of a long phrase cluttered with circumstantial details: "We should not be mistaken, if we say that the very structure of this phrase muffles the terrible shot, detracts from its strength, and turns it into almost pantomimic gesture [or] a hardly noticeable movement of thought, while the emotional coloring of this event is extinguished, pushed aside, eliminated".[47]

The hidden key to the plot of the novella lies, so to speak, on the surface: it is given in the title "The Gentle Breath". Throughout the text there are several hints about this other reading of events and circumstances, but the discovery comes only with the last lines of the novella. The teacher remembers how she had overhead Olya talking about "the old funny book" that described the "gentle breath" as the most essential and exquisite element of female beauty. And after this reminiscence by the teacher comes the final sentence: "Now this gentle breath evaporated in the world, in this cloudy sky, and this cold wind of spring . . .". Vygotsky perceived this as the cathartic point of the novella. The plot dominated by the theme of the gentle breath finally overcomes the material, and as a result, instead of a realistic account of a short and muddled life, we get an almost religious feeling of "purification". The only aftertaste is that of this gentle breath, this promise of life evaporated, disappeared into the cloudy sky. All previous events reveal their second nature when experienced through the prism of the gentle breath. For example, the pictures of nature, the description of elements cease to be perceived as a mere "frame" for human actions but instead acquire a new meaning within the dominant rhetorical figure of gentle breath—life—life's disappearance.

Vygotsky concluded that the well-worn statement that the material and the form should be harmonized in a work of art is essentially wrong. Esthetic feeling comes with catharsis, and catharsis comes because there is a series of dramatic confrontations between the form and the material with the former ultimately overcoming the latter. The objective properties of the text should therefore guarantee this dual attraction—one toward material embodied in the story, the other toward form embodied in the plot and other literary devices. Implicit in this position is the rejection of both extremes of the literary continuum: chronological realism and complete formalism. To achieve catharsis the reader must be able to pursue both dimensions, material as well as formal. When one aspect is too weak—when, for example, the whole work is a parade of formal devices—then there is nothing to overcome and no tension to discharge. This approach also presupposes the active participation of the reader, who is not only assumed to be sensitive enough to be influenced by the formal devices, but also experienced enough to be able to assemble the realistic aspect out of the events provided by the author.

There is an interesting addendum to Vygotsky's study of Bunin's novella, which is typical of him. To get a physical equivalent of the influence of a plot on a reader, Vygotsky and his colleagues undertook a pneumographic study of a reader's breathing while reading different types of texts. Not surprisingly, the pneumogram of the reading of the Bunin's novella presented a smooth curve of the "gentle breath", unperturbed by the brutality of the events described.

Once the first step is made, and the objective characteristics of a work of art that evoke esthetic feelings are tentatively identified, there must be a turn toward the study of the subjective part of the equation. The general formula offered by Vygotsky was that "art is a social technique of feelings".[48] This understanding fits quite accurately into Vygotsky's later theory of symbols that serve as barriers and "transformers" of human natural impulses. Art is therefore one of the most complex systems of symbols which helps to transform the original human feelings into what Vygotsky called an esthetic reaction. But where are the original impulses coming from? Vygotsky's answer was unequivocal: from the unconscious. "It does not require any special perceptiveness to grasp that the immediate source of the esthetic effect lies in the unconscious and that only by reaching out to this area can one approach the problem of art".[49]

To posit the unconscious as an immediate source of artistic creativity and esthetic feelings does not mean to accept the Freudian system as a whole. Vygotsky joined other critics in the attack on Freud's alleged pansexualism, and criticized psychoanalysis for the lack of a proper elaboration of the relationship between unconscious and conscious processes. The crucial element in Vygotsky's disagreement with psychoanalysts is their respective evaluation of the role played by artistic form. Vygotsky reviewed the pertinent works of Freud, Otto Rank and Hans Sachs and concluded that form is relegated in psychoanalysis to the role of "bait" (*Vorlast*). This bait attracts the reader, who is then relieved of the psychological tension by the therapeutic effect of the *material* of a work of art rather than its form. From this perspective there is nothing specifically "artistic" in the mechanism of the esthetic reaction, since it becomes just another mechanism of incomplete revelation of hidden complexes. Likewise, the author appears in psychoanalysis as a neurotic whose creativity could barely be distinguished from the work of dreams, fantasies and the symptoms of psychological maladaptation.

From Vygotsky's point of view psychoanalysts were reluctant to develop the very theme they had first suggested, namely that art reflects a transformation of unconscious processes into such behavioral and cognitive manifestations that have social form and meaning. The unconscious could thus be a source of artistic creativity but until it is filtered through the semiotic mediatory mechanism it will remain beyond art: "Art as the unconscious is merely a problem; art as a social resolution of the unconscious—this is the most likely answer to this problem".[50]

To give a tentative answer to the question of the psychodynamics of an artistic experience, Vygotsky first inquired into the "economy" or energy distribution associated with this experience. He refuted on both empirical and theoretical grounds the then-popular doctrine of the "mental economy", which stipulated that all well-organized mental processes (the experience of a work of art among them) are organized along energy-saving lines. Vygotsky argued that, on the contrary, the prime function of a work of art is to release energy. This is, however, as he called it, a *central* release. Instead of actually releasing energy in a form of action or physiological abreaction on the periphery, the spectator or reader discharges his affect with the help of fantasy.

Vygotsky's second observation concerned the essentially ambivalent nature of esthetic experience. This could be recognized in such "lower" verbal forms as jokes, as well as in the "higher" forms of a tragedy. This ambivalence stems from the contradictory nature of esthetic affect, which could include the almost physical pain of watching a tragic event, and at the same time the feeling of unique triumph evoked by the tragedy as a whole.

Such affective transformations do not happen spontaneously, but only under the influence of specific semiotic devices that distinguish a particular artistic genre and grant it its esthetic value. Thus a tentative schema of esthetic experience is the following: the unconscious impulses of the author are encoded in social, semiotic forms that appear in the text as its material and its formal devices. The reader experiencing this double structure of the text develops conflicting affective tendencies, one of which is associated with material, the other with the formal side. The original source of these affects may also be the unconscious. The tension mounts and at a certain moment the reader achieves a catharsis, when the formal, artistic aspect finally overcomes the material aspect of the text. The discharge of the affect takes place in a form of intensive fantasy that restructures the reader's entire inner experience.

From the vantage point of the present it is easy to see how this tentative schema of esthetic experience corresponds to Vygotsky's theory of "psychological tools". Vygotsky drew parallels between material tools and symbolic, "psychological tools" that help to transform natural cognitive functions into cultural ones. *The Psychology of Art* suggests a somewhat similar analogy between the material tools and semiotic devices used by the artist: "The amalgamation of feelings", concluded Vygotsky, "occurs outside us with the help of social affect which is objectivized and materialized in the artistic devices which become the tools of society."[51]

NOTES

1. Information on Vygotsky's family and his childhood comes almost exclusively from the memoirs of his friend Semion Dobkin, "Ages and days". In K. Levitin, ed., *One Is Not Born a Personality* (*sic*). Moscow: Progress, 1983.
2. B. A. Kraver, *Gomelskii Process* (*Gomel's Trial*). St Petersburg: Obschestvennaya Polza, 1907, p. 840.
3. See G. W. F. Hegel, *Introduction to the Philosophy of History*. Indianapolis: Hackett, 1988. For a review of Hegel's philosophy written from a position congenial to the Marxist interpretation later shared by Vygotsky, see Herbert Marcuse, *Reason and Revolution: Hegel and the Rise of Social Theory*. Boston: Beacon Press, 1960 (original work published in 1941), and Alexandre Kojeve, *An Introduction to the Reading of Hegel*. Ithaca, NY: Cornell University Press, 1980 (original work published in 1947).
4. Hegel, *Introduction*, p. 58.
5. The notions of objectivation and disobjectivation are introduced by Hegel in his preface to *The Phenomenology of Spirit*:

   > The spirit, however, becomes an object, for the spirit is this movement of becoming something other for itself, i.e. an object for its self, and then to sublimate this otherhood. And experience is the name we give to just this movement in which the immediate, the unexperienced, i.e. the abstract, whether of sensible being or of a bare, simple thought, becomes estranged and then returns to itself from estrangement, and is only then presented in its actuality and truth and becomes the property of consciousness. (Walter Kaufmann, *Hegel: Texts and Commentary*. Notre Dame: University of Notre Dame, 1977, p. 56).

   In Marxist tradition the notion of objectivation became linked to the phenomenon of reification and the alienation of human activity in the form of commodities. See Georg Lukacs, *History and Class Consciousness*. Cambridge, MA: MIT Press, 1971 (original work published in 1923).

   In contemporary social science the notion of objectivation is used to describe social institutions as objectivation of human activity. See Peter Berger and Thomas Luckmann, *The Social Construction of Reality*. New York: Doubleday, 1966, and

Serge Moscovici and Robert Farr, *Social Representations*. Cambridge: Cambridge University Press, 1984.

6. The term "method" is used in Vygotsky's writings to designate a general epistemological position informing a particular inquiry. This understanding of method and methodology derives from René Descartes' *Discourse on Method*.

7. Lev Vygotsky, *Istoricheskii Smysl Psikhologicheskogo Krizisa* (*Historical Meaning of the Crisis in Psychology*). In *Sobranie Sochinenii* (*Collected Papers*), vol. 1. Moscow: Pedagogika, 1982, pp. 291–436.

8. See Lev Vygotsky, *Mind in Society*. Cambridge, MA: Harvard University Press, 1978.

9. Alexander Potebnya, *Mysl' i Iazyk* (*Thought and Language*). Kharkov: Gosudarstvennoe Izdatel'stvo Ukrainy, 1913 (original work published in 1862).

10. Wilhelm von Humboldt, *Linguistic Variability and Intellectual Development*. Coral Gables, FL: University of Miami Press, 1971 (original work published in 1836).

11. Ibid, p. 130.

12. Ibid, p. 27.

13. See Lev Vygotsky, "Traurnye stroki: 9 ava" ("The lines of mourning: 9th ava"), *Novy Put'*, No. 27, 1916, pp. 28–30; "Literaturnye zametki" ("Notes on literature"), Ibid, No. 47, 1916, pp. 27–32; "Avodim hoinu", Ibid, No. 11–12, 1917, pp. 8–10. See also David Vygodsky, "Novaya evreiskaya poeziya" ("New Jewish poetry"). In A. L. Volynsky, ed., *Parthenon*. St Petersburg: Parthenon, No. 1, 1922, pp. 92–7.

14. The relationships between the poetics of the Symbolists and the Futurists are discussed in Krystyna Pomorska, *Russian Formalist Theory and its Poetic Ambience*. The Hague: Mouton, 1968.

15. See G. W. F. Hegel, *The Phenomenology of Spirit*. London: Clarendon Press, 1977.

16. Boris Pasternak, *Safe Conduct*. New York: New Directions, 1958, pp. 44–5 (original work published in 1930).

17. See Thomas Kuhn, *The Structure of Scientific Revolutions*. Chicago: University of Chicago Press, 1962; Paul Feyerabend, *Against Method*. London: Verso, 1971.

18. Osip Mandelstam, "On the nature of the word". In *The Critical Prose of Osip Mandelstam*. Ann Arbor, MI: Ardis Press, 1979 (original work published in 1922). For Vygotsky's use of Mandelstam's poetry and ideas, see Lev Vygotsky, *Thought and Language*. Cambridge, MA: MIT Press, 1986, ch. 7.

19. Victor Shklovsky, "The resurrection of the word". In L. Matejka

and K. Pomorska, eds, *Readings in Russian Poetics: Formalist and Structuralist Views*. Ann Arbor, MI: Ardis Press, 1978, p. 12 (original work published in 1914).

20. Velemir Khlebnikov, "Nasha Osnova" ("Our basis"). In *Sobranie Proizvedenii (Collected Works)*. Leningrad: Izd. Pisatelei, 1933, vol. 5, p. 229.

21. Vygotsky, *Thought and Language*, p. 251.

22. See Pomorska, *Russian Formalist Theory*, p. 84.

23. Thomas Mann, *Doctor Faustus*. New York: Knopf, 1948, pp. 191–2.

24. For a critical analysis of Formalist theories, see Peter Steiner, *Russian Formalism: A Metapoetics*. Ithaca, NY: Cornell University Press, 1984.

25. Boris Eichenbaum, "The theory of the formal method". In L. T. Lemon and M. J. Reis, eds, *Russian Formalist Criticism: Four Essays*. Lincoln, NE: University of Nebraska Press, 1965, p. 102 (original work published in 1927).

26. Roman Jakobson, *Noveishaia Russkaya Poeziya (Modern Russian Poetry)*. Prague, 1921, p. 11.

27. Roman Jakobson, "Linguistics and poetics". In T. Sebeok, ed., *Style in Langauge*. Cambridge, MA: MIT Press, 1960.

28. Vygotsky, *Thought and Language*, pp. 252–3.

29. Ibid, p. 221.

30. Victor Shklovsky, "Art as technique". In L. T. Lemon and M. J. Reis, eds, *Russian Formalist Criticism: Four Essays*. Lincoln, NE: University of Nebraska Press, 1965, p. 12 (original work published in 1917).

31. Victor Shklovsky, "Sterne's *Tristram Shandy*: Stylistic commentary." In Lemon and Reis, eds, *Russian Formalist Criticism*, pp. 27–8 (original work published in 1921).

32. Ibid, p. 29.

33. Ibid, pp. 56–7.

34. Yuri Tynyanov, "On literary evolution". In L. Matejka and K. Pomorska, eds, *Readings in Russian Poetics: Formalist and Structuralist Views*. Ann Arbor, MI: Ardis Press, 1978 (original work published in 1927).

35. Ferdinand de Saussure, *Course in General Linguistics*. New York: McGraw-Hill, 1959 (original work published in 1916).

36. Lev Jakubinsky, "O dialogicheskoi rechi" ("On verbal dialogue"). In L. V. Scherba, ed., *Russkaya Rech (Russian Speech)*. St Petersburg, 1923 (for an abridged translation see *Dispositio*, vol. 4, pp. 321–36. Ann Arbor, MI: University of Michigan Press, November 1979).

37. Vygotsky's essays on Jewish culture are listed in note 13. See also the review of Bely's *Petersburg* in *Letopis'*, No. 12, 1916; review of Ivanov's book of essays in *Letopis'*, No. 10, 1916; review of Merezhkovsky's play in *Letopis'*, No. 1, 1917.
38. *The Psychology of Art* was first published in Russian in 1965 in abridged form. Here I use the second, revised edition: Lev Vygotsky, *Psikhologiya Iskusstva* (*The Psychology of Art*). Moscow: Iskusstvo, 1968. All quotes from *The Psychology of Art* and from Vygotsky's Collected Papers were translated from Russian by the author.
39. Ibid, p. 15.
40. Ibid, p. 38.
41. Ibid, p. 75.
42. Roman Jakobson and Yuri Tynyanov, "Problemy izucheniya literatury i yazyka" ("Problems of the study of language and literature"), *Novy Lef*, No. 12, 1928.
43. Vygotsky, *Thought and Language*, ch. 5.
44. Vygotsky, *Psikhologiya Iskusstva*, p. 188.
45. Ibid, p. 194.
46. Ibid, p. 199.
47. Ibid, p. 202.
48. Ibid, p. 17.
49. Ibid, p. 95.
50. Ibid, p. 113.
51. Ibid, pp. 316–17.

CHAPTER TWO

The Psychology of Tragedy

VYGOTSKY'S essay on *Hamlet* is probably the most beautiful sample of his writing from the period before he became fully involved in academic psychology. The first sketch of this essay was written while he was attending the gymnasium, and the final draft in 1916.[1] This essay leaves the impression of an almost unbearable intensity of thought and feeling, the sort of intensity that can be achieved only in youth and which only very infrequently manages to express itself in literary form. Vygotsky's essay seems to express the entire culture of the early twentieth century, with its newly emerging art, literature and style of thinking. In this essay one finds, side by side, a reflection upon the problem of altered states of consciousness inspired by William James, a literary critique of the Russian poet-Symbolists, and innovations in the dramatic arts brought about by British theater director Gordon Craig. Moreover, there is also a deep presaging of a new type of thinking, associated nowadays with the philosophical hermeneutics of Martin Heidegger and Hans-Georg Gadamer, and the existentialism of Jean-Paul Sartre.

THE READER'S CRITIQUE AS EXISTENTIAL ANALYSIS

Written by Vygotsky as a twenty-year-old student, this essay continues to puzzle researchers and critics, who have found that it resists easy categorization such as "immature youthful work", or "the first step towards Vygotsky's future psychological theory". If the genre is easily recognizable (this is a long essay), the field is not. It is neither a scholarly literary analysis, nor a philosophical tract. It is more likely a case of phenomenological or existential psychology *par excellence*. Vygotsky himself defined it as a "reader's critique": "There is a sphere of immediate, non-scientific creativity, a sphere of subjective critique, and to this sphere all of the following belongs. This type of criticism is nurtured neither by scholarly knowledge, nor by philosophical thought, but by an immediate esthetic impression. This is an explicitly subjective critique which makes no claims [for objectivity]; it is a reader's critique".[2]

Vygotsky proceeded to show that a deliberately subjective critique is by no means an arbitrary one. The fact that such a critique is not constrained by the state of literary or psychological scholarship only amplifies its dependence on the analyzed text itself. This implies that the reader's critique is always an immanent one. It should not leave the sphere of the chosen work, and this work should not become a mere pretext for unrelated speculations. This type of critique is constrained by its own subjective perspective, and should not be turned into a survey of someone else's views: "While objectively accepting the equal rights and freedom of all interpretations, subjectively a critic must take into account only his own interpretation, which for him must be the only veritable one".[3]

The tacit assumption of the reader's critique is that the work under scrutiny has a superior artistic value. This critique is not interested in analytical muckraking, which is the prerogative of literary journalism. It must be clear from the above that the reader's critique is not an attempt at conclusive explanation; rather, it is a dialogue. When explanation is achieved there is no reason for further reading. A reader-critic accepts the irrational character of any work of art and has no intention of *explaining* it. Vygotsky quoted the Russian poet Appolon Grigoriev, who wrote: "My theory is obscure—dear reader—isn't it? But what can I do, it corresponds to the [obscurity] of the subject".[4] The obscurity of the reader's feelings borders on the mystical experience mentioned by James: "Most of us can remember the strangely moving power of passages in certain poems read when we were young, irrational doorways as they were through which the mystery of fact, the wildness and the pang of life, stole into our hearts and thrilled them. . . . We are alive or dead to the eternal inner messages of art according to whether we have kept or lost this mystical susceptibility".[5]

But while a professional critic is able to cast his or her feelings in precise words, the reader-critic is "mute"—the work of art remains figuratively inside his or her head. Between the reader's impressions and the inner word of those who read his or her critique there is the written word which the reader-critic often fails to master. That is why this type of critical writing has no value if it is detached from the subject of the study: "They are like notes indicating how to read the work of art, but they have no meaning apart from this work and its reading".[6]

All these principles for a reader's critique were formulated by Vygotsky as the justification for his own "dilettantic" analysis of *Hamlet*. The only required starting point for such an analysis is a good knowledge of the text of Shakespeare's tragedy. Vygotsky deliberately abandoned all attempts to explain *Hamlet*. Traditional critique sought to reveal the clear meaning of this tragedy, which, as has been always admitted, is rather obscure. Vygotsky turned the tables, and suggested considering this obscurity not as an obstacle, but as the essence of *Hamlet*. This tragedy's mysterious and puzzling character is not an enveloping cover that must be removed in order to make the tragedy visible. This mystery is the very core, the inner focus of the tragedy. This means that neither the characters nor the ideas could serve as a starting point for the interpretation of the tragedy, but the tragedy itself must be accepted as a *myth*. *Hamlet* is primarily the myth of Hamlet and all the characters, images and ideas are to be derived from this original mythological core. With this Vygotsky defined the subject of his essay as the "myth of the tragedy of Hamlet, Prince of Denmark. *Myth as a religious truth* (in an epistemological sense) *revealed in the work of art* (i.e. in the tragedy)".[7]

Vygotsky pointed to two different meanings of the ineffability of the essence of *Hamlet*. On the one hand, there is an essential obscurity about the tragedy which cannot be comprehended, but only experienced. And this ineffability should remain with us because without it *Hamlet* would cease to exist. On the other hand, there is the problem of expression inherent in the position of reader-critic who is only too aware of the imperfection of his or her words. This latter problem is due to the chasm between thought and words, between spiritual experience and its public expression. And yet a reader-critic is luckier than a lyric poet for whom there is no help beyond poetic genius. Unlike a poet, a reader-critic has the text of the tragedy, and a reader of his or her comments can attend to the tragedy's spiritual words *accented* by the experience of the critic. What the critic supplies to the reader is the *intonation* that corresponds to his or her own inner intonation.

Before proceeding to examine Vygotsky's critique of *Hamlet*, let us first pause for a moment and consider what is at stake here. Vygotsky's text is not a scholarly treatise but rather a case study of the inner experiences of a concerned person—Vygotsky himself—who encounters a cultural phenomenon of mythological proportions. In a word, this is an existential or phenomenological analysis of a borderline situation, that is, an inquiry into the heart of human life. To preserve this existential attitude Vygotsky cleared his text of all references and scholarly remarks and put them into supplementary notes. These notes give some idea of the intellectual background of Vygotsky's study which included, beyond Shakespeareana, James's analysis of mystical experiences, numerous critical works of the Russian Symbolists, the philosophical writings of Lev Shestov and Vladimir Soloviev, and the novels of Dostoevsky.

Vygotsky's existential analysis is based not on real-life situations, but on the specific text of the tragedy. For us this poses the question of what literature of Shakespearean caliber meant for Vygotsky. He alluded to this problem quoting Vecheslav Ivanov's maxim that in a mythological text a symbol is not allegory but reality. A text, therefore, is as real as life, or better; it is life. This line of thought linked Vygotsky to a wide circle of humanistic ideas dominant in the twentieth century. On the Russian scene his position could be compared to that of his contemporary Mikhail Bakhtin who developed a concept of verbal creativity based on the assumption that a text is the primary reality of human thought and feelings: "Verbal expression is never just a reflection of something existent beyond it which is given and 'finished off'. It always creates something absolutely new and unique, something which is always related to life values such as truth, goodness, beauty, etc."[8] A reader's critique is thus an expression of the capacity of human language taken at its highest point—in the interaction between the inner word of a concerned reader and a text of superior value. In terms of Western counterparts to Vygotsky's position one cannot but mention Ernst Cassirer and his inquiry into the mythological foundations of human consciousness for which the world is a phenomenon of pure expressivity.[9] And from here it is just one step to the philosophical hermeneutics of Martin Heidegger with its claim that "Language is the house of Being. Man dwells in this house. Those who think [*die Denkenden*] and those who create poetry [*die Dichtenden*] are the custodians of the dwelling".[10] One may also notice that in his later works Heidegger focused on the interpretation of selected poetic and philosophical texts in which "the tale of Being" is preserved.

Vygotsky's quest for the existential problems brought him to the issue of limits: the limits of life, and the limits of art. *Hamlet* became a testing ground for the problems of boundaries. What is a legitimate sphere of art, and where does it become a mythological foundation for life? Or, as his favorite poet Boris Pasternak put it, "And here the art ends,, and everything is just a breath of fate and ground". What does it mean to speak *sub specie mortis* versus *sub specie vita*? And thus the theme of the death and its comprehension in life. It seems significant that Vygotsky praised Freud's *Beyond the Pleasure Principle* exclusively because "it is important to master the notion of death".[11]

The complex structure of Vygotsky's essay requires a special expository technique. To achieve greater clarity I will assume the first person voice, speaking for Vygotsky, while placing my own comments in the notes.

THE TRAGEDY OF HAMLET

"In the daily circle of time, in the chain of ever changing light and dark hours there is one moment, the most obscure and indefinite—a fleeting edge between night and day."[12] At this moment all objects acquire a double existence—they continue their nocturnal life, but they already see the first light of day; the fragile cover of time is wearing off. This is the most gruesome and mysterious hour, fearful and enigmatic. This is the hour of *Hamlet*—the most obscure and enigmatic of all tragedies, the tragedy that causes the heart of the reader to sink and his head to become dizzy. *Hamlet* has a double life: the "surface story" is rather common and easy to comprehend, whereas the deeper tragedy is enigmatic and ineffable. *Hamlet* appeals to the very essence of the human tragic experience, and this experience is rooted in the very fact of human existence. Everything is tragic in human life: "the very fact of human life which is given to man, his solitude and loneliness in the universe, and his feeling of being thrown from the world of the unknown and abandoned in the world of knowledge thus belonging to both of them".[13] *Hamlet* touches the very essence of the human tragic experience and in this sense it is a *tragedy of tragedies*.

Hamlet reveals what is tragic in any tragedy. Any tragedy is ineffable, and this is particularly true of *Hamlet*. *Hamlet* includes a number of separate dramas and individual tragedies, each of them essentially incomplete and sketchy because all of them depend on the central focus which remains ineffable. Behind the surface drama there is the inner one, behind the overt dialogue there is an inner one which is conducted in silence. All of this makes *Hamlet* a borderline tragedy: its action is suspended on a web of invisible threads leading to what is happening *over there*, in the world of death.

> And therefore as a stranger give it welcome.
> There are more things in heaven and earth, Horatio
> Than are dreamt of in your philosophy. (1.5)

Hamlet himself might have spoken of a real, or better unreal drama, but he cannot for he is dead: "I am dead, Horatio." And Horatio will tell only a "surface story" about "carnal, bloody and unnatural acts", "casual slaughters" and "purposes mistook" (5.2). Hamlet, whose soul has become a depository for the "deep tragedy" dies and thus takes the key to *Hamlet* to his grave. This deep tragedy is not present in the text of *Hamlet* directly, but only as a shadow, as an echo.

Of course the issue of the tragic essence of life can be approached directly, but in this case *Hamlet* as a work of art would have to take a back seat: "This is a special topic, which is mystical and metaphysical (as is the meaning of the tragic experience itself), and which allows only a religious approach, thus transcending the esthetic perception of the tragedy".[14]

For a reader-critic the task is therefore to find the influence of this second meaning—which is indirect—in the overt text of the tragedy. This can be achieved by analyzing the plot of the tragedy and its characters and discovering what lies *between* them. *Hamlet* is strange because it lacks action, which seems to be a condition *sine qua non* of any tragedy. *Hamlet* is built on words, not action. The original cause of the drama—the murder of Hamlet's father—occurs before the tragedy begins, and only its last scene is filled with action. The rest is presented through the stories told by different characters. Thus *Hamlet* is a tragedy of projections. These projections are embodied in the theater within a theater of *The Mousetrap*, in Hamlet's verses, Ophelia's songs, and above all in the perspective of the entire tragedy as a *story* told afterwards by Horatio. So by its own structure this is a tragedy of reflections, shadows and echo.

Although the "surface story" is simple, the "surface tragedy" is not and should be reconstructed. First, the role of the Ghost is not that simple. The Ghost is not merely a technical device used to show Hamlet the truth about his father's death; this could be done by any other authoritative character. The Ghost is important because it becomes a real factor in the tragedy by bringing with it the horrors of Hell. It not only tells the real story of the past, but also serves as a harbinger of future misfortunes:

And even the like precurse of feared events,
As harbingers preceding still the fates
And prologue to the omen coming on,
Have heaven and earth together demonstrated
Unto our climatures and countrymen. (1.1)

It is remarkable that Horatio, the scholar, skeptic and representative of the rational mind, immediately recognizes the importance of the Ghost, and feels that the Ghost would like to speak to Hamlet. Horatio thus recognizes that the origins of the strange political and practical events of the present should be sought in the world of shadows. In terms of the tragedy's structure the Ghost is not a character but a dramatic device, a part of the plot: "The Ghost is an other-worldly source of the tragedy, it is a force acting from behind the grave, the link between two worlds, their mediator through which the other world influences what is happening in this one. . . . [The Ghost] dominates this actionless play by its own inactivity".[15]

Now, we should reassess the role of Hamlet or, more precisely, the role of the shadow of the Ghost in *Hamlet*. "Biographically", Hamlet is very much a person of the world. The favorite of the court, a scholar and a chevalier, he is versed in letters and dexterous with the sword. But from the moment we first encounter him, he already has a strong foreboding about the tragic events of the future. The shadow of the Ghost is already cast on his soul before he actually sees the Ghost. The vividness of this foreboding is extreme: "Seems, madam? Nay, it is. I know not 'seems' " (1.2). At the same time Hamlet's own mind, the rational, "daily" part of his self cannot explain his own irrational feelings. These feelings also seem strange and unnatural for others, even threatening in a certain unspecified way. Here the double life of the tragedy shows itself. The king and the queen ask Hamlet to stay in Elsinor and to abandon his idea of returning to Wittenberg. And Hamlet, who is psychologically prepared to disobey and to depart, suddenly agrees: "I shall in all my best obey you madam" (1.2). At this moment all the characters act according to the signals sent to them along the invisible wires from the world of shadows. The king unwittingly prepares his own downfall, while Hamlet carries the will of the Ghost who has not yet spoken to him. The double stage of the tragedy is already set up: the characters act or abstain from action apparently for their own psychological reasons, but actually because the tragedy as such demands it. Stylistically, the double stage is marked by heteroglossia, that is, a mixture of mundane and mystical elements in Hamlet's speech. On the surface there is small talk with Horatio about drinking, and even an ironic mentioning of the thrift in using funeral baked meats for the marriage tables. And at the same time: "But break my heart, for I must hold my tongue" (1.2).

Probably nowhere is the irrational feeling of Hamlet's second role so obvious as in his letter to Ophelia. "Thine evermore, most dear lady, whilst this machine is to him, Hamlet" (2.2). Hamlet honestly offers his love but only "whilst this machine"—what a wonderful word to express the entire determinism of the tragedy—obeys him. But once the mechanism of the tragedy is set in motion all Hamlet's promises become meaningless. This inner lack of freedom on the part of Hamlet is somehow felt by others. They explain it, however, in terms of the surface story. Thus Laertes tries to reason with Ophelia pointing to the fact that Hamlet's will "is not his own. For he himself is subject to his birth" (1.3). Laertes means of course the quite mundane fact of Hamlet's higher social position and responsibilities, but, as all other characters do, he unwittingly alludes to the second meaning of Hamlet's determination by his birth.

Finally the period of foreboding ends, Hamlet meets the Ghost, and he actually steps forward to approach it. Hamlet is not afraid in the ordinary sense, because

> Why, what should be the fear?
> I do not set my life at a pin's fee
> And for my soul, what can it do to that
> Being a thing immortal as itself? (1.4)

Horatio, however, warns him of another possibility, that the Ghost will deprive him of his "sovereignty of reason". And this is what actually happens, because Hamlet, after he meets the Ghost, is no longer the master of his life and reason. The tragedy itself steps in and Hamlet, escaping from the last bonds of his mundane life, rushes to the Ghost: "My fate cries out . . . I am called . . . Go on, I'll follow thee" (1.4). And Hamlet resolutely crosses the line between this world and the other.

His encounter with the Ghost, that is, with the other world, leads to his "second birth": "After that Hamlet for the rest of the tragedy is an entirely different person, he is no longer an ordinary man, he is born again".[16] This new state is seen already in Hamlet's first monologue.

Yea, from the table of my memory
I'll wipe away all trivial fond records,
All saws of books, all forms, all pressures past
That youth and observation copied there,
And thy commandment all alone shall live
Within the book and volume of my brain,
Unmixed with baser matter. . . . (1.5)

Hamlet changes physically and psychologically; his actions and his inaction are directed by this new meaning, as well as his speech. The encounter with the other world leads to the feeling of the abyss of time: "The time is out of joint" (1.5) In this development the path is from the psychological to the metaphysical: first comes the psychological trauma of encountering the other world, then the metaphysical problem of "a cursed spite that ever I was born to set it right" (1.5). The path is therefore from Hamlet's psychological tragedy to the metaphysical tragedy of Hamlet. The essence of this second tragedy is the fate of being born to serve as a link between two worlds. This is neither a choice nor a calling; it is something that is given. Hamlet physically and genetically is related to his father and this is a given, but he is also related to the world of the Ghost, and this is also a given.

All the characters recognize that Hamlet is no longer the same person, and thus the topic of madness is introduced. Although all agree that something is wrong with Hamlet's psyche, they hesitate to pronounce it a simple, "natural" madness. The sacred character of Hamlet's madness somehow transpires to them, and thus Polonius remarks on "A happiness that often madness hits on, which reason and sanity could not so prosperously be delivered of" (2.2).[17] Born again, Hamlet becomes a bearer of mystical experience and borderline existence, so his behaviour cannot but be strange or transformed. In a sense it is wrong to speculate whether his madness is genuine or fake, for Hamlet does not know this himself; he is no longer the master of his own reason. Hamlet's "pathological" melancholy is the melancholy of death. This is a reflection of the world of death onto the surface of the world of life. That is why melancholy always contains a shade of mystery. Hamlet starts looking at and commenting about life events *sub specie mortis*.

Hamlet's melancholy is complemented by his famous (or infamous) lack of action which renders the tragedy its peculiar pace. The mystical, other-worldly commitment of Hamlet is the key to his so-called passivity: "A mystic feels that his will is paralyzed; since there is something other-worldly in mystical conditions, and this 'something' represents their very essence, the element of will is missing . . .".[18] That is why Hamlet's lack of action is not strictly speaking a psychological trait of character, but a projection of what is required by the tragedy itself. And when Hamlet acts this is not an action caused by the awakened will, but again a reflection of the command coming from the other world: "This lack of will or submission to someone's command relates this condition to psychological automatism and the trance state of mediums".[19] Hamlet is a mystic because of his state of mind, and a medium because of his position in the tragedy. His case is that of a tragic automaton. The highest drama is achieved because Hamlet, being a medium of other-worldly forces, cannot comprehend his own lack of resolve. He may act as a tragic automaton, but he is a man and not a machine. His puzzlement expresses itself when he sees the troops led by Fortinbras, who is ready to slaughter thousands for a strip of land devoid of any significance, while he who has reason, strength and means still hesitates. After his trip to England and the killing of Rosencrantz and Guildenstern, Hamlet's mystical anticipation of the end reaches the ultimate vividness. But it is still not a state of making decisions, but the state of the highest alertness: "The readiness is all" (5.2).

Now a few words about the relationships between Hamlet and the other characters in the tragedy:

> If we compare Hamlet, his position and his role in the tragedy with the needle of a compass affected by the forces of a magnetic field, i.e. the invisible lines crossing the tragedy and guiding it, then the other characters should be compared to simple iron needles that found themselves in the same field. The guiding force is behind the scene and affects Hamlet, but through him it is also transmitted to others; as the needle of a compass magnetizes other needles, Hamlet infects others with the [feeling] of the tragedy.[20]

The roles of the other characters are not independent but reflect the central tragedy of Hamlet; they are the tragic victims of his drama. Ophelia is connected to Hamlet in two ways. She is the daughter of a tragically killed father, like Hamlet, like Fortinbras. All of them are related to the other world by this genetic link. But through her love for Hamlet she also becomes related to the specific tragedy of Hamlet's family, and the sin of Hamlet's mother finds its punishment in Ophelia's inability to be loved and to bear children. Ophelia comes the closest to the world of Hamlet and the result is predictable—insanity. She ceases to be the mistress of her own mind, and her death is as ambivalent as Hamlet's life—half-incident and half-suicide. Ophelia seems to impart to the tragedy the only position that is relevant to Hamlet's world, that of prayer. She prays for the soul of Hamlet, and this is the only position mortals may have when they encounter the enigma of death.

During the last scene all the characters become involved in the world of Hamlet. They are dying and already speak from "over there", that is *sub specie mortis*: "Here an impossible moment is taken: all these people, the Queen and Laertes, are already mortally wounded, poisoned, they *are not here* any more; they have just half an hour to live, and they act in this prolonged minute, which is the minute of dying".[21] The tragedy ends, death reigns over it, and only Horatio is left to tell the "surface story", the rest is silence.

The question is: to what does the above reading of the tragedy bring us? If we manage to exhaust—admittedly very subjectively and one-sidedly—the artistic or literary meaning of the tragedy, what is left beyond it? It becomes clear that *Hamlet* is neither a tragedy of characters, nor even a tragedy of fate, since in both cases the plot is determined by the actions of the heroes. It seems that the true subject of *Hamlet* is the eternal melancholy of human existence: "Melancholy is in the eternal solitude of man, in his own 'I', in that I am not you, and not others, that a man, a stone, and a planet are alone in the great silence of eternal night".[22] *Hamlet* starts where ordinary tragedy ends, in touching the original sorrow of Being. The meaning of the tragedy is thus in its religious sense: "The tragedy is a certain religion of life, i.e. a religion of life *sub specie mortis*, and thus the religion of death; that is why the tragedy exits into death and its meaning merges with the secrets of the grave".[23] *Hamlet* therefore marks the limits of art, and the beginning of religious types of experience. The feeling that "tragedy requires" a certain course of events is a religious feeling. When Hamlet speaks about the higher forces that govern our lives as well as the life of a sparrow, this is "the religion of a tragedy which has only one ritual—death; one virtue—readiness; and one prayer—mourning".[24] In a sense an esthetic reading of Shakespeare's tragedy is a "worried reading" because it stops before reaching the last "pages", for they are too fearful to be conceived of in such an art form. The silence and the mystery, therefore, are necessary complements of the text, they alone make the tragedy complete.

This returns us to the idea of *Hamlet* as a myth. Like almost all mythological heroes Hamlet is called upon to perform the most fundamental connection in human existence: the connection between Being and Nothingness. However, unlike the mythological heroes of antiquity, he is the hero of a Christian, and moreover a Renaissance, play. He is the hero in a culture that has already developed a highly elaborate Christian mythology, which has created such a hybrid of a ritual and an art as a passion play, and which has already started to demythologize itself via Renaissance anthropocentrism and psychologism. The depth of *Hamlet* is found exactly in this juxtaposition of the fundamental, mythological foundations of life which are beyond art, and the art form which presupposes an historically particular cultural and psychological experience.

Two comments should be made about the prospective and retrospective frameworks of Vygotsky's essay. With respect to its antecedents, Vygotsky's essay seems to have been influenced by the philosophy of "art as a mystery" espoused by the Russian Symbolists, and by the mythological interpretation of *Hamlet* put forward by Gordon Craig who staged it at the Moscow Art Theater.

The idea of the fusion of life and art, and the achievement of quasireligious salvation through art was enormously popular in Russia in the 1910s. Although one of the major theoretical proponents of this idea was the poet Vecheslav Ivanov, the composer Alexander Scriabin actually worked on a synthetic art form that was to include music, light effects and ritual movements and which with the force of mythological ritual was supposed to change the lives and mentality of the participants and viewers. In a broad sense, the whole Symbolist movement sought to interpret life as art, and not without mythological and religious overtones.

A more specific influence, acknowledged by Vygotsky in his essay, came from the revolutionary interpretation of *Hamlet* by the British theater director Gordon Craig.[25] Craig aimed at breaking the nineteenth-century stereotype of presenting *Hamlet* as a psychological drama of hesitation, and staged it along the lines of a passion play. The mythological element, as well as the portrayal of Hamlet as a mystic, was very much present in Craig's interpretation. Some details of Craig's production antecede Vygotsky's analysis: for example, Craig wanted Hamlet to be present in the background of each scene, arguing that he is the only real character of the tragedy while all the others are merely his reflections. Stage sets that were quite modernistic in design downplayed all psychological or concrete historical associations and elevated *Hamlet* to the level of a timeless mystery.[26]

The problem of the prospective influence of Vygotsky's essay is a more delicate matter. A direct impact is improbable, because there is no reason to believe that the essay, which remained unpublished until 1968, could have influenced anyone. At the same time there seems to exist an intriguing affinity between Vygotsky's perception of *Hamlet* and that of Boris Pasternak who was translating *Hamlet* into Russian in the 1930s. This affinity was somehow felt by V. V. Ivanov, the editor of Vygotsky's essay, who considered it necessary to use Pasternak's translation because in Vygotsky's manuscript all quotes were in English; moreover, he supplemented the text of the essay with Pasternak's own poem "Hamlet", which links the melancholy Prince to Christian mythology. In his brief remarks about the task of translating *Hamlet*, Pasternak espoused a philosophy that seemed congenial to that of Vygotsky.[27] He mentioned that rhythm plays a superior role in *Hamlet*, giving it a clairvoyant quality. Pasternak rejected the interpretation of *Hamlet* as a psychological drama of inactivity. "What is important is that chance has allotted Hamlet the role of judge of his own time and servant of the future. *Hamlet* is a drama of a high destiny, of a life devoted and preordained to an heroic task".[28] Pasternak's interpretation likened the myth of Hamlet to Christian myth, that Hamlet is carrying the will of the Other who sent him. The sense of the tragic in Hamlet is also infused with religious meaning. According to Pasternak, Hamlet's foreboding about his fate in its intensity of sorrow are on a par with Jesus' experience in the Garden of Gethsemane.

Most probably the affinity between Vygotsky's and Pasternak's perceptions of *Hamlet* is a reflection of an even deeper affinity in their cultural positions. Their "Hamlets" could not have been written either earlier or later—they are characteristic products of the cultural discoveries made during the first thirty years of this century. What had been "discovered", among other things, was the possibility of a direct dialogue with some fundamental mythological schemas conceived of not as relics of the past but as addressed to the present. Thus Pasternak took extraordinary liberties in his rendition of Shakespeare into Russian, arguing that since the original text gives an impression of life rather than of literature, the same should be true in the translation. This shared vision of twentieth-century culture *vis-à-vis* not only Shakespeare but also the culture of the past in general may explain what appears to be an even more mysterious "influence" of Vygotsky on Pasternak's own poetry and prose.[29]

THE CRISIS

The essay on *Hamlet* marked a high point in Vygotsky's early career as a humanistic writer. In 1917, the year of the Russian Revolution, he graduated from Moscow University and returned to his native town of Gomel. There he experienced the full measure of the misery of the Civil War and famine. For a while he was employed as a teacher in a local school, and later obtained a position as lecturer at a newly established teacher's college. There is circumstantial evidence that sometime between 1921 and 1923 Vygotsky experienced a serious crisis. His preoccupation with the theme of death, which revealed itself so poignantly in the essay on *Hamlet*, had very real roots in his own life. There was a history of tuberculosis in Vygotsky's family and he experienced one of his first attacks in 1920. A friend remembered that Vygotsky was quite pessimistic about his prospects and had collected his manuscripts to be delivered to his literary mentor Yuli Aichenwald for possible posthumous publication.[30] The irony of the situation was that while Vygotsky recovered from his attack, Aichenwald was exiled from Russia in 1922 with a group of pre-Revolutionary intellectuals considered undesirable by the new regime. One may assume that Aichenwald's exile was a severe blow for Vygotsky; it was a symbol of the fate of the humanistic intelligentsia with whom Vygotsky presumably identified himself. After all, only a few years earlier Vygotsky had written that "You cannot build the life of a nation on the foundation of positivism and rationalism" and that "culture cannot be created by the calculated actions of political parties".[31]

Aichenwald's position was very similar: he abhorred any political regulation of an author's works and was a severe critic of the pragmatic view of literature as an instrument of social change. Aichenwald earned his reputation primarily because of his extremely popular book *Silhouettes of Russian Authors*.[32] Several ideas advanced in this book undoubtedly had a profound impact on young Vygotsky. One of these ideas, which found its way into *The Psychology of Art*, is that the sociological approach to literature is misleading at best. "We were taught", wrote Aichenwald, "to consider a work of art as a means of smuggling political ideas under the innocent flag [of literature]".[33] For Aichenwald, the author is the center of an historical epoch rather than a sponge that absorbs its social problems. This position is related to another, that of the relationship between art and life, word and deed: "Art creates life, rather than reflecting it. Literature antecedes reality; word comes ahead of deed".[34] Vygotsky later struggled with the same problem in his *Thought and Language*, and came to the conclusion that although action precedes word, it is only in a sense of developmental precedent, and not in terms of metaphysical superiority.

Vygotsky's ideas about the unconscious as a true source of creativity could also have come from Aichenwald, who claimed that the unconscious is the major channel of artistic creativity. The acceptance of the leading role of the unconscious casts doubt on the rationalistic notion of the author as an omniscient interpreter and as best critic of his or her own writings: "Usually the author is not the best of his own readers. He is not always capable of translating his own 'poetry' into 'prose' [of critique]".[35] According to Aichenwald the esthetic vision of the world is inherent in the human mind: "Our own psyche has an esthetic character. The human being is inherently artistic. Who is not creative, who is not original in his own dreams?".[36] This fact creates a rather special type of relationship between the author and the reader, between the text as it is written and as it is experienced: "The author and the reader are mutually corresponding notions. . . . In fact, the author as some definite, objective and conclusive entity does not exist. He does not have a life of his own; he lives with us and in us".[37]

Aichenwald's thesis is important for understanding certain parallels in the thinking of Vygotsky and Bakhtin, each of whom, in his own way, struggled with the problem of the universality of the word versus its seemingly idiosyncratic origin in the mind of the author (see Chapter Five).

Apart from the symbolic importance of Aichenwald's exile, Vygotsky made a "gesture" of his own: he changed his family name. For a person so preoccupied with the importance of signs and symbols to human behavior this could not have been a merely technical operation. The original spelling of his family name was Vygodsky, and his numerous relatives retained this spelling. Lev, however, changed it to Vygotsky. He justified this by his discovery of the true origin of his family name, which he claimed originally derived from the name of the village Vygotovo.[38] This act seems to be symbolic of the way Vygotsky was seeking self-identification both as a person and also as a scholar. On the surface the change of name is a rather typical way for a young man to set himself apart, to distance himself from his past and from his family. But the justification Vygotsky offered is characteristic of him: he was not interested in severing ties with the past; rather, he was interested in re-establishing a connection with the real past rather than being associated with its habitually accepted image. And this is also true of Vygotsky as a thinker: Vygotsky's whole psychological system appears to have been an attempt to build a *new* system through a careful analysis of the fundamental and in this sense truly *traditional* problems of psychology. This quality of Vygotsky's scholarship becomes particularly pronounced when viewed against the background of that of his contemporaries, reflexologists and "Marxist psychologists" who were ready to change any names and to ignore any past in their chase for the utopian new science and society. What later distinguished Vygotsky was his ability to accept the task as it was posed by the turbulent Soviet social reality of the 1920s, but to approach it with methods informed by the Western intellectual tradition.

If there had been a crisis in Vygotsky's life between 1921 and 1923 its most explicit reflection could be found in *Educational Psychology*.[39] This textbook, according to Luria, was written in exactly those years and included lectures delivered by Vygotsky at Gomel's teachers' college. The textbook leaves one with an uneasy feeling that it is a "chimeric" work. One part of it is hardly compatible with another, and the author seems to be speaking in a number of different voices. The book was intended as an introductory psychology text for a new generation of Soviet teachers, those who were to replace the pre-Revolutionary educational establishment. Certain sections of the text, particularly those devoted to human creativity, are indistinguishable in style and content from *The Psychology of Art*. Other sections look like a straightforward and rather impersonal review of European and American experimental psychology. Yet another section presents the Pavlovian theory of conditional reflexes in apologetic terms, claiming that reflexes ought to become the foundation of the new psychology. In addition, the text is occasionally peppered with quotations from the influential party leader and Marxist theoretician, Leon Trotsky. At times the text is so un-Vygotskian that it looks like a page lifted from a popular communist propaganda brochure. For example, in explaining that educational systems reflect the class interests of the dominant groups in society, Vygotsky suggested that these systems should be studied from the class position.

Educational Psychology will probably remain an enigma. Why should Vygotsky have published it in 1926 when his views on reflexology and the uses of Marxism seemed to be incompatible with those espoused in the text? Does it mean that he was not fully responsible for the publication? Was this text the result of an early compromise between Vygotsky as a scholar and Vygotsky as a young man who wanted to survive in the new social environment? All these questions will probably remain unanswered, since there is little hope that the last survivors of that era will share with us their memories.

NOTES

1. According to V. V. Ivanov, who prepared Vygotsky's manuscript for publication, the final draft was written between February 14 and March 28, 1916. It was first published in Lev Vygotsky, *Psikhologiya Iskusstva* (*The Psychology of Art*), pp. 340–496. Moscow: Iskusstvo, 1968.
2. Vygotsky, *Psikhologiya Iskusstva*, p. 342.
3. Ibid, p. 336.
4. Ibid, p. 348.
5. William James, *The Varieties of Religious Experience*. London: Longman, 1906, p. 383.
6. Vygotsky, *Psikhologiya Iskusstva*, p. 350.
7. Ibid, p. 353.
8. Mikhail Bakhtin, *Estetika Slovesnogo Tvorchestva* (*The Esthetics of Verbal Creativity*). Moscow: Iskusstvo, 1979, p. 299 (original work written in the 1920s).
9. See Ernst Cassirer, *The Philosophy of Symbolic Forms*. New Haven, CT: Yale University Press, 1953.
10. Martin Heidegger, quoted in George Steiner, *Heidegger*. Brighton, UK: Harvester Press, 1978, p. 127.
11. Lev Vygotsky, *Sobranie Sochinenii* (*Collected Papers*). Moscow: Pedagogika, 1982. Vol. 1, p. 336. Vygotsky also wrote an introduction to the Russian translation of Freud's *Beyond the Pleasure Principle*.
12. Vygtosky, *Psikhologiya Iskusstva*, p. 362.
13. Ibid, p. 363. This phrase reads as a catalogue of twentieth-century existentialist ideas, from the "abandonment"—a Sartrean term—to the idea of life as "given" to man developed in the philosophy of Max Scheller.
14. Ibid, p. 368.
15. Ibid, p. 385.
16. Ibid, p. 409. The concept of "second birth" is borowed by Vygotsky from James's *The Varieties of Religious Experience*, p. 157. In introducing the notion of second birth James refers to Lev Tolstoy's religious conversion at the age of fifty, and quotes an appropriate paragraph from Tolstoy's autobiographical writing.

Vygotsky also mentions several characters in Dostoevsky's novels who discuss the issue of the human experience of the other world. This experience is incompatible with originary psychology and even physiology. Kirillov, from Dostoevsky's novel *The Possessed*, says that to experience such a state a person should change physically, and that human childbearing has no sense in view of this experience. This seems to parallel Hamlet's words to Ophelia that there should be no more marriages and childbirth.

17. Vygotsky mentions that in Dostoevsky's novels insanity is closely related to the subject of "messages" from the other world. Consider the following episode:

> They say, "You are ill, so what appears to you is only unreal fantasy." But that's not strictly logical. I agree that ghosts only appear to the sick, but that only proves that they are unable to appear except to the sick, not that they don't exist. . . . Ghosts are as it were shreds and fragments of other worlds, the beginning of them. A man in health has, of course, no reason to see them, because he is above all a man of this earth and is bound for the sake of completeness and order to live only this life. But as soon as one is ill, as soon as the normal earthly order of the organism is broken, one begins to realize the possibility of another world . . . (Feodor Dostoevsky, *Crime and Punishment*. New York: Random House, 1947, p. 283)

18. Vygotsky, *Psikhologiya Iskusstva*, p. 431.

19. Ibid, p. 431. Here, in addition to James's influence, there seems to be a clear reference to Pierre Janet's study of psychological automatism, *L'Automatisme psychologique*. Paris: Alcan, 1889.

20. Vygotsky, *Psikhologiya Iskusstva*, pp. 459–60.

21. Ibid, p. 488.

22. Ibid, p. 492.

23. Ibid, p. 494.

24. Ibid, p. 495.

25. Ibid, p. 537.

26. For more on Craig's *Hamlet*, see Laurence Senelick, *Gordon Craig's Moscow Hamlet*. Westport, CT: Greenwood Press, 1982.

27. Boris Pasternak, "Translating Shakespeare". In Boris Pasternak, *I Remember*. New York: Pantheon, 1959.

28. Ibid, p. 131.

29. The following remarks are intended as a preliminary and plainly speculative analysis of the deeper affinity between the cultural positions of Vygotsky and Pasternak. The original impulse toward such an analysis was given by the fact that not only do Vygotsky's and Pasternak's perceptions of *Hamlet* seem to have much in common, but that Pasternak's major work *Dr Zhivago* (New York:

Pantheon, 1958) in some mysterious way realized the esthetic and existential principles outlined in Vygotsky's unpublished essay.

The fate of *Zhivago* bears a peculiar resemblance to that of *Hamlet*. Both works are rather obscure, offering no easy interpretation, baffling critics and readers alike. Both have a deceptively simple "surface story". In the case of Pasternak's novel this is a story of the loves and misfortunes of a physician and poet named Zhivago during the Civil War of 1918–22. Critics, particularly in the West, tended to misinterpret *Zhivago* as a political novel about the atrocities of the Russian Revolution. There is no doubt that the political scandal caused by the publication of *Dr Zhivago* abroad, its prolonged ban in the Soviet Union, and the punitive actions against Pasternak only reinforced this superficial interpretation.

If one looks at *Zhivago* through the lenses of Vygotsky's *Hamlet*, however, an entirely different drama emerges. First, *Zhivago* is filled with endless coincidences, with characters meeting or being related to each other in the most artificial ways. This usually baffles and annoys the readers who takes *Zhivago* for a realistic, psychological novel. If, however, one considers *Zhivago* as a myth, as a tragedy with a will of its own, all these coincidences would be justified. As in *Hamlet*, they are not a product of the characters' activities but a projection of the spirit of the tragedy itself.

Second, as in Vygotsky's *Hamlet*, *Zhivago* has a double, if not a triple structure. The main text portrays the lives of the characters in what seems to be a quite realistic setting. But this prose is complemented by the second text level consisting of poems allegedly written by Dr Zhivago. One needs not have great analytical skills to realize that the poems provide the key to the understanding of the prose. The poems, however, far from serving as a mere lyrical accompaniment to the prose, have their own themes and subjects. They alternate between lyrical themes and the evangelical story; the circle of poems starts with "Hamlet" and ends with "the Garden of Gethsemane". Looking for the keys to the main text, one should not miss the message in the first chapter of *Zhivago* in which through one of the characters an original version of Orthodox Christian ideology is presented. Both "keys" provide a connection to the hidden second meaning of the novel.

Finally, the so-called realistic prose of *Zhivago* is not very realistic after all. It is rather strange, if not careless if judged by the canon of the classical psychological novel. Many events are simply named and situations sketched without elaboration. This allowed some harsh critics such as Vladimir Nabokov to dismiss

Zhivago as a sloppy work devoid of any esthetic value. From the point of view espoused here, this predominance of paradigmatic "signposts" over the syntagmatic cohesion of the narrative is not a defect, but a deliberate literary device aimed at reaching the outer limits of the novelistic genre. *Zhivago* is not only a religious, but also an experimental novel. In his "experiment" Pasternak attempted to reach for the personal, nonliterary memory of his readers. The unit of the reader's apperception in this novel is not a literary episode, but a relevant episode from the real life of the reader. That is why many things and events are simply named. Pasternak is not interested in describing them, but just in pressing the necessary key on the keyboard of the reader's own memory. The esthetic effect of *Zhivago* is then achieved by reliving the reader's life experiences cued by Pasternak's prose, freshly accented by religious themes provided by Zhivago's poetry and philosophical passages. The reader's own experiences provide the "material" for his or her reading of the novel. This "material" is then decoded or accented with the help of poetic and religious keys supplied by Pasternak. The reader thus becomes a participant in the novel, to the same extent that a true believer participates in the passion play, his or her life being "accented" by the Christian myth. One may notice that the dialectic of material and form outlined above corresponds to their interpretation in Vygotsky's *The Psychology of Art*.

The above schema for reading *Zhivago* along the lines suggested by Vygotsky's analysis of *Hamlet* is only preliminary, and it certainly does not aspire to a comprehension of the whole of Pasternak's novel. *Zhivago* is much richer than the literary and philosophical devices mentioned here. The reason for this lengthy note was to suggest that Vygotsky's analysis of *Hamlet* is not a personal document of Vygotsky's youth, and not even an original sample of existential analysis, but a multidimensional work that touches the main "power lines" of twentieth-century thought and artistic imagination.

30. See Semion Dobkin, "Ages and days". In K. Levitin, *One is not Born a Personality*. Moscow: Progress, 1982, p. 36.

31. Lev Vygotsky, "Abodim Hoinu" ("We worked as slaves"). *Novy Put'*, Nos 11–12, 1917, p. 9.

32. See Yuli Aichenwald, *Siluetty Russkikh Pisatelei (Silhouettes of Russian Authors)*. The Hague: Mouton, 1969. Vygotsky probably read the revised edition of 1911, which included a theoretical introduction.

33. Ibid, p.12

34. Ibid, p. 8.
35. Ibid, p. 22.
36. Ibid, p. 6.
37. Ibid, p. 19.
38. See Dobkin, "Ages and days", p. 24.
39. Lev Vygotsky, *Pedagogicheskaia Psikhologiya (Educational Psychology)*. Moscow: Rabotnik Prosvescheniya, 1926. See also Alexander Luria, "Biographical note on L. S. Vygotsky". In L. Vygotsky, *Mind in Society*. Cambridge, MA: Harvard University Press, 1978; Mikhail Yaroshevsky, *Lev Vygotsky*. Moscow: Progress, 1989, p. 72.

CHAPTER THREE

The Crisis in Psychology

L ITTLE IS KNOWN about the last years Vygotsky spent in
Gomel. His job at the teachers' college apparently drew
him closer to academic psychology, and some connections were
probably established with colleagues in Moscow or Leningrad.
Still it is not clear what prepared Vygotsky's appearance at the
Second Psychoneurological Congress convened on January 6,
1924 in Leningrad. Most probably his independent work had
simply reached a stage when it was imperative for him to share
his ideas with an audience. Taking into account the less than
established status of Soviet psychology at that time it was not
impossible for a young teacher interested in psychological problems to get his paper accepted at the congress.

In this chapter I first discuss the paper "Methodology of
reflexological and psychological research", which Vygotsky presented to the congress, and after that I will provide some background information on Soviet psychological doctrines dominant
at the time.[1] Vygotsky's central thesis was simple: if reflexology
was to become a general theory of behavior it must first accept
the existence of consciousness and must incorporate the methods
of psychological investigation. In the process of such incorporation the demarcation between reflexology and psychology will
disappear, and a new scientific psychology of mind *and* behavior

will emerge: "Mind [*psichika*] without behavior does not exist, but behavior without mind does not exist either, because they are one".[2]

Vygotsky pointed out that while reflexology made an important contribution to the study of the foundations of behavior, its claims for explaining more complex forms of behavior as aggregates of conditional reflexes is schematic and declarative. He further revealed the lack of consistency in the reflexological doctrine, which admits the spoken word as one possible "response" of an organism, but denies the existence of thought. Vygotsky reminded his opponents that the founding fathers of Russian reflexology, Ivan Sechenov and Vladimir Bekhterev, had suggested that thought is nothing but a reflex that is inhibited after it travels two-thirds of its way. So if it is legitimate to study a fully expressed verbal reflex, why is it wrong to study it in an inhibited state?

Another weakness in the reflexological doctrine lies in its refusal to consider a systemic relationship between different groups of reflexes. The expression of reflex in a form of movement or endocrine secretion inevitably becomes a stimulus for another system of reflexes. So the real subject of "enlightened" reflexology is the functional organization of different systems of reflexes and the mechanism of their "communication". In this context the notion of thought can be rendered in a form potentially acceptable for reflexologists: "The act of thought, from our point of view, is not a reflex, i.e. it cannot serve as a stimulus, but it is a transmitter mechanism between [different] systems of reflexes".[3] Vygotsky here apparently approached one of the aspects of thought, namely thought as an *organization* of behavioral acts.

From the theoretical limitations of reflexology, Vygotsky turned to methodological problems. He reiterated that it is wrong to ignore such obvious components of human conduct as speech and thinking. This did not mean, however, that behavioral science must surrender to introspective methodology. Drawing on his favorite criminological metaphor, Vygotsky explained: "The human subject is no longer a witness who testifies about the crime he has witnessed, he himself is a perpetrator and—what is more important—the perpetrator who is observed at the very moment of the crime".[4] So instead of ignoring the phenomenon of consciousness, as reflexologists do, and instead of taking the subject's introspective report as a true copy of conscious processes, as introspectionists did, Vygotsky suggested placing the subject in such experimental circumstances as would provoke an observable manifestation of inner mental processes.

We do not know how many participants of the congress were swayed by Vygotsky's arguments. The subsequent reviews were not exactly favorable.[5] But it appears that Vygotsky's challenge left a deep impression. Alexander Luria remembers:

> Instead of choosing a minor theme, as might befit a young man of twenty-eight speaking for the first time to a gathering of the greybeards of his profession, Vygotsky chose the difficult theme of the relation between conditional reflexes and man's conscious behavior. . . . Although he failed to convince everyone of the correctness of his view, it was clear that this man from the small provincial town in western Russia was an intellectual force who would have to be listened to. It was decided that Vygotsky should be invited to join the young staff of the new, reorganized Institute of Psychology in Moscow.[6]

In the fall of 1924 Vygotsky moved to Moscow and found himself close to the epicenter of controversies that were shaking Russian psychology in the 1920s.

THE PSYCHOLOGIES OF THE 1920S

The Moscow Institute of Psychology, which Vygotsky was about to join, was founded by Georgy Chelpanov in 1912.[7] It was the only institution in Russia dedicated exclusively to research and training in the field of psychology. Chelpanov served as the director of the Institute from the moment it was founded until 1923 when he was dismissed by the new Marxist leadership. This dismissal and an attack on Chelpanov's psychological views were very much talked about at that time.

Chelpanov had appeared on the Russian psychological scene in the 1890s as an enthusiastic advocate of psychology as an independent empirical science. He identified materialistic reductionism and traditional metaphysical psychology as two major foes of the new, empirical psychology. His popularly acclaimed *Brain and Soul* (1900) contained a systematic critique of nineteenth-century physiological reductionism, including critical remarks directed at the leader of Russian reflexology, Ivan Sechenov. For a positive program Chelpanov took as a model the psychology of Wilhelm Wundt and his students at Würzburg University.[8] Chelpanov will probably be remembered not so much for his views and writings, as for his efforts on behalf of academic psychology in Russia. He worked tirelessly to establish first a psychology program within the framework of the philosophy department at Moscow University, and then to raise funds for the Institute of Psychology. Chelpanov's liberal views and pluralistic attitude greatly influenced the activity of the Institute. Studies that bridged Wundt's mental chronometry with American functionalism and ultimately behaviorism were conducted by one of Chelpanov's students, Konstantin Kornilov; while another, Gustav Schpet, inquired into Husserl's phenomenological method, Humboldtian cross-cultural studies of language, and sketched an outline of philosophical hermeneutics. Chelpanov did not find it necessary to change his views with the coming of the Revolution. In the years of Civil War (1918–22) he managed to preserve the Institute, which was no easy task, and to keep some studies going.

The first post-Revolutionary Psychoneurological Congress (1923), which was organized with Chelpanov's active support, indicated that Russian psychology had entered a new era. Chelpanov's views on psychology as presented at the congress were the same—he advocated an independent, empirical psychology free from physiological or philosophical reductionism. This time, however, Chelpanov faced formidable opponents: reflexologists and the new "Marxist psychologists" whose challenge was not confined to academic issues but extended toward the subject of the social and political usefulness of psychology. Kornilov presented a blueprint for Marxist psychology in which he claimed that "Marxism fundamentally breaks ties with the mentalism which infiltrated the whole body of modern psychology. Marxism aims not only at the explanation of the human mind but also at its mastery".[9] Reflexologist Vladimir Bekhterev, who had always attacked what he perceived to be the subjectivism of

Wundtean psychology, continued his charge. This time, however, his call for an "objective psychology" was perceived in a new ideological framework, that of a fundamental dichotomy of "materialists" and "idealists". While Bekhterev and Kornilov were judged to be materialists, Chelpanov with his Wundtean program and his use of the introspective method was inevitably branded as an "idealist". If one adds to this that many of Chelpanov's former colleagues, professors of Moscow and St Petersburg universities, had been exiled to the West in 1922, it comes as no surprise that soon after the 1923 congress Chelpanov was relieved of his duties as director of the Institute.

With Chelpanov's departure, reflexology and "Marxist psychology" became dominant trends in Soviet behavioral science.[10] Even before the Revolution reflexologists had been suspicious of the kind of psychology advocated by Chelpanov, but their opposition had been confined to the framework of purely academic debates. Pavlov, who had banned the use of mentalist terms in his laboratory, had welcomed the establishment of Chelpanov's Institute and sent his congratulations. After the Revolution, reflexology received a not unexpected boost because it was perceived to be compatible more with the materialist dialectics of Marxism than with Chelpanov's inquiry into the workings of the mind. Reflexology, however, encompassed a number of mutually antagonistic scientific trends, the best known of which is Pavlov's theory of conditional reflexes.[11] Working on the salivary reflex in dogs and being primarily concerned with the brain mechanisms of reflex-like behavior, Pavlov had been a world-renowned scientist since 1904 when he was awarded the Nobel Prize. Although Pavlov did not work with human subjects, on a number of occasions he suggested that the whole domain of human behavior can—at least potentially—be subsumed under the notion of higher nervous activity: "Conditional reflexes are phenomena of common and widespread occurrence: their establishment is an integral function in everyday life. We recognize them in ourselves or animals under such names as 'education', 'habits', and 'training', and all of these are really nothing more than the results of the establishment of new nervous connections during the postnatal experience of an organism".[12] In the 1920s Pavlov, still at the stage of theoretical generalization rather than experimental study, extended the notion of reflex toward the sphere of verbal activity.[13]

If Pavlov was ready to make such broad generalizations, his students, both genuine and self-styled, went much farther in claiming an exclusive status for reflexological research. They argued that the theory of conditional reflexes was not only the best scientific approach to human behavior, but that it was best prepared to carry on a radical transformation of human behavior envisaged by the Revolutionary idea of a "new Soviet man".

In their effort to dominate the field of behavioral science, Pavlovians were opposed by the students of Vladimir Bekhterev. Bekhterev—neurologist, psychiatrist, and a man of many other talents—had been Pavlov's major rival since the turn of the century. Unlike Pavlov whose scientific agenda, at least in the beginning, was rather narrow, Bekhterev always sought to capture human behavior in its multifaceted manifestations. His laboratory was the first to experiment with human "associative" motor reflexes. And Bekhterev immediately realized some applications of reflexological methodology, such as tests for a simulated or "functional" deafness, blindness and anesthesia. Beyond the experimental study of reflexes, Bekhterev inquired into the mechanism of hysterical neuroses, developed a system for the clinical and experimental use of hypnosis, and ventured into the then obscure fields of social behavior, industrial psychology and the psychology of art.

A charismatic leader, Bekhterev established in 1907 the Psychoneurological Institute in St Petersburg which combined the function of a college with that of a research center where studies ranged from theory of personality to neuropsychology. Although widely eclectic in his methods, Bekhterev insisted on what he called an "objective" study of human behavior defined in terms of stimuli and responses: "The new science which we call reflexology has for its aim the study of personality by means of objective observation and experiment, and the registration of all its external manifestations and their external causes, present and past, which arise from the social environment and even from the framework of inherited character. In other words, the aim of reflexology is the strictly objective study, in their entirety, of the correlations of the human being with the environment . . . ".[14] He dismissed the method of introspection as unreliable, and was suspicious of consciousness, arguing that many behavioral acts are performed unconsciously. Bekhterev attracted even more followers than Pavlov, and they were only too eager to use Bekhterev's reflexology as a tool for the revolutionary transformation of human behavior.

Finally, Konstantin Kornilov, whose pre-Revolutionary career had not been spectacular, came to the scene as the author of the new Marxist psychology. The focus of his research was the human sensory-motor reaction, which he explained by mixing the elements of what Wundt called "mental chronometry", with the ideas of American functionalists and the nascent principles of behaviorism. Unlike many other psychologists, however, Kornilov had been a Communist Party member—a difference that apparently became quite important after the Revolution. Without changing in any significant way the experimental methods he employed, Kornilov embarked upon an ambitious campaign of creating the new "Marxist psychology". The idea itself was not unique: in the 1920s many enthusiasts of the Marxist method made many hasty attempts to create a "Marxist biology", a "Marxist physics" and a "Marxist agricultural science". The recipe in most cases was very similar: some existing experimental methods were combined with a number of quotes from Marx, Engels or Lenin, and the resultant text was presented as an example of a new science.

Kornilov surveyed the classic Marxist texts and selected what from his point of view was relevant to psychology. He pointed out that Marxism, though built on the foundation of Hegelian dialectics, decisively breaks with the Hegelian idealist interpretation of development as the unfolding of the Mind.[15] Asserting the philosophical materialism of the new psychology, Kornilov identified its major foes as the classical metaphysical idealism of Hegel, as well as the modern "pseudomaterialism" of Ernst Mach and Richard Avenarius. Kornilov took "the law of the transformation of quantity into quality", "the mutual penetration of opposites", and "the law of the negation of negation" as the fundamental laws of Marxist philosophy. He then used psychological examples to underscore the validity of these laws. He claimed, for example, that the qualitative changes in perception of "wholes" described in Gestalt psychology reflect the law of the relationship between quality and quantity.[16]

79

Unlike the radical reflexologists, Kornilov retained the notion of consciousness in his system: "In living creatures with highly organized nervous systems, we find the clear expression of those internal reactions of the activities of the brain which we call consciousness, thought, psyche. . . . Thus, that which we call consciousness or psyche from this point of view is indistinguishable in its nature from matter . . . and is not more than one of the properties of the most highly organized matter".[17] At the same time, Kornilov pointed out that psychological phenomena are not identical with physiological processes, and concluded that psychology should be a unity of "subjective and objective". Kornilov suggested that "reaction", defined as a response of the organism to physical as well as social stimuli, should be considered as a methodological unit of psychological research. Building on his pre-Revolutionary work, Kornilov distinguished between the rate of reactions, their intensity and their form, to which he added the "social significance" of the reaction.

Kornilov's "reform" in psychology resulted in the abandonment of the terminology of mental states and processes and in the almost ritualistic clearing of the psychological house of all vestiges of Chelpanov's past. This is how Luria described this bizarre process:

> For a while the reform [*perestroika*] of psychology was taking two forms, renaming and removing. Perception, as far as I remember, we started calling the reception of a signal for reaction, attention [became] the limitation of reaction, memory—the preservation with reproduction of reaction, emotions—emotional reactions. Wherever possible (and impossible) we added the term "reaction" honestly believing that we were doing something serious and important. At the same time we were constantly moving desks from one room to another; I clearly remember that when moving a desk upstairs I believed that exactly in this way we would reform [psychological] work and create a new foundation for Soviet psychology.[18]

THE PROBLEM OF CONSCIOUSNESS

Vygotsky's presentation at the Psychoneurological Congress of 1924, when judged against this background, was bold indeed. Vygotsky's program for the study of consciousness was further developed in the paper published the following year in a volume edited by Kornilov, entitled *Psychology and Marxism*.[19] On the first page of this paper Vygotsky defined the problem that would remain the focus of his entire career as a psychologist, the problem of what is uniquely human behavior: "Among all these [reflexological] principles we find not even one psychological law of human behavior that would express the relationship or interdependence of phenomena that would characterize the uniqueness of human behavior".[20]

To understand what is unique in human behavior, Vygotsky suggested considering the *historical* character of human behavior and learning: "Man makes use not just of physically inherited experience: throughout his life, his work and his behavior draw broadly on the experience of former generations, which is not transmitted at birth from father to son. We may call this historical experience".[21]

The second component is the *social* nature of human experience. The social character of human existence and the availability of interpersonal communication allow an individual to rely on the almost infinite pool of experiences of others. This reliance, however, changes the entire nature of what is called "individual experience". Individual experience in a narrow sense becomes just one element in the field of experiences available for the individual. We literally live in the experiences of others. Speech plays the decisive role in this transformation of the experiential field. Speech is a special kind of stimulus that can be reproduced by individuals and thus through it they can identify themselves with others. "In a broad sense", wrote Vygotsky, "speech is the source of social behavior and consciousness".[22] This discussion had a direct bearing on the old psychological problem of knowing another person's mind. Vygotsky suggested that "We are aware of ourselves, for we are aware of others, and in the same way as we know others; and this is as it is because we in relation to ourselves are in the same [position] as others are to us".[23] With this statement Vygotsky arrived at his thesis of the primacy of the social component in psychological development: "The social dimension of consciousness is primary in time and in fact. The individual dimension of consciousness is derivative and secondary".[24]

The last component of uniquely human behavior is its *twofold* nature as a mental activity and as an external action. Vygotsky pointed out that while animals adapt to their environment, man actively adapts the environment to himself; hence the importance of work and tool action. What distinguishes the human use of tools from that of birds who build nests and bees who construct honeycombs is that while the latter follow an unchangeable instinct, humans follow in their overt activity a constantly changing mental design. In this context Vygotsky recalled Marx's saying that even a poor architect differs from the best bee in that he first envisages the project in his mind. The twofold nature of human behavior which involves the inner, mental plane as well as the outer, actional plane, not only requires consciousness, but actually posits it as a fundamental premise of human behavior.

In developing his ideas Vygotsky relied on intellectual sources which look rather unexpected in the volume *Psychology and Marxism*. Vygotsky's points of reference were William James, Sigmund Freud, neo-Kantian philosopher Paul Natorp, and physiologist C. S. Sherrington. Vygotsky approvingly referred to the psychoanalytic attempt to account for the inner processes on the basis of unintentional, yet objective manifestations such as slips of the tongue and free associations. He was also fascinated by James's concept of emotions as a secondary conscious perception of one's own affective-physiological reactions. Sherrington armed him with the notion of the integrative function of the nervous system, which is not merely an aggregate of reflexes but a highly organized system.

There is, however, one author who was never mentioned by Vygotsky, but whose views on the social nature of behavior were probably the closest to his own: the "social behaviorist", G. H. Mead. Consider the following passages:

> The difficulty is that Wundt presupposes selves as antecedent to
> the social process in order to explain communication within this

process, whereas, on the contrary, selves must be accounted for in terms of the social process, and in terms of communication.[25]

> Gestures become significant symbols when they implicitly arouse in an individual making them the same responses which they explicitly arouse, or are supposed to arouse, in other individuals, the individuals to whom they are addressed. . . . The same procedure which is responsible for the genesis and existence of mind or consciousness—namely, the taking of the attitude of the other toward one's self, or toward one's own behavior—also necessarily involves the genesis and existence at the same time of significant symbols, or significant gestures.[26]

The affinity between these two thinkers escaped the attention of their contemporaries. It became apparent only forty years later and caused developmental psychologists to engage in a comparative analysis of Vygotsky's and Mead's approaches to language as an instrument of the "external" regulation of individual behavior.[27]

Another aspect of Vygotsky's work that becomes apparent only with the wisdom of hindsight concerns his critique of the "substantialist" one-sidedness of both classical mentalistic and reflexological positions. For reflexologists, not only is everything a reflex, but also the nervous system appears as a sort of metaphysical "substance" from which reflexes emanate physically and by reference to which are explained theoretically. The same happens with traditional mentalist psychology, which explained the phenomenon of consciousness through reference to the theoretical notion of consciousness. Both trends are caught up in a vicious circle where the *subject of psychological study* is indistinguishable from the *explanatory principle*. Reflexes are defined as a subject of study, but they also serve as an explanatory schema, and the same was held to be true for mental states. As recent interpretations suggest, the distinction between the subject of study and the explanatory principle is probably the most important epistemological contribution made by Vygotsky in his early psychological papers. The implicit conclusion is that if consciousness is to become a subject of psychological study, some other layer of reality should be referred to in the course of the explanation: "It is necessary to search for this stratum of reality, a stratum whose *function* is consciousness".[28] Socially meaningful activity, then, may serve as such a layer and as an explanatory schema.

A full-scale epistemological analysis of the critical issues in psychology was undertaken by Vygotsky in his next major work, *The Historical Meaning of the Crisis in Psychology*. It was completed in 1927 and, for a while, was considered as an historical and a philosophical introduction to a planned larger volume on the development of higher mental functions. Like many of Vygotsky's other works, however, *Crisis* was not published until 1982.[29]

THE CRISIS IN PSYCHOLOGY

Crisis appeared as Vygotsky's assessment of the situation in contemporary psychology and at the same time as a metatheoretical (or "methodological", as Vygotsky called it) critique of psychology's perspectives. The first task was immediately related to Vygotsky's attempt to find a place for his own positive psychological program in the overall system of psychological scholarship as he found it. The second task stemmed from Vygotsky's belief that no headway could be possible for psychology as a positive science without defining the epistemological position of psychology *vis-à-vis* its subject, human behavior and mind, and its powerful rivals, philosophy and physiology. The epistemological problem revealed itself in the urgent need for a *general psychology*, which was conceived of by Vygotsky as a metapsychological theory that takes as its subject concrete, historically specific manifestations of psychological research: "Through the analysis of scientific reality we wish to come to a clear understanding of the essence of individual and social psychology as two aspects of one science; [we also wish to understand] their historical destiny".[30]

Stylistically, *Crisis* looks like a stream of Vygotsky's consciousness projected onto paper, with all the abrupt turns, leaps and elliptic pauses characteristic of inner dialogue. This peculiar quality of Vygotsky's work was recently noticed by an historian, David Joravsky, who concluded that Vygotsky's pitting of the faith in unified psychology against the incoherent pluralism of contemporary culture had "an acrid flavor of modernist absurd-ity".[31] In many respects *Crisis* is an unusual work for a psycho-logist, if only because it is not typical of psychology as an inductive science to offer a metatheoretical critique *before* a positive research program has been formulated. It should be said, however, that the atmosphere of the 1920s was favorable for all sorts of general projects to be put ahead of concrete research. A good portion of all psychological debates was about what ought to be, rather than what really is. A disagreement about the perspective of the discipline was often much more important for the parties involved, than an agreement in research practices. This is probably true for the entire ethos of the 1920s, when social projects were valued more highly than economic achievements, and when, for example, architectural concepts were judged by their drawing-board versions rather than their bricks-and-mortar realizations.[32]

Vygotsky began his analysis of the crisis in contemporary psychology by pointing to an important role played by the change in what is taken to be a "type" and what is taken to be a "variation". In classical mentalistic psychology a study of subjective responses to objective stimuli was conducted with a tacit agreement that the healthy adult male constitutes the "type", while children, women and the mentally ill represent a "variation". In terms of the theory this roughly meant that a child is an underdeveloped adult whose mental functions, though qualitatively the same as those of an adult, are quantitatively inferior. The child's mental level, therefore, can be estimated by the distance to be covered before it reaches the adult level. Similarly, a mentally ill person is one whose cognitive and behavioral processes represent a variation of the normal type.

With the advent of the new psychological systems such as reflexology, behaviorism and psychoanalysis, the tacit agreement about type had changed. In psychoanalysis the female hysteric became a type and the theory was built in such a way that the behavior of healthy adult males became a variation of this type. The reversal of the role of psychopathology with respect to normal psychology became particularly pronounced in Ernst Kretschmer's theory of "physique and character".[33] Kretschmer took psychopathological typology as a foundation for the typology of normal characters. Schizoid character, for example, was no longer seen as a deviation from the normal type but, on the contrary, some features of normal cognition were perceived as derivatives of the cognition of a schizoid character type.

Similar processes were taking place in reflexology and in behaviorism. In both of these trends animal behavior was taken as a foundation for the understanding of human behavior. Pavlov claimed that while the progress of behavioral physiology is decisive for the understanding of psychological functions, the reverse is not true: "Pavlov is not only seeking independence for his own field of research, but he also wishes to extend the influence [of his model of science] on all fields of psychological knowledge. . . ".[34] The salivary reflex in the dog became a paradigm for understanding human behavior; animal behavior was taken as a type while human behavior appeared as a variation. What was important in this change of types was that a tacit agreement had been broken and different schools of psychology started promoting their respective types as natural research paradigms, while dismissing alternative types as unscientific.

It seems relevant to mention here that the proliferation of types did not stop with the psychopathological and animal models described by Vygotsky. The animal model, in due course, has been superseded by the computer or information-processing model.[35] Historically, this change took the form of a fierce battle between Pavlovians who did not want to give up the physicalist interpretation of behavior as a physiological response to physical stimuli, and the proponents of a new model for whom the central notion was a notion of information processing and the prototype of behavior was computer simulation.[36] With the information-processing group finally victorious, computer operations became a type while human equivalents of these operations are the variations. Currently the computer type is under continuing attack by those who perceive it as too impoverished to serve its function, and who believe that the notion of information processing is a poor approximation of what can be achieved by human language. Some tentative steps have been made toward the formulation of a new type—that of a creative process and possibly, in a more restrictive way, as a "faculty of writing". In this new perspective an ordinary communicative language, for example, will be perceived as a "variation" of the literary language type.[37]

These developments have a direct relevance to what Vygotsky defined as two alternative methodological approaches: from the top down and from the bottom up in which "top" and "bottom" stand for more and less advanced processes. To start from a reflex in order to explain the whole of human behavior is to move from the bottom up. But the opposite top-down movement, from more complex functions to more primitive, is also legitimate. Noting that to interpret animal behavior as a variation of human behavior is not necessarily anthropomorphic, Vygotsky argued that "Often methodological reasons suggested this direction of research. Subjective psychology sought a key to animal behavior in the behavior of the human type, i.e. in the higher forms of behavior it sought an answer to the problems of the lower forms. The researcher, however, should not necessarily follow the historical path of nature; sometimes a reverse movement seems more advantageous".[38] In support of this thesis Vygotsky quoted a well-known idea of Marx that the study of historically more advanced social and economic systems is a key to the understanding of less advanced ones. The more advanced system, such as the capitalist economy, contains relics of the already vanished social and economic relations of feudalism on the one hand, and on the other capitalism fully develops those capacities that were in their budding stages in precapitalistic society. When we start with the end point it is much easier to understand the whole development and the significance of each of its stages. Vygotsky submitted that the top-down method had already benefited a number of disciplines; its applicability in psychology was still a subject of controversy. Only a future general psychology will resolve this controversy between animal and human models, and how it resolves it will be decisive for the entire destiny of this science.

The route to this future general psychology leads through the metapsychological critique of the existing schools of psychology, each of which claims to possess an explanatory system adequate to become the basis for a general psychology. Traditional mentalistic psychology claims that such a basis is provided by the notion of subjective psychological states accessible only by the individual him or herself. Reflexology in its turn claims that the basis is established by the notion of reflex which serves to explain the whole of human behavior. Psychoanalysis claims that general psychology must rest on the foundation of unconscious impulses. Vygotsky observed that "any behavioral or mental act being expressed in terms of these three systems would acquire three entirely different meanings, which indicate three different aspects of this fact, or more precisely, three different facts".[39]

It is not only the conclusions that are different for introspectionists, reflexologists and psychoanalysts, but actually the very facts with which they are operating. The Oedipus complex is an empirical fact for psychoanalysts, but for many child psychologists it is no more real than the calculations of astrologers. For behaviorists, what mentalists call "thinking" is a secondary reflection of the original motor behavior; the existence of this empirical link, however, is denied by mentalists. For Pavlov it is impossible to say that a dog remembers something, because in his scientific theory memory is an empty word and not an empirical fact.

The reality of conflicting psychological theories and facts reveals a fundamental scientific and philosophical problem of the origin and development of scientific fact. Vygotsky posed this problem in a deliberately paradoxical way. On the one hand, "each natural scientific concept, whatever the degree of its abstraction from the empirical fact, still retains the residue of the concrete reality from which it has emerged in the course of scientific inquiry", but on the other, "in any immediate, 'raw' and the most empirical of scientific facts there is always something of the original abstraction".[40] Vygotsky further pointed to the difference between the empirical reality given to a person in its immediacy, and the same reality interpreted as a scientific fact. Physics operates with such "facts" as physical matter, bodies and movements, all of which are scientific abstractions. The "energy of steam formation" is believed to be a physical, that is, an empirical entity, but who can claim that he has encountered it? Vygotsky went even further and posed a fundamental question about the role of speech in the perception of the world. Once a word is used there is already a generalization present. "A word is already a theory", said Vygotsky, remembering a maxim he had read in Potebnya's book. Vygotsky's line of thinking here followed that of the American linguist Edward Sapir whose works exerted a considerable influence on Vygotsky's interpretation of language. For Sapir, "it is obvious that language has the power to analyze experience into theoretically dissociable elements and to create that world of the potential intergrading with the actual which enables human beings to transcend the immediately given in their individual experiences and to join in a larger common understanding".[41]

The difference between immediate experience and scientific fact not only lies in the linguistic and conceptual nature of the latter, but it also reflects the fundamental disparity between experiential and scientific worlds. For example, chemical forms of perception discovered in some animals cannot be experienced by the human being, that is, they cannot become an experiential fact of human life. But they can become a scientific reality and they are treated as scientific facts. The most revealing example of this disparity is the phenomenon of sunrise and sunset, universally experienced as the movement of the sun around the earth. The scientific fact that it is the earth that rotates around the sun, not only contradicts the experiential fact of sunrise, but it is also powerless to change human perception. Without actually using these terms, Vygotsky exposed the confrontation between the phenomenological approach for which the primary source of psychological knowledge is experiential fact, and the scientific-conceptual approach that operates only with scientific facts.

The disparity between experiential and scientific facts and principles, and the different rates of their acquisition by children, became one of the major themes of Vygotsky's *Thought and Language*. The same problem, obscured for a while by other psychological and educational issues, was restated recently by the Soviet educational psychologist Vasili Davydov.[42] Davydov's analysis of scientific facts appears in a very specific context: the struggle to reform the Soviet school curriculum and methods of instruction. Traditional methods, Davydov claimed, rely on the everyday experiences of a student, and these have to be grouped and abstracted to yield scientific notions such as the notions of number or energy. Davydov argued that such an approach is essentially erroneous, because it obscures the fundamental difference between experiential and scientific reality. The only logic of generalization available for the traditional forms of instruction was the empiricist logic of the seventeenth-century philosopher John Locke. Since the task of education, from Davydov's point of view, is to develop in a student a scientific world-view, it follows that theoretical scientific facts and principles should be taught from the very beginning of classroom instruction. The correct path, therefore, is from scientific abstraction and scientific fact to their everyday counterparts. This problem will be discussed later, but for the moment it is sufficient to note that an early methodological remark of Vygotsky concerning scientific versus experiential facts received an important rejoinder fifty years later.

Another important parallel to Vygotsky's idea that scientific facts are "theory laden" appeared in the context of the philosophy of science debate that stirred the American scientific community in the 1960s and 1970s. The target of critique at that time was a positivist theory of knowledge and the definition of science as an accumulation of experimentally proven facts. The major challenge in this instance came from Thomas Kuhn's notion of scientific revolutions and Paul Feyerabend's anarchistic theory of knowledge.[43] Kuhn pointed to the utter impossibility of interpreting scientific facts out of the context of the dominant mindset of the scientific community, designated by the catchword "paradigm". For example, the discovery of "new" stars, which had of course been observable previously, happened immediately after the transition from the physical paradigm of unmovable earth to the heliocentric paradigm championed by Copernicus. These stars became a scientific and empirical fact only following the change in the entire scientific world-view.

Feyerabend also explored the result of the fusion of empirical facts ("appearances") with certain statements about them that yielded "natural interpretations": "Eliminate all natural interpretations, and you will also eliminate the ability to think and perceive".[44] Theoretical views are organically fused with so-called empirical data. The acknowledgment of such a state of affairs leads to a new interpretation of how scientific research should be done. Scientific research at its best is an interaction and confrontation between a new, explicitly stated theory and older views that penetrate the language of observation and facts. Facts themselves depend on changing ontologies. Because of that some problems—and this seems to be particularly true of psychology and other social sciences—are never resolved but rather disappear. Feyerabend mentioned such problems as the trajectory of electrons and the behavior of demons, both of which have disappeared because of the changing ontologies of the physical world.

Systems of knowledge that are based on different ontologies are "incommensurable" and their dispute cannot be resolved empirically. As will be shown later, Vygotsky was quite aware of the tendency of different psychological systems to develop into all-embracing world-views, which presuppose that their own ontologies are incommensurable with others.

The acknowledgment of the theory-laden character of psychological facts helped Vygotsky to expose the hollowness of modern psychology's claim that it is strictly empirical. First, he pointed to the fact that historically the definition of psychology as an empirical discipline appears as a negative rather than a positive definition. Empiricism defined its psychology as "psychology without a soul" or "psychology without metaphysics", that is, negatively, as something that is not based on a metaphysical foundation. In certain historical contexts, such as that of the struggle with metaphysical psychology, or that of the opposition between rationalism and empiricism, such a definition has its merits. But in the 1920s, when all psychologies claimed to belong to the empirical trend, the notion of empiricism became hollow and misleading. It obscured dramatically the different non-empirical postulates upon which each of the competing schools had built its scientific practice. Vygotsky observed that while psychoanalysis at least openly acknowledged its metapsychological component, other schools refused to inquire into their own metapsychological, nonempirical foundations. The use of empiricist logic, and the refusal to reflect upon its own theoretical position, led psychology to an absurd situation when it should have been defined as a "natural science of non-natural phenomena". Empiricist psychology tried to hide behind facts, but each fact betrayed its own theoretical foundation and context.

What Vygotsky sketched as an unfortunate general trend became an elaborate reality in American behavioral science married to logical positivism. This is how this reality was reconstructed by Stephen Toulmin and David Leary: "First, psychologists had to cut themselves loose from all the verbiage of earlier philosophical speculation; next, they had to create for themselves a theoretical *tabula rasa*—an empty field or flat conceptual space, awaiting the erection of some vast and disinfected scientific emporium; and finally, they had to throw up new 'logical constructions' *de novo*, as building material become available from controlled experiments".[45]

The problem of multiple psychologies was resolved by refusing admission to all those facts that did not fit into the logical positivism schema. But, as Vygotsky correctly predicted, the cult of empirical facts did not relieve neobehaviorism from the necessity of developing its own rules regarding the interpretation of facts. Much of what American psychologists did in the 1930s and the 1940s was about scientific decision procedures, rather than actual behavior.[46] The close affinity between neobehavioristic methodology and logical positivism made the transition from purely behavioral problems to philosophical generalizations look quite natural. And this is precisely the point made by Vygotsky: empirical fact is always only a starting point; the general principle "hidden" in this fact will inevitably reveal itself as the scientific notion evolves from its empirical "beginning" to its philosophical "end". The detailed account of this process is one of the central themes of *Crisis*.

Tracing the evolution of such psychological systems as reflexology, psychoanalysis and Gestalt psychology, Vygotsky revealed a uniform pattern in their development, from their initial discovery to their becoming all-embracing world-views.

The development of each of these systems starts with an initial empirical discovery or observation that proves to be important for the revision of the views existing in a given field of psychology. This moment begins the first stage in the development of an idea in which the idea appears in an empirical form, such as the discovery of conditional salivary reflex in dogs, the observation of apparent motion by Gestalt psychologists, or the treatment of hysterical neurosis by Freud.

In the second stage of its development, the initial idea acquires a conceptual form and thus becomes a generalized concept. As such it starts to lay claim to related psychological phenomena and fields of knowledge. At this stage the ties between the generalized concept and the initial discovery are already weakened. The idea that is becoming an "independent" generalized concept exists, however, only because the initial discovery continues to nurture its scientific reputation and to lend it its scientific legitimacy. At this stage it becomes possible to distinguish between an idea as an original generalized concept and as an explanatory principle. For example, in reflexology the generalized concept of behavior is accompanied by the explanatory principle of reflex, and in psychoanalysis the concept of the unconscious is explained through the principle of the libido.

At the third stage the generalized concept acts in accordance with the explanatory principle and becomes applicable to all problems within a given discipline. The concept now resolutely severs its connection with the initial discovery. In ranging over the whole of psychology it transforms the discipline, but in doing so it itself becomes transformed. The generalized concept and the subject matter of psychology are captured by the expanding explanatory principle: all behavior becomes a sum of conditional reflexes, or a transformation of the libido, or a change of Gestalts.

At the fourth stage, a new disengagement of the generalized concept and the explanatory principle takes place: "The idea serves as an explanatory principle [only] until it coincides with the basic generalized concept; to explain means to go out in search of an external cause. As soon as the idea as an explanatory principle coincides with the basic concept it ceases to explain anything".[47] As a result the explanatory principle disengages itself from the subject matter of psychology and becomes an ideology or a world-view. At this moment, Vygotsky observed, the idea usually collapses under the weight of its enormous intellectual debt. It ceases to exist as an independent intellectual principle and merges with one of the dominant philosophies of the time.

Psychoanalysis originated, according to Vygotsky, in the specific discoveries belonging to the field of the psychopathology of neuroses. It was shown that "some psychological phenomena can be defined through reference to the unconscious sphere" and that "some phenomena which have not been considered as belonging to the sexual sphere revealed their sexual underpinnings".[48] Gradually the generalized concept related to this particular discovery, being supported by the success of corresponding therapeutic techniques, was extended to cover other subjects such as the psychopathology of everyday life and child psychology. In its expansionist movement psychoanalysis reached such remote corners of psychology as ethnopsychology and the psychology of art. But this expansion led psychoanalysis outside psychology: "... sexuality became a metaphysical principle like all others, psychoanalysis became a world-view, and [its] psychology became a meta-psychology. Psychoanalysis has its own theory of knowledge and its own metaphysics. ... Communism and totem, religion and Dostoevsky's writings, occultism and commercials, myth and Leonardo da Vinci's inventions—all of them are just a libido in disguise and nothing else".[49]

A similar pattern is discernible in the evolution of the idea of reflex. The starting point here was Pavlov's experimental research of salivary reflexes in dogs. Then the idea of conditional reflex left its original sphere of applicability and was applied to other behavioral phenomena. In Bekhterev's system it had already been extended toward the phenomena of language behavior, sleep, thinking and creativity. Various fields of psychology, including social, educational and clinical psychology, became subsumed under the name of reflexology: "Anna Karenina and kleptomania, class struggle and landscape painting, language and dreams—are reflexes".[50] As in the case of psychoanalysis, where all types of behavior appeared to be derivations of libidinal impulses, reflexology presented the same behavioral phenomena as derivatives of conditional reflexes. Reflexology thus ceased to be a mere scientific theory and became a world-view, with its own social projects, epistemology and even esthetics.

Vygotsky believed that all the above-mentioned metatheoretical claims of different schools of psychology were nothing than revealing symptoms of the crisis in psychology. Although the symptoms themselves were often grotesque, they expressed, in this distorted form, the genuine and legitimate desire of psychologists to establish a psychological metatheory and to formulate an immanent method of psychological inquiry. What on the surface appeared as a caricature fight between different schools for supremacy, on a deeper level corresponded to a serious concern with psychology's lack of coherence as a science.

Before proceeding to an analysis of Vygotsky's response to this crisis in psychology, let us first make a leap of fifty years and check what has happened to the idea of a unified and methodologically coherent psychology. The authoritative text assessing psychology's current status as an independent scientific discipline is Sigmund Koch's "The nature and limits of psychological knowledge".[51] Koch's analysis reveals two significant moments. First, that a unified methodological base for psychology had almost been achieved by American neobehaviorism in the 1930s and 1940s, but only at the cost of ignoring alternative approaches and producing what Koch calls an a-meaningful knowledge. Second, that since the beginning of the decline of neobehavioristic theory a strong tendency toward theoretical and substantive fractionation is observed, rather than integration.

According to Koch there was good reason for this course in psychology's development. At different times different aspects of behavior, mind and personality appeared at the forefront of psychological inquiry, but the ultimate aim of explaining the whole of the human individual always lurked behind these more limited goals. To restate Koch's point in somewhat different terms, psychology repeatedly attempted to understand the human being—this presumably universal subject—with remarkable limited and certainly nonuniversal means of inquiry. The unsatisfactory results of such attempts could be easily foreseen. To solve the paradox of universal subject versus particular means, American neobehaviorism seemed to be ready to dispense with human universality. This had to be achieved by "bracketing" the human being, and focusing on "behavior" as a subject of its own. Even this limited goal was difficult to achieve. As Koch's penetrating analysis shows, the neobehaviorists failed to conform to the very rules of logical positivism that they proclaimed to be the metatheoretical premise of any scientific inquiry. The next step was the radical empiricism of B. F. Skinner who declared that he rejected any theoretical ordering devices. The decline of neobehaviorism and the resurgence of fragmentation in psychology stems, I believe, not from the failure of behavioral theory to achieve logical-positivistic purity, but from a sometimes unconscious, but nevertheless very real dissatisfaction on the part of psychologists with what they had produced. Data about "behavior" that are divorced from the important issues related to human universality became a-meaningful not only for critical outsiders, but also for the psychologists themselves. Certain "compensatory" mechanisms evoked by this a-meaningfulness closely resemble those described by

Vygotsky. B. F. Skinner, for example, more often than not leaped from the empirical data derived from operant conditioning in laboratory animals to sweeping social and educational projects. The first, empirical component seems to guarantee the scientific status of the idea and the second its human relevance. The paradoxical coexistence of these two components allowed operant conditioning to serve as a world-view without abandoning its status as a particular scientific approach.

Koch's solution to the problem of psychology's particularity versus human universality was to reaffirm the universality of a human being, and simultaneously to absolve psychology from being either a unified or a scientific discipline.

> My position suggests that the noncohesiveness of psychology finally be acknowledged by replacing it with some such locution as "the psychological studies". . . . Moreover, the conceptual ordering devices, technical languages ("paradigms", if you prefer), open to the various psychological studies are . . . perspectival, sensibility-dependent relative to the inquirer, and often non-commensurable . . . . Different theories will—relative to their different analytical purposes, predictive or practical aims, perceptual sensitivities, metaphor-forming capacities, and pre-existing discrimination repertoires—make asystematically different perceptual cuts upon the same domain. They will identify "variables" or markedly different grain and meaning contour selected and linked on different principles of grouping. The cuts, variables, concepts will in all likelihood establish different universes of discourse, even if loose ones.[52]

Koch further hinted that the above "universes of psychological discourse" would generally gravitate toward two distinctive poles: one of them being a discourse of biology and natural sciences, and the other a specific discourse of the humanities.

After this brief incursion into psychology's self-reflection in the 1980s, let us return to Vygotsky's analysis of different responses to the crisis in psychology in the 1920s. The first type of response was a denial of the crisis. Such a denial was possible for those who were insensitive to theoretical contradictions and for whom psychological theory is by definition an exercise in eclecticism. Vygotsky named Chelpanov as a representative of this type. Chelpanov was ready to accommodate any idea and any approach, and he seemed to be unperturbed by their mutual incommensurability. Vygotsky believed that such eclecticism is incompatible with genuine scientific progress. Eclectics could be good "professors, organizers and kulturtriggers", but they fail to produce any significant scientific results. One may wonder whether Vygotsky would have stuck to his low opinion of eclectics like Chelpanov if he had known how rigid noneclectic scientific opinion could be. One may also wish that Vygotsky had dwelled in greater detail on the difference between eclecticism as a theoretic position and pluralism as a scientific policy. Taking into account Chelpanov's record as a scholar and as an organizer, it seems plausible that what Vygotsky took as his theoretical position was Chelpanov's attitude toward scientific policy, which allowed his assistants and students to pursue many different types of psychological research. One may further wonder whether pluralism à la Chelpanov is not the only real guarantee against the single-principle imperialism successfully exercised by neobehaviorists and Pavlovians alike.

The second type of response to the critical situation in psychology was to divide all theories into "my theory and the wrong ones". This, according to Vygotsky, was the position taken by J. B. Watson and other behaviorists in the United States and Bekhterev in Russia. For them the crisis was a dividing line between the forces of the past, which were wrong, and the psychology of the future—their own—which was right. Vygotsky ridiculed this self-centered interpretation of the crisis, but he seemed to be largely unaware of the destructive potential of such an "egocentrism" in psychology. The subsequent developments in Pavlovian behavioral science in the Soviet Union and in neobehaviorism in the United States showed how harmful the existence of "only one correct" and "self-correcting" methodology can be.

An important source of information about the crisis in psychology is the language of psychology. Vygotsky believed that terminology is not an "external" attribute of little consequence, but a true mirror of the state of psychology: "The word giving the fact its name simultaneously gives its philosophy, its theory and system. When I say 'the awareness of color' I create a definite set of scientific associations, the fact is placed in a definite series of phenomena and it is given a definite meaning; when I say 'reaction to white' all these aspects are different".[53] According to Vygotsky, psychological language in the age of crisis revealed a conglomerate of: (*a*) words belonging to everyday speech, (*b*) vestiges of philosophical language, and (*c*) borrowings from the natural science lexicon. He mentioned Gestalt psychologist Kurt Koffka as a scholar who clearly recognized the existence of different psychological vocabularies and discourses. Human behavior, according to Koffka, has two aspects: one of them is open to natural scientific inquiry, which in turn presupposes functional concepts; the other aspect is experiential and presupposes descriptive language.[54] The everyday language so often used in psychological writings obscures this important dichotomy between explanatory and descriptive discourses.

The terminological dichotomy is important not in itself, but as a sign of the essential division between two large groups of psychological theories gravitating toward two different types of knowledge. Competing schools that reveal their tendency to develop into all-embracing world-views should not be mistaken for potentially reconcilable approaches. The positions taken by different schools are based on different, mutually exclusive types of knowledge. Vygotsky concluded that in the last account the multiplicity of psychologies can be reduced to just two types: a natural-scientific explanatory psychology and a descriptive, philosophical-phenomenological psychology.[55] The actual development of psychological ideas in the age of crisis pointed to the necessity for a psychological metatheory, which inevitably would be either natural-scientific or phenomenological-humanistic.

Vygotsky acknowledged that this dichotomy has a long history, appearing under different names, such as the "nomothetic" versus "idiographic" approach, or natural versus historical knowledge, or causal versus intentional theory, in the works of W. Windelband, H. Rickert, W. Dilthey, and more recently in those of Hugo Münsterberg and Ludwig Binswanger. The Swiss psychoanalyst Binswanger attracted Vygotsky by his clear understanding of the necessity of a metatheory in psychology, as an epistemology of psychological knowledge.[56] Binswanger also did not hesitate to identify the dividing line between the two major psychological camps as the criterion of the natural-scientific approach to psychological phenomena. Another protagonist of Vygotsky's *Crisis* was German-American Hugo Münsterberg, who was a fascinating figure for Vygotsky because he seemed to personify the split nature of psychology. Münsterberg as a theoretician claimed that causal psychology was able to provide answers only to artificially formulated questions, and that the human experience required understanding, rather than explanation. At the same time Münsterberg as a pioneer of applied and industrial psychology acknowledged that only a causal-explanatory method of natural sciences is suitable for the applied and industrial problems.[57] Thus Münsterberg as a consistent theorist continued to develop two mutually exclusive approaches to human behavior.

Vygotsky's own position was primarily that of a chronicler and critic of the crisis. When it came to taking sides, he seemed to be on that of scientific, explanatory psychology, but he did so with the following far-reaching reservation: "We leave the question open of whether psychology is indeed a natural science in an exact sense of this word. . .".[58] Vygotsky proceeded to explain that since psychology had not yet been understood as a social and cultural theory, scientific psychology was identified as a natural science. But it would be the task of the future metatheory to elucidate how psychology would be possible as a materialistic, scientific and at the same time social and cultural form of knowledge.

Vygotsky directed a considerable amount of his critical temper against those of his colleagues, including his "boss", Kornilov, who suggested that "Marxist psychology" was a viable alternative to both natural-scientific and phenomenological psychologies. First of all, Vygotsky objected to their uses of Marxism. In his opinion Soviet psychologists sought Marxist support "in the wrong places", that they assimilated "the wrong material", and that they used this material "in a wrong way".[59] Vygotsky's critique deserves some attention if only because the practices he criticizes were destined to become a standard feature of Soviet psychological theory from the 1920s to the 1950s and beyond.

Vygotsky ridiculed the popular method of selecting fortuitous quotations from the works of Marx and Engels and presenting them as a Marxist *position* regarding psychology. Vygotsky pointed to the fact—and for him this was a fact—that neither Marx himself nor his followers ever possessed any notion of psychological method. Even an epistemological component of psychological theory can not be found in their writings. "Marxist psychologists", he stated, were looking for the wrong material, because what they sought was a ready-made Marxist *formula* applicable to psychological phenomena. But such a "formula" could only be reached at the end of a theoretical process that had not yet begun. Finally, Vygotsky believed that Marxist ideas were misused because "Marxist psychology" adopted an authoritarian and dogmatic posture that stiffened critique and prevented the free search for scientific truth.[60]

All these abuses of Marxism, according to Vygotsky, stemmed from one root, from the misunderstanding of the nature of the crisis in psychology. No one philosophical system, including Marxism, could be a substitute for a psychological metatheory, and the only legitimate contribution of Marxism would be to help in developing such a metatheory. This applied not only to psychology but to all fields of knowledge; there was no Marxist magic formula to solve their problems: "Immediate application of the theory of dialectical materialism to the problems of science, in particular to biology and psychology, is impossible, as it is impossible to apply it immediately to history or sociology".[61]

Vygotsky argued that if psychology were to learn from Marx, it should write its own *Capital*, in the same sense as *Capital* served as metatheory of nineteenth-century economics. For the rest of his life Vygotsky sought this new metatheoretical approach, which would make psychology scientific, but not at the cost of the naturalization of human consciousness, and which would make use of the Marxist method without degenerating into "Marxist psychology".

PHILOSOPHY OF PRACTICE

But if neither a-theoretical empiricism nor "Marxist psychology" could provide an escape route from the crisis, then where would it come from? To this question Vygotsky gave a dialectically paradoxical answer: from the crisis itself! For this purpose, however, the crisis should be reconsidered as a positive, rather than negative phenomenon. To comprehend the crisis as a positive development one should first uncover the basic contradiction—in a creative, Hegelian sense of this term—that underlay all symptoms of the crisis.

According to Vygotsky two major forces stood behind the apparent dispute over general psychological theory in the 1920s: *epistemology* and *practice*. To comprehend the crisis an epistemological critique was needed of the fundamental research philosophies revealed by the crisis, and the critical program realized in Vygotsky's *Crisis* was a first step in this direction. But the second major force—practice—should also be taken into account. It was in the 1920s that psychology first became fully conscious of the practical aspects associated with industrial, forensic, educational and mental health tasks and problems. Vygotsky believed that this encounter with practical tasks would force psychology to reconsider its own principles along the lines dictated by the requirements of practice. The practical approach would broaden the horizons of psychology and force her to take a fresh look at the wealth of practical psychological knowledge accumulated through the ages by religion, politics, industry and the military. In all these spheres of life the task of organizing and controlling human behavior was of paramount importance and a wealth of psychological principles has been amassed. Analytical procedures should be used to "extract" and identify these principles. According to Vygotsky any practical situation, from industrial work to writing a lyric poem, could be used as a cultural experiment staged on human mind and behavior. What in a "real" experiment is accomplished by controlling stimuli and responses, in such a cultural experiment could be achieved by theoretical procedures of analysis and synthesis. It would be erroneous, therefore, to perceive practical psychology as an application of previously established theories. The relationship should be reversed, with practice selecting its own psychological principles and ultimately creating its own psychology.

The practical and epistemological components of the crisis should not be viewed as two unrelated issues; both of them have a common center—a *philosophy of practice*. Vygotsky believed that while searching for a general method of psychological inquiry we would inevitably come to the issue of practice: "Method [from the Greek *meta*—after, and *hodos*—way] means to pursue, to go after; we understand method as the means of the pursuit of knowledge; but this pursuit at all of its stages is determined by the goal. That is why practice [as a goal] transforms the entire methodology of science".[62]

The above constitutes the high point of Vygotsky's analysis of the crisis in psychology. Further discussion goes beyond Vygotsky, but it is inspired by his idea of practice as a driving force of the crisis. The central issue now becomes a critique of the philosophy of practice. If psychological theory is supposed to correspond to certain practices, the fundamental question is: what kinds of practice? It is significant that in working with psychological theory, Vygotsky encountered the same problems that social scientists had discovered and continue to discuss in the context of the general theory of human social activity. The starting point in Marxist social theory is that material production should become the basic paradigm for the analysis of human activity. "The mode of production of material life conditions the general process of social, political, and intellectual life", wrote Marx.[63] Furthermore, there is supposed to be a close correspondence between human practice (understood as a material production) and scientific method. A prominent theoretician of Soviet Marxism and Vygotsky's contemporary, Nikolai Bukharin emphasized that "*historically*, the sciences grow out of practice, the production of ideas differentiates out of production of things; *sociologically*, social being determines social consciousness, the production of material labor is the constant *force motrice* of the whole social development".[64]

A more sophisticated analysis of the relationship between the system of material production and the principles of scientific theory was offered by another contemporary of Vygotsky, the social philosopher Georg Lukacs.[65] Lukacs explored what he believed to be an affinity between the rationality existing in the system of material production and rationality upheld by the natural sciences. The logic behind this contention is that both nature as a subject of scientific inquiry and human activity as a source of material production appear as an *objective* reality that can be grasped in abstract laws and principles pertaining to the relations between *things*. Human activity assumes the form of production and acquisition of things as commodities. And ultimately this activity itself becomes a commodity measured by so-called exchange value. The type of knowledge that corresponds to this objectivized world is scientific knowledge: "What is important is to recognize clearly that all human relations (viewed as the objects of social activity) assume increasingly the objective forms of the abstract elements of the conceptual systems of natural science and of the abstract substrata of the laws of nature".[66] Lukacs also quoted another social philosopher, Tonneis, who observed that "A special case of abstract reason is *scientific* reason and its subject is the man who is objective, and who recognizes relations, i.e. thinks in concepts. In consequence, scientific concepts . . . behave within science like commodities in society. They gather together within the system like commodities in society. The supreme scientific concept which is no longer the name of anything real is like money".[67]

So, if one develops a psychological science relevant to human practice, which in turns finds its paradigm in the system of material production, then this psychology is destined to be of the same mold as a classical natural science. Human beings will appear in this science as subjects of purposive-rational action attuned to the needs of survival in the world of things-commodities. This science can be social or cultural only in so far as social and cultural relations are considered to be derivative of the relations of material production. Since the 1920s a considerable number of critiques have been written about the "reified", commodity-like form of human activity.[68] It has been suggested that the objectification of human activity detracts from what are traditionally perceived as essential human qualities such as freedom, creativity and understanding. Moreover, it has been suggested that many negative phenomena of psychological life, sometimes subsumed under the notion of "alienation", originate from the extension of commodity relations into the interpersonal sphere of life. It now appears that the paradigm of material production when applied to the whole of human activity, would point to what is pathological in the human condition, rather than to what is "normal". Psychology which corresponds to the practice understood as material production thus becomes a study of sociopathology rather than of normal development: "Thus it makes sense to ask whether the critique of the incomplete character of the rationalization that appears as reification does not suggest taking a complementary relation between cognitive-instrumental rationality, on the one hand, and moral-practical and aesthetic-practical rationality, on the other, as a standard that is inherent in the unabridged concept of practice, that is to say, in communicative action itself".[69]

Before discussing how practice can be conceived of as communication, let us go over those changes that occurred in the twentieth-century philosophical understanding of the human subject and the consequences these changes had for psychology. No doubt the changes have been germinating for a long time, at least since the age of Hegel and the German Romantics, but they became a pervasive intellectual reality only in the twentieth century.

First, the idea of the homogeneous and rational mind that had been popular among the Rationalists and Empiricists alike, had been replaced by the notion of multilevel and heterogeneous consciousness, with rational cognition representing just one of its aspects, leading to the twentieth-century psychology preoccupation with unconscious motives, regressive states of mind, and prelogical thought of children and "primitive" people.

Second, the Cartesian notion of an idealized human being— "the thinker"—who is the *subject* of activity and the natural starting point of any theoretical inquiry, had lost its intuitive appeal. The human subject was no longer seen as a self-conscious mind confronting nature, but appeared instead as a *construction* that emerges at the crossroads of sub- and super-individual structures of human life. The slogan of psychology became "from action to thought"; consciousness and self-awareness were seen as the end result of activity which in its original form did not include the element of self-reflection. Developmental psychology focused on the internalization of actions, social psychology on the internalization of roles, and psycholinguistics on the influence of verbal activity on thought.

Third, the human subject lost all his objective, finished characteristics and turned into a pure "becoming". In the words of Spanish philosopher Ortega-y-Gasset: "A man is not object but drama, his life is pure and universal happening".[70] Psychology became interested in unique creative experiences and such states of mind, which are not reproducible by definition. Psychotherapeutic experience is often aimed at opening new perspectives in life that are not predictable in a scientific sense.

The revision of the notion of practice has been intertwined with these changes in philosophical anthropology. Thus if in the material production paradigm the tool action and the purposive-rational behavior associated with it is taken as a model of human conduct, then in the communicative action paradigm this role is played by a symbolic interaction rooted in the intersubjectively shared culturally dependent language. This returns us to Vygotsky's contention that practice is the key to the future of psychology. At first glance, it seems that Vygotsky made no distinction between different types of human practice, lumping together industrial labor, religious rituals and the writing of lyric poetry. If, however, instead of looking for a precise quote we take Vygotsky's writings as a whole, we would immediately recognize that he distinguished between a purposive-rational behavior considered within the paradigm of a material tool action, and a cultural cognition that depends on intersubjective communication and which can be grasped in the change in word *meanings*. Practice then becomes divided into material production and human cultural production. When Vygotsky reminded his readers that any lyric poem is a ready-made psychological experiment, that is, a "snare" for psychological functions, he was obviously referring to a kind of practice that cannot be derived from material tool action.

The fact that Vygotsky's theoretical program was interpreted differently by various groups of his followers reflects the dissimilarities in their philosophies of practice. One of these philosophies is rooted in the classical Marxist interpretation of practice as material production. It sought to amplify Vygotsky's idea that the use of tools, and the emergence of the division of labor, was responsible for the transformation of natural mental processes into human psychological functions. Interpersonal communication was seen as a derivative moment, secondary to that of tool-mediated interaction with the world. This line of reasoning was fully developed in Leontiev's theory of psychological activity.[71]

An alternative "reading" of Vygotsky's theory—which has been undertaken only recently—focuses on the role of language and other symbolic mediators. These mediators, though dependent on the overall system of human practice, possess a remarkable ability to become independent of this system, and to create their own symbolic construction of reality. In this interpretation, Vygotsky's theory would be allied with twentieth-century philosophical hermeneutics, and with a psychology that takes the humanities rather than the natural sciences as its model. These conflicting (but in a certain way also complementary) interpretations of Vygotsky's theory will be discussed at some length in Chapter Seven.

NOTES

1. Lev Vygotsky, "Metod reflexologicheskogo i psikhologicheskogo issledovaniya" ("Methodology of reflexological and psychological research"). In L. Vygotsky, *Sobranie Sochinenii* (*Collected Papers*), vol. 1. Moscow: Pedagogika, 1982 (original work published in 1926).
2. Ibid, p. 57.
3. Ibid, pp. 51-2.
4. Ibid, p. 51.
5. See review in *Novoe v Reflexologii*, No. 1, 1925.
6. Alexander Luria, *The Making of Mind*. Cambridge, MA: Harvard University Press, 1979, pp. 38-9.
7. Alex Kozulin, "Chelpanov and the establishment of the Moscow Institute of Psychology". *Journal of the History of the Behavioral Sciences*, vol. 21, 1985, pp. 23-32.
8. For an appraisal of Wundt's school and his followers, see Arthur Blumenthal, "A reappraisal of Wilhelm Wundt". *American Psychologist*, vol. 30, 1975, pp. 1081-8.
9. Kornilov, quoted in Pauline Efrussi, *Uspekhi Psikhologii v Rossii* (*Advances in Psychology in Russia*). Petrograd, 1923, p. 26.
10. See Raymond Bauer, *The New Man in Soviet Psychology*. Cambridge, MA: Harvard University Press, 1968; Alex Kozulin, *Psychology in Utopia*. Cambridge, MA: MIT Press, 1984; David Joravsky, *Russian Psychology*. Oxford: Blackwell, 1989.
11. Ivan Pavlov, *Conditioned Reflexes*. Oxford: Oxford University Press, 1927.
12. Ibid, p. 26
13. Kozulin, *Psychology in Utopia*, pp. 44-9.
14. Vladimir Bekhterev, *General Principles of Human Reflexology*. New York: International Publishers, 1932, p. 81.
15. Konstantin Kornilov, "Psychology in the light of dialectical materialism". In C. Murchison, ed., *Psychologies in the 1930s*. Worcester, MA: Clark University Press, 1930.

16. Ibid, p. 255.
17. Ibid, p. 247.
18. Luria, quoted in K. Levitin, *Mimoletniy Uzor (Ephemeral Pattern)*. Moscow: Znanie, 1978, p. 49.
19. Lev Vygotsky, "Consciousness as a problem of the psychology of behavior". *Soviet Psychology*, vol. 17, 1979, pp. 5–35 (original paper published in 1925).
20. Ibid, p. 5.
21. Ibid, p. 13.
22. Ibid, p. 29.
23. Ibid, pp. 29–30.
24. Ibid, p. 30.
25. G. H. Mead, *Mind, Self, and Society from the Standpoint of a Social Behaviorist*. Chicago: Chicago University Press, 1974, p. 49 (original work published in 1934).
26. Ibid, p. 48.
27. L. Kohlberg, J. Yaeger and E. Hjertholm. "Private speech", *Child Development*, vol. 39, 1968, pp. 691–736. See also Jaan Valsiner and Rene van der Veer, "On the social nature of human cognition: An analysis of the shared intellectual roots of G. H. Mead and L. Vygotsky". *Journal for the Theory of Social Behavior*, vol. 18, 1988, pp. 117–36.
28. V. V. Davydov and A. Radzikhovsky, "Vygotsky's theory and the activity-oriented approach in psychology". In J. Wertsch, ed., *Culture, Communication, and Cognition*. New York: Cambridge University Press, 1985, p. 46.
29. Lev Vygotsky, *Istoricheskiy Smysl Psikhologicheskogo Krizisa (The Historical Meaning of the Crisis in Psychology)*. In *Sobranie Sochinenii (Collected Papers)*, vol. 1. Moscow: Pedagogika, 1982 (original work written in 1925–27).
30. Ibid, p. 296.
31. David Joravsky, "Vygotsky: A muffled deity of Soviet psychology". In M. Ash and W. Woodward, eds, *Psychology in Twentieth Century Thought and Society*. New York: Cambridge University Press, 1988.
32. A study of the ethos of the 1920s as reflected in architectural projects is reviewed by A. Kozulin, *Studies in Soviet Thought*, vol. 34, 1987, pp. 111–16.
33. Ernst Kretschmer, *Physique and Character*. London: Paul, Trench, Traubner, 1925.
34. Vygotsky, *Crisis*, p. 295.
35. For a history of the transition to the information-processing paradigm in American psychology, see Roy Lachman, J. L. Lachman

and E. C. Butterfield, *Cognitive Psychology and Information Processing*. Hillsdale, NJ: Erlbaum, 1979.

36. See Kozulin, *Psychology in Utopia*, ch. 3.

37. For more about this alternative, see Alex Kozulin, "Life as authoring: The humanistic tradition in Russian psychology". *New Ideas in Psychology* (in press).

38. Vygotsky, *Crisis*, p. 294.

39. Ibid, p. 299.

40. Ibid, pp. 312–13.

41. Edward Sapir, *Culture, Language, and Personality*. Los Angeles: University of California Press, 1970, p. 7 (original work published in 1933).

42. Vasili Davydov, "The concept of theoretical generalization and problems of educational psychology". *Studies in Soviet Thought*, vol. 38, 1988, pp. 169–202 (original work published in 1972).

43. Thomas Kuhn, *The Structure of Scientific Revolutions*. Chicago: University of Chicago Press, 1962; Paul Feyerabend, "Against method". In M. Radner and S. Winokur, eds, *Analysis of Theories and Methods of Physics and Psychology*. Minnesota Studies in the Philosophy of Science, vol. IV. Minneapolis, MN: University of Minnesota Press, 1970.

44. Feyerabend, *op. cit.*, p. 50.

45. Stephen Toulmin and David Leary, "The cult of empiricism in psychology". In S. Koch and D. Leary, eds, *A Century of Psychology as Science*. New York: McGraw-Hill, 1985, p. 608.

46. A thorough critique of the neobehaviorist theory was written by Sigmund Koch, Epilogue in *Psychology: A Study of a Science*. New York: McGraw-Hill, 1959, vol. 3, pp. 729–88.

47. Vygotsky, *Crisis*, p. 303.

48. Ibid, p. 306.

49. Ibid, p. 307.

50. Ibid, p. 307.

51. Sigmund Koch, "The nature and limits of pscyhological knowledge". In S. Koch and D. Leary, eds, *A Century of Psychology as Science*. New York: McGraw-Hill, 1985.

52. Ibid, p. 93.

53. Vygotsky, *Crisis*, p. 358.

54. See Kurt Koffka, *The Growth of the Mind*. New York: Harcourt, Brace & Co., 1928, pp. 7–11.

55. See Vygotsky, *Crisis*, p. 381.

56. Ludwig Binswanger, *Einführung in die Probleme der allgemeinen Psychologie*. Berlin, 1922.

57. See Hugo Münsterberg, *Grundzüge der Psychotechnik*. Leipzig: Barth, 1914.
58. Vygotsky, *Crisis*, p. 384.
59. Ibid, p. 397.
60. Ibid, p. 398.
61. Ibid, p. 419.
62. Ibid, p. 388.
63. Karl Marx, *A Contribution to the Critique of Political Economy*. Moscow: Progress, 1970, p. 21 (original work published in 1859).
64. Nikolai Bukharin, "Theory and practice from the standpoint of dialectical materialism". In J. Needham, ed., *Science at the Crossroads*. London: Cass, 1971, p. 15 (original paper published in 1931).
65. See Georg Lukacs, *History and Class Consciousness*. Cambridge, MA: MIT Press, 1971 (original work published in 1923).
66. Ibid, p. 131.
67. Quoted in Lukacs, *History*, p. 131 (original work published in 1887).
68. For a review, see Jürgen Habermas, "Technology and science as ideology". In *Toward a Rational Society*. Boston: Beacon Press, 1970.
69. Jürgen Habermas, *The Theory of Communicative Action*. Boston: Beacon Press, 1984, pp. 363–4.
70. J. Ortega-y-Gasset, "History as a system". In R. Klidansky and J. H. Patton, eds, *Philosophy and History*. Oxford: Clarendon Press, 1936, p. 303.
71. Alexei N. Leontiev, *Activity, Consciousness, and Personality*. Englewood Cliffs, NJ: Prentice Hall, 1978.

CHAPTER FOUR

Tool and Symbol in Human Development

VYGOTSKY'S positive psychological program, taken in its most global plane, was an extension and amplification of his early statement that the social dimension of the human mind is primary and that psychology should focus its attention on uniquely human higher mental processes.[1] In developing this rather abstract thesis into a full-scale research program, Vygotsky was first helped by two young members of the Institute of Psychology, Alexander Luria and Alexei N. Leontiev. Together they formed a now famous "troika". By the age of twenty-three, Luria had already revealed himself as an energetic researcher seeking to integrate the psychoanalytic technique of free associations with the study of sensory-motor responses and thus to establish an "objective" approach to unconscious emotional processes.[2] Leontiev, who was accepted as a doctoral student by Chelpanov, was allowed to continue after the latter was dismissed from the Institute and eventually became a member of the troika. Vygotsky, who had no apartment in Moscow at the time he joined the Institute, lived for a while in the basement room of the Institute that housed the philosophy department archives.[3] Luria remembers that their troika would meet once or twice a week in Vygotsky's room and plan the next step in developing their research program.

If anything, this program was not a detached theoretical progression of ideas. Vygotsky's group was deeply immersed in the
turbulent life of the 1920s, with all its enormous social problems.
One of the most acute problems was that of homeless and handicapped children—direct and indirect victims of the Civil War;
another major problem was the establishment of a psychological
service for the emerging system of compulsory secondary education. Members of the troika held a number of concurrent
appointments—all of them at almost symbolic pay—lecturing
in different colleges and conducting research at a number of
laboratories and research stations, which was almost a norm in
those days. Luria was the head of the psychological laboratory
at the Academy of Communist Education, while Vygotsky had
already made the first steps toward the establishment of a center
for the study of handicapped children by 1925.

The troika soon attracted new members and thus became a
"magnificent eight", including Lidia Bozhovich, Roza Levina,
Natalya Morozova, Liya Slavina and Alexander Zaporozhets.
The work of the group was truly collective. All of the members
accepted Vygotsky's theoretical leadership and each was free to
use Vygotsky's ideas in his or her own research. This commune-
like attitude toward intellectual property creates a number of
problems for a historian and a critic. On the one hand it is clear
that such a large work as *The History of the Development of Higher
Psychological Functions*, which was completed in 1931, was based
on a number of studies done by different members of the group,
theoretically integrated by Vygotsky.[4] There are, however, less
clear cases, such as Luria's article "Problems of the cultural
behavior of the child". [5] The English version of this article was
published in 1928; the Russian version is unknown, and the
content does not allow one to distinguish it from other works in
which Vygotsky is listed as a sole author.

There is also considerable confusion when it comes to determining a chronology for the development of Vygotsky's research
program.[6] There are a number of ways to distinguish different
themes and layers in Vygotsky's writings. One may reasonably
speak about his shifting priorities and abandoned approaches,
but it seems counterproductive to attempt to impose a rigid
temporal sequence on the development of his research program.
Such rigid temporalization becomes almost impossible to prove

because of the delays in publication for some papers and the rather speedy appearance of others. For example, Lev Sakharov's study of experimental concept formation was published in 1930, and became integrated in Vygotsky's *Thought and Language* in 1934, thus placing it among the "late" studies, but Sakharov had died in 1928 and the project therefore had to have been formulated early in the activity of the group. Thus the thematic approach is more advantageous than a chronological one. In what follows, Vygotsky's theory of higher mental processes is presented in the form it took in works such as "The problem of the cultural development of the child" (1929), "Tool and symbol in child development" (1930), and *The History of the Development of Higher Psychological Functions* (1931).[7]

Vygotsky's theory was based on a number of interlocking concepts, such as the notion of higher mental processes, the notion of mediated activity, and the notion of psychological tools. Human higher mental processes, according to Vygotsky, are *functions of mediated activity*. Let us examine the constituent elements of this theoretical "formula".

1. *Higher mental processes.* The higher mental processes such as verbal thought, logical memory and selective attention differ qualitatively from the lower, natural processes of memory, attention and intelligence, with which they share their names. The higher mental function does not develop as a direct continuation of the corresponding elementary function, thus constituting a new type of psychological formation. In ontogenesis, both types of functions are closely intertwined. This fact has often misled researchers because it creates the illusion of higher mental functions being a direct extension of their lower counterparts.[8] To illustrate this point Vygotsky offered some data on the development of elementary arithmetic notions in children. In the early stages of cognitive development the child's operations with quantities reflect a spontaneous and perceptual attitude. The child is not counting in the proper sense of this term but immediately perceives the quantity. For example, when asked to count a number of pieces forming a cross, a young child makes a systematic mistake by counting the central piece twice. In older children this primitive type of "arithmetic" is replaced by a

more sophisticated approach, making use of such mediators as the fingers and of self-directing speech. In the above-mentioned task older children subordinate their perception of the cross to the method of counting that analyzes the cross into sections and counts the constituent pieces of one section after another.[9]

The study of higher mental processes calls for a revision of the entire nomenclature of psychological functions. Traditional experimental psychology, which paid little attention to the distinction between elementary and higher mental processes, considered activities such as counting or writing as secondary formations, as derivatives of more fundamental processes of perception, memory and learning. Vygotsky, in contrast, suggested that the psychological components of the activities such as drawing, counting and writing traditionally regarded as derivatives of intelligence or imagination, should be granted full rights as higher mental functions.

> The concept of the "development of higher mental functions" and the subject of our study include phenomena, which at first glance may seem unrelated, but which actually represent two main branches, or two streams in the development of the higher forms of behavior. . . . The first group consists of the processes of mastering the external means of cultural development and cognition, e.g. language, writing, counting, drawing. The second group [includes] the processes of the development of the higher mental functions, which so far have failed to be precisely identified and defined, and which still pass traditionally under such names as selective attention, logical memory, concept formation, etc. These two groups of processes, taken together, represent what we are calling the processes of the development of higher mental functions.[10]

2. *From action to thought.* Rather than a simple extension of a natural process originating in human biology, the higher mental process is a function of socially meaningful activity. This emphasis on the generative aspect of activity is theoretically significant, because it distinguishes Vygotsky's position from that of the "substantialists" who envisaged the material substance of the brain or the spiritual substance of Mind as the true seat of mental functions. Vygotsky's position was the opposite: higher mental function is created through activity, it is an objectivation

of action. The traditional rationalist formula, from thought to action, is thus reversed, and becomes, from action to thought.

Consider the following reconstruction of the development of an indicatory gesture in an infant. At first it is simply an unsuccessful grasping movement directed at a desired object. Vygotsky designated this as a "gesture-in-itself". The grasping movement is a result of a natural, unmediated impulse. When the mother comes to the aid of the infant, the "gesture-for-itself" becomes a "gesture-for-other". The other—the mother in this case—interprets the infant's grasping movement as an indicatory gesture. What started as a simple act of grasping has become, because of the mother's mediation, a socially meaningful, communicative act. The infant begins to address his gesture to his mother rather than to the desired object. It is important, however, that the infant is the last person to consciously realize the true meaning of his gesture. Only at this later stage does his gesture become a "gesture-for-himself". The conscious use of the movement of a hand as a gesture comes late in development; the starting point is not an "idea of gesture", not even a gesture as a deliberate behavioral "message", but simply a grasping movement that becomes a message only because of the interpretative function of the other.[11] Development is therefore not an unfolding or maturation of pre-existing "ideas"; on the contrary, it is the formation of such ideas—out of what originally was not an idea—in the course of socially meaningful activity.

3. *Mediation*. The above case brings us to the issue of mediation. An activity that is generative of higher mental processes is a socially meaningful mediated activity. The source of mediation is either in a material tool, in a system of symbols, or in the behavior of another human being. Vygotsky paid particular attention to semiotic mediators, from simple signs to complex semiotic systems such as works of literature, which act as "psychological tools" in transforming natural impulses into higher mental processes.

One aspect of such development is the transformation of unmediated, impulsive behavior aimed at a desired object into the "instrumental" behavior mediated by a material tool. Vygotsky pursued this line of reasoning in his discussion of the similarity and difference between instrumental behavior in apes as reported by W. Köhler and the behavior of human infants.[12] The issue of material tools is crucial because it provides an opportunity to link Vygotsky's theory of higher mental processes with the Marxist theory of material praxis.[13]

Vygotsky himself warned that parallels between material and symbolic tools should be drawn with the utmost caution. The only reliable foundation for such an analogy is the mediatory nature of both instrumental and symbolic action. Whereas in instrumental action the tool mediates human action directed at nature, in the symbolic act a psychological tool mediates man's own psychological processes: "The most essential feature distinguishing the psychological tool from the technical tool, is that it directs the mind and behavior whereas the technical tool, which is also inserted as an intermediate link between human activity and the external object, is directed toward producing one or another set of changes in the object itself".[14] Vygotsky indicated that the psychological aspects of material instrumental activity and symbolic mediatory activity are intertwined: "The mastery of nature and the mastery of behavior are mutually related, [because] in the course of man's transformation of nature, his own nature changes as well".[15]

Finally, Vygotsky pointed to yet another form of mediation—mediation through another person. Here he invoked Pierre Janet's statement that "in the process of development, children begin to use the same forms of behavior in relation to themselves that others initially used in relation to them".[16] Vygotsky also mentioned Piaget's study, which suggested that an argument between children is an original form of mental argument: "We could formulate the general genetic law of cultural development as follows: Any function in the child's cultural development appears twice, or on two planes. First it appears on the social plane, and then on the psychological plane. First it appears between people as an interpsychological category, and then within a child as an intrapsychological category".[17] In this statement Vygotsky comes very close to the position of the social behaviorist, G. H. Mead: "I know of no way in which intelligence or mind could arise or could have arisen, other than through the internalization by the individual of social processes of experience and behavior, that is, through this internalization of the conversation of significant gestures, as made possible by the individual's taking the attitude of the other individuals toward himself or toward what is being thought about".[18]

4. *Internalization.* The essential element in the formation of a higher mental function is the process of internalization. What first appears as an external sign-mediator or an interpersonal communication later becomes an internal psychological process: "Any higher mental function necessarily goes through an external stage in its development because it is initially a social function. This is the center of the whole problem of internal and external behavior. . . . When we speak of a process, 'external' means 'social'. Any higher mental function was external because it was social at one point before becoming an internal, truly mental function".[19]

The idea of internalization was certainly not Vygotsky's invention. He mentioned Karl Bühler's understanding of psychological development as a gradual internalization of adaptively useful actions. One may also think of the psychoanalytic notion of the internalization of the relationships with and images of "significant others". And finally, there is Piaget's theory of the internalization of sensory-motor schemas. What seems to be original in Vygotsky's approach is his elaboration on the theme of the social character of an "external" function which is preserved when that function becomes internalized. There is also an interesting dynamic in the relationship between natural psychological processes and higher processes in the course of internalization. Vygotsky suggested that the internalization of the higher function, such as the mnemonic process based on external memory aids, leads to the following changes: (*a*) the natural mnemonic process is replaced by the mediated type of storing and retrieving; (*b*) the natural process does not disappear, but it is dislocated from the center of activity and becomes its subordinate element; and (*c*) the higher forms of mnemonic activity represent a functional system, rather than a single function, a system that may involve conceptual thinking and verbal analysis.[20]

Vygotsky also pointed to the elusiveness of the social dimension in human mental processes. Psychologists seem to be unable to establish a connection between, for example, the development of logical memory or voluntary action and the social development of a child. This connection is elusive because the "beginning" and the "end" of the developmental process has an individualized form. But although in its biological beginning and in its intrapsychological end of development, a psychological function appears as an individual process, analysis shows that it passes through a stage of being a particular form of social collaboration. Only in the later stages does it acquire an individualized form, carrying "inside" the essential symbolic aspects of its previous structure.[21]

The process of internalization is by no means automatic; the processes involved change their mode of operation. The transition from a collective to an individual form of behavior at first lowers the level of the whole activity. The social forms of behavior are more complex and more advanced, and when individualized they first acquire a simpler mode of operation. For example, egocentric speech is more primitive in its structure than communicative speech, yet as a stage in the development of thought it is higher than the socialized speech of a child of the same age.[22] The significance of the above for the understanding of the disagreement between Vygotsky and Piaget about the role of egocentric speech will be discussed in Chapter Five; what is important now is that the transition from explicitly social type of activity, to its internalized and individualized form may involve a moment of functional regression.

5. *"Primitive" processes.* One of the important advances made by Vygotsky's group was the discovery of intermediate forms situated "between" higher mental processes and natural functions. These intermediate forms testify to the dynamic nature of the developmental process: higher mental processes are acquired neither through a one-time insight, nor through the copying of adult behavior. Symbolic operations emerge from behavior which initially is not symbolic. Taking as an example a child's acquisition of the function of mediated memorization, Vygotsky showed how an auxiliary picture card, which in the future will serve as a psychological tool affecting the structure of the child's mnemonic process, is still perceived by the child as just another stimulus juxtaposed with the target one. The child fails to appreciate the arbitrary nature of a sign-mediator and looks for

a picture card that already has some relationship to the word to be memorized.

In another experiment, meaningless objects were offered as memory aids. Instead of creating a deliberate association between the target word and an auxiliary object-aid, the children attempted to interpret these objects as direct "referents" of the word. In both cases the potential mediatory role of psychological tools was overlooked, and tools themselves were perceived as belonging to the same syncretic whole as the target word.

Vygotsky's notion of "primitive" processes is directly related to Heinz Werner's theory of syncretic forms of behavior and cognition. Vygotsky and his co-workers often referred to an early work of Werner, published in German.[23] Werner, however, focused on the phenomenology of development, rather than on its driving forces. He catalogued the changing forms of mental organization, but was reluctant to speculate about the processes that generate this change. For Vygotsky the "primitive" forms were of interest primarily because they help to explain the dynamics of the emergence of the mediated type of mental process from the syncretic one.

Before proceeding to a systematic examination of Vygotsky's study of the history, structure and dynamics of higher forms of attention, memory, problem solving and decision making, it seems relevant to inquire into the wider theoretical context of his position. This context seems to be dominated by two major issues: the issue of *mediation* as formulated in the Hegelian philosophical system, and the notion of the *social nature* of human cognition as developed in the French sociological school of Emile Durkheim.

THE PROBLEM OF MEDIATION

Vygotsky explicitly acknowledged his dependence upon the Hegelian system of reasoning at least twice. On one occasion, while discussing the issue of psychological tools, he mentioned that mediation (*Vermittlung*) is considered by Hegel as a central characteristic of human reason. The cunning of reason is in the mediating activity which, by causing objects to act upon and react to each other in accordance with their own nature, carries reason's intentions without any direct involvement in the process.[24] On another occasion Vygotsky revealed his acquaintance with Hegel's dialectics of historical development cast in terms of the interaction between the Master and the Slave. The primitive form of the division of labor presupposes the division of the function of supervision and that of practical execution between the supervisor and the worker. In more advanced systems these two roles are integrated in one individual who is the Master and the Slave at one and the same time, that is, someone who makes a decision and implements it as well. Similarly, human mental processes undergo a transition from the "external" form when they are supervised from "outside" and are only executed "inside", to their internalised form when the moment of decision making and execution are integrated inside the psychological apparatus.[25]

The notion of mediation is central to the Hegelian dialectic because it presents all interactions as necessarily mediated by one of the terms involved. For example, the Master and the Slave can not exist in isolation. The Slave is a slave because he is enslaved by the Master and in this way is defined through him. But the Master is a master only because he has succeeded in overcoming and enslaving the other. In this way the Master is also defined only through the Slave.

Moreover, the notion of mediation is essential in distinguishing between animal and human attitudes toward life. Natural impulse or desire (*Begierde*) is essential for both the Man and the Animal, but in the Animal activity engendered by Desire is extinguished at its satisfaction. The Animal does not transcend its own body, it has no distance with respect to itself. But to become human, to have self-consciousness, one must be able to transcend oneself as a given. This transition to self-consciousness becomes possible for the Slave because he satisfies the Desire of the other, and therefore his relationship to the world and to himself becomes mediated:

> Only action carried out in another's service is *Work* [*Arbeit*] in the
> proper sense of the word: an essentially human and humanizing

action. . . . The being that acts to satisfy its *own* instincts, which—as such—are always *natural*, does not rise above Nature: it remains a *natural* being, an animal. But by acting to satisfy an instinct that is *not* my own, I am acting in relation to what is not—for me—instinct. I am acting in relation to an *idea*, a *non*biological end. And it is this transformation of Nature in relation to a *non*material idea that is *Work* in the proper sense of the word: Work that creates a nonnatural, technical, humanized World adapted to the *human* Desire. . . . [26]

Work not only transforms the World, which then becomes "humanized", but it also transforms human nature. Man is no longer dependent on the immediate natural conditions in the World, but on conditions mediated by human civilization. Man continues to be determined by the real World, but since this World has been changed, he changes as well: "Work is *Bildung*, in the double meaning of the word: on the one hand, it forms, transforms the World, humanizes it by making it more adapted to Man; on the other, it transforms, forms, educates man, it humanizes him . . .".[27]

The notion of Work as a source of universal mediation was borrowed from Hegel by Marx and eventually became a central category in Marxist philosophical anthropology. Work is what creates a universal system of "communication" based on the exchange of commodities:

The activity of mediation is no other than activity of labor. Through his labor, man overcomes the estrangement between the objective world and the subjective world; he transforms nature into an appropriate medium for his self-development. When objects are taken and shaped by labor, they become part of the subject who is able to recognize his needs and desires in them. Through labor, moreover, man loses that atomistic existence wherein he becomes a member of a community. The individual, by virtue of his labor, turns into a universal; for labor is of its very nature a universal activity: its product is exchangeable among all individuals.[28]

But whoever accepts material production as a paradigmatic form of human activity must also accept the consequences of such a paradigm. Specifically, it may lead to the identification of human existence as "reified". The phenomenon of reification points to such a mode of human activity when products of this activity are perceived as independent natural "things" rather than as the actual result of human effort. Moreover, human activity itself becomes reified and perceived as a commodity. The issue of Marxist social theory in general and the notion of reification in particular is raised here because Vygotsky's emphasis on tools as mediators creates a possibility for interpreting material production as an explanatory principle of his theory. This very position has been adopted by some modern students of Vygotsky who claim that "in Vygotsky's opinion, the mind is determined by labor activity and the category of practical activity is the general explanatory principle of his theory".[29] This evaluation is not surprising; after all, Vygotsky more than once emphasized the role of practice in psychology (see Chapter Three).

Moreover, Vygotsky's followers, particularly Leontiev, did develop a theory of psychological activity based on the paradigm of material production as it is interpreted in traditional Marxism. In Leontiev's psychological theory human motives and objects of activity are determined by the division of labor in society, while more concrete actions are related to practical goals.[30] What is problematic in Leontiev's attempt to link the study of psychological activity with Marxist social theory was his reluctance to elaborate on the applicability of the material production paradigm and to face up to the phenomenon of reification. Instead of explaining how the phenomenon of reification is accounted for in his psychological theory of human action, Leontiev offered a highly ideological "sermon" about the alienation of human activity under capitalism and its free development in socialist society.[31] Leontiev and his followers also seem to have been determined to show that human interpersonal relations and communication are derivatives of the activity of material production.[32] But this again begs the question of *how* communication conceived in such a way is related to the real system of the division of labor and the exchange of commodities that exist in a given society. Later I will return to the problem of the two paradigms — material production versus interpersonal communication — in the context of a comparison of Vygotsky's ideas with those developed by his students in the late 1930s.

COLLECTIVE REPRESENTATIONS

Now it is time to assess the intellectual context of Vygotsky's claim that human mental functions are social in origin and in content. Taking into account an overall social orientation of Marxism one might assume that it was Marxist theory that provided an intellectual guideline for Vygotsky. This assumption holds no water, however; as Vygotsky showed in his *Crisis*, Marxist theory in the 1920s failed to develop any of the concepts required for a psychological study of human behavior and cognition.[33] The only sufficiently developed theory of human cognition as socially determined was offered by the French sociological school of Emile Durkheim, and was discussed in the related works of Lucien Lévy-Bruhl, Charles Blondel and Maurice Halbwachs.

The sociological school brought about a radical denaturalization of the notion of human cognition. This was achieved with the help of the notion of "collective representations". A collective representation is either a concept or a category of thought held in essentially similar form by a number of individuals to allow effective communication. Moreover, collective representations have a supra-individual character and in this capacity they are imposed upon individual cognition:

> . . . collective ways of acting and thinking have a reality outside individuals who, at any moment of time, conform to it. These are things which exist in their own right. The individual finds them already formed, and he cannot act as if they did not exist or were different from how they are. . . . Of course, the individual plays a role in their genesis. But for a social fact to exist, several individuals, at the very least, must have contributed their action; and it is this combined action which has created a new product. Since this synthesis takes place outside each one of us (for a plurality of consciousness enters into it), its necessary effect is to fix, to institute outside us, certain ways of acting and certain judgements which do not depend on each particular will be taken separately.[34]

Such presumably *a priori* categories of human thought as space and time can be conceived of as functions of collective existence. Historically the first notion of the spatial organization of the world is said to be derived from the idea of a social space, while time is said to represent the rhythm of collective activity: "The division into days, weeks, months, years, etc., corresponds to the periodical recurrence of rites, feasts, and public ceremonies. A calendar expresses the rhythm of the collective activities, while at the same time its function is to assure their regularity".[35]

An interesting first attempt to apply Durkheim's notion of collective representations to a particular mental function was undertaken by Halbwachs in his study of collective memory, *Les Cadres sociaux de la mémoire*, which was published in 1925 and was apparently available to Vygotsky and his colleagues. Halbwachs made an observation coinciding with Vygotsky's views, that what we call memory is not an immediate revival of some immutable image, but rather an active process of *reconstructing* a certain event. Thus memory, far from being a natural function of image retention, appears as an intellectual mnemonic activity. This process of reconstructing an event, according to Halbwachs, is mediated by the group experience contemporary with this event. Halbwachs contended further that—contrary to individual intuition—an event pertaining to group memory is easier to recollect than a highly personal memory: "The idea we most easily picture to ourselves, no matter how personal and specific its elements, is the idea others have of us. The events of our life most immediate to ourselves are also engraved in the memory of those groups closest to us. Hence, facts and conceptions we possess with least effort are recalled to us from the common domain. These remembrances are 'everybody's' to this extent. We can recall them whenever we want just because we can base ourselves on the memory of others".[36]

Halbwachs also astutely observed that many so-called childhood memories are mediated by the activity of adults who select specific episodes from their child's life and then feed them back into the child's memory by way of repeating their own, adult recollection of these events. The resultant childhood memories should rather be called "family memories", even though the child retains them as his or her own.

Halbwachs took one further step and inquired into the possible influence of a nation's historical memory on the autobiographical memories of individuals. He started with the phenomenon of the living historical memory that is preserved by older members of the family and is transmitted to the younger generation. Then comes the formal historical memory of society as a whole. What is important here is that individual memory seems to be constantly shaped in its content and its organization by the social and cultural "frames" or *cadres*, as Halbwachs calls them.

In his later works Halbwachs touched upon another topic relevant to Vygotsky's program, namely the phenomenon of historical change in the recollection of ideologically important information. In his earlier work Halbwachs was concerned with the influence of official history on the organization of the biographical memory of the individual (compare to popular self-identification terms such as the "lost generation", or the "Vietnam generation", etc.), but in his later work he inquired into the process of change in historical memory under the influence of changing value configurations. He showed, for example, how the locations revered by Christians in the Holy Land shifted according to historically significant doctrinal and political changes.[37]

Although Halbwachs' studies are alarmingly essayistic to modern psychological tastes, their broad cultural focus is attractive when compared with more recent cross-cultural studies of memory. In the latter, the spotlight is rather rigidly directed at the alleged benefits of the logically mediated memory when compared with spontaneous and unmediated memorization. There are indications, however, that social life in so-called "primitive" societies compels people to attach different "weights" to memories of different objects, and that these objects will then be remembered in accordance with their social importance or weight, rather than on the basis of their position in an abstract classification schema.[38] Such a memorization can hardly be called unmediated, but the mediating mechanism here is more socially contextual than in a case of abstract classification. Halbwachs' attention to different types of mediation processes and to different socially important types of memorization compares favorably with this recent preoccupation with the categorization process alone.

The issue of the cognition of "primitive" peoples constituted one of the centerpieces of Durkheim's theory. Much of what Vygotsky and Luria wrote about the historical transformation of mental functions was in response to the challenge presented in the works of Durkheim and Lévy-Bruhl. On the surface, the well known and much-criticized notion of "primitive mentality" advanced by Lévy-Bruhl pitted the prelogical forms of cognition characteristic of "primitive" society against the logical thought of modern, Western educated people.[39] On a deeper, epistemological level, "primitive" peoples provided researchers with a model of a "total" society in which objective-behavioral and symbolic-ideological components of human conduct are perfectly integrated. All forms of behavior and cognition in such a society seem to be determined by the mythological and ritualistic core of the people's life-world. Any socially meaningful act is ritualistically completed to resemble the paradigmatic act of the mythological hero. In this way, a total integration of life is achieved, and no act is idiosyncratic or "atomistic" because, by definition, any act has a mythological history as its natural environment and context. The entire history and "philosophy" of the tribe is present in every act of its members through reference to the appropriate act of a mythological hero. In a sense, the "primitive" society is an ideal case fitting Durkheim's notion of "collective representations".

"Primitive" society also displays in a pure form some of the mechanisms of social mediation that have become obscured in more "advanced" societies. One of the fundamental problems in any society is how it is presented as a whole to an individual member. Durkheim discussed this problem in his study of totemism. The totem is conceived as a spirit of the clan represented by a totemic animal or plant. According to Durkheim the totem is nothing but the clan itself taken in its hypostatic form as a deity. The worship of a totemic animal is an affirmation of the individual's belonging to the clan itself. This affirmation is achieved, however, not through intellectual comprehension of one's "membership", but through concrete identification with and "participation" in the totemic animal. The totem is thus a material-symbolic formation which, while remaining a real animal, at the same time serves as a symbol of the clan and as the family name of its members. The mechanism of participation allows the part to stand for the whole, and one element to be present in a number of systems without contradiction. This mechanism, which is certainly prelogical, serves an important function of social cohesion in the tribe and extends the social type of relationship toward nature as well.[40]

Vygotsky was fascinated by the mechanism of totemic identification, which he believed was also present in children's thinking. The identification of a member of a clan with a totemic red parrot, for example, may seem illogical when considered in terms of conceptual identification, but it is quite consistent with the logic of participation, in the same way that different members of a family are identified by one name.[41]

The totem is probably one of the simplest systems of social mediation that evolved historically into the complex ideologies of "advanced" societies. But it is important to remember that a number of participatory practices, such as a salute to the flag (as well as its burning), are retained in modern society and continue to play an important psychological role.

The notion of collective representations allowed for the social interpretation of human cognition, but it also revealed what is problematic in such an interpretation, namely the issue of individuation. Since collective representations are by definition similar in all members of a given group, the question is how does the individual acquire his or her own concepts and representations? This question is of paramount importance because it applies not just to Durkheimian theory but to any social theory of human cognition. Durkheim answered this question by reverting to the mind–body dualism:

> There are in [the man] two classes of states of consciousness that differ from each other in origin and nature, and in the end toward which they aim. One class merely expresses our organisms and the object to which they are most directly related. Strictly individual, the states of consciousness of this class connect us only with ourselves, and we can no more detach them from us than we can detach ourselves from our bodies. The states of consciousness of the other class, on the contrary, come to us from society; they transfer society into us and connect us with something that surpasses us. Being collective, they are impersonal; they turn us toward ends that we hold in common with other men; it is through them and them alone that we can communicate with others. . . . In brief, this duality corresponds to the double existence that we lead concurrently: the one purely individual and

rooted in our organism, the other social and nothing but an extension of society.[42]

Durkheim further remarked that the dualism of human nature is just another instance of the more fundamental division of things into the sacred and the profane. The issue of individuation resurfaced in the dispute between Durkheim, Halbwachs and Blondel regarding who is the subject of the theory of "primitive mentality".[43] If the subject is identified as the bearer of the prelogical and often even magic collective representations, then it is hard to understand how such an illogical person copes with practical problems that require realistic and logical solutions. The dualistic answer to this question would presume the coexistence of the two subjects in one: the subject of the practical relationship with nature who is realistic, and the subject of social life who depends on myth and magic. This dualistic solution was questioned by Blondel who pointed out that practical skills can hardly be acquired separately from the social group, and that social communication is positively required for the transmission of these skills to the next generation. Moreover, it is difficult to imagine practical intelligence without certain generalizations, but the generality of human concepts, according to Durkheim, is rooted in their social and communicable origin. It seems impossible to divide a "primitive" person into an illogical "ideologue" who lives in the realm of the sacred, and a practical realist whose body guides him in the realm of the profane.

The problem of individuation became one of the central issues in the discussion between Vygotsky and Piaget regarding the paths of a child's development and the role of socialization. The theoretical experience of the French school seems indispensable in understanding the problems of any social theory of cognition. As we shall see later, Vygotsky's students, particularly Leontiev, experienced considerable difficulty in explaining the phenomenon of individuation, which bemused the French thinkers. It is also significant that the most sophisticated Soviet critic of Vygotsky's theory, Sergei Rubinshtein, revealed a deep and genuine interest in the work of the Durkheimians.[44]

THE CULTURAL-HISTORICAL THEORY

One of the first, and rather straightforward, attacks Vygotsky's group made on the issue of the social determination of speech and reasoning was Luria's study of urban, rural and homeless children. Luria formulated his fundamental assumption thus: "The social circumstances in which a child grows up will inevitably leave their mark on the mechanisms underlying complex psychological processes, not just on the content of those processes".[45] That is, different social experiences are expected to stimulate different types of mental processes, not just to supply different knowledge. To test this hypothesis Luria undertook a study of simple associations in three groups of children, who presumably had had very different social experiences. One group comprised children reared in a big city (presumably Moscow), the second group included children from a remote rural village, and the third group represented homeless urchins, altogether some 130 children between nine and twelve years of age. Luria used a simple experimental design, with children responding with the first association to the target word. He suggested that such first, "spontaneous" associations are more revealing of the social experience of a child than are "prepared" answers to psychological questionnaires.

The data obtained allowed Luria to assess the degree of homogeneity of responses, defined as a percentage of children in a given group who produced the same association to a target word. On the other hand, the index of idiosyncrasy allowed him to assess the number of unique responses in a given group. An inter-group comparison showed a sharp difference in terms of the homogeneity between rural children on the one hand, and urban and homeless children on the other. Unique responses were infrequent in rural children, and the degree of homogeneity was very high. Luria interpreted these results as an indication of the influence of the impoverished rural environment on a child's associative abilities: "Even though the rural child may think that the word association he gives as a response is out of his own head, in actual fact it is merely environment speaking through him; and he himself unconsciously responds in a way typical for his group as a whole".[46]

Next Luria inquired into the degree of homogeneity of

responses which depended on the experiential category of the target word. It turned out that the homogeneity of responses to the words related to the immediate environment, such as home and school, was much higher in rural than in urban children; the number of unique responses grew in rural children when the target word referred to city life or social phenomena. At the same time urban and homeless children gave about the same number of unique responses to all categories of target words. Luria interpreted this as an indication of the immediate character of the experience of a rural child, who responded with a social cliché to the question pertaining to a familiar sphere of life and improvised with a unique answer when responding to the word representing the unfamiliar one. For the urban children the difference in categories of the target words was less important because their experience was mediated by verbal information: "For the city child the world of immediate impressions begins to give way to more mediated forms of experience, to a world of facts assimilated through communication, books, and cultural influences".[47]

This becomes particularly clear if one compares the responses of rural and urban children to such words as "cart" and "union". For rural children a cart is a familiar detail of their everyday experience, to which they respond in a very homogeneous way: almost two-thirds of the responses was "to ride". Urban children, on the other hand, failed to display any uniform answer to the word "cart", and produced a number of literary associations. The word "union" seemed to be interpreted by rural children in the context of their experience with cooperative unions that have their own shops; the most frequent association was "shop". In contrast, urban children responded to "union" as a social notion often encountered in newspapers, producing such associations as "workers", "youth" and "councils".

After this rather straightforward attempt to assess the influence of sociocultural milieu on a child's mind, Vygotsky and Luria embarked on a much more ambitious project to study the changes occurring in human cognition associated with changes in the cultural environment. Here I only briefly discuss this project because it has been described in considerable detail by Luria himself and has already generated a number of critical replications by American psychologists.[48] At the heart of the project was the opportunity offered by the rapid change in the sociocultural environment of Soviet Central Asia in the late 1920s and the early 1930s.

The Uzbeks, a central Asiatic national group, were almost overnight brought from a medieval, feudal society into a nascent socialist republic. This rapid transition included considerable changes in economic practices—from that of family-based farming or cattle breeding to the planned economy of the collective farms. Concurrently, a massive education and propaganda campaign had been launched, with formerly disenfranchized groups, such as women, gaining access to elementary school education and previously forbidden social activities.

Vygotsky and Luria hypothesized that such a rapid cultural transition, which affected some people but left others untouched, was the closest thing to a cultural-historical experiment. Some Uzbeks continued living in a traditional society, while others, indistinguishable from the first "baseline" group, experienced, in one short leap, a cultural change that normally would have taken centuries. Cultural-historical theory did not distinguish specifically between changes in economic practices and in educational standards, considering them to be mutually related. In the most general terms the idea behind the cultural-historical project was the following. In those peasants who continued to maintain their traditional way of life, Vygotsky and Luria expected to find "primitive" forms of cognition mediated by everyday experience. These "primitive" forms, it was argued, should be not unlike those discovered in young children by Piaget, Werner and Vygotsky himself. At the same time people engaged in a new, modern form of economy requiring considerable collective planning and communication, as well as some abstractive reasoning, were expected to display verbally and logically mediated forms of cognition. This second group of subjects had been exposed to some schooling, and they were expected to respond to psychological tests in a way similar to that of older, educated children.

The study included a number of tests to assess the subjects' perceptual and memory strategies, classification, problem solving, and self-analysis. The use of tests was accomplished by in-depth interviews during which Luria tried to assess the subjects' rationale for giving this or that answer. To get some idea of how the study was conducted consider the following vignettes.

One subject, an illiterate peasant from a remote village, was shown a hammer, a saw, a log and a hatchet and asked to tell which of the objects could be called by the same word. At first the peasant rejected the very idea of a common name, arguing that you cannot call different objects by the same name. When prompted by the suggestion that "one fellow said that the hammer, saw and hatchet are alike", the subject responded that the log also belongs to the same group. When the experimenter suggested that hammer, saw and hatchet are tools, the subject responded: "Yes, but even if we have tools, we still need wood—otherwise, we can't build anything".[49]

Another illiterate peasant was given the following syllogism. In the far north all bears are white. Novaya Zemlya Island is in the far north. What color are the bears there? The subject refused to speculate about bears he had never seen: "We always speak only of what we see; we don't talk about what we haven't seen". When Luria directed the subject's attention to the meaning of the words of the syllogism, the peasant replied: "Your words can be answered only by someone who was there, and if a person wasn't there he can't say anything on the basis of your words".[50] From tests and conversations such as these Luria concluded that illiterate, traditionally oriented people cannot transcend their everyday experience. For them any mental problem always appeared to be related to some practical situation encountered in real life.

An entirely different attitude was revealed by those subjects who had received some schooling and were employed on a collective farm. They used abstractive classification and solved simple syllogisms easily. Interesting results were obtained from an intermediate group of subjects who were involved in some sort of collective work, but who were barely literate. These subjects displayed a certain ability to think categorically, but they often reverted to the contextual logic of practical situations. One such subject correctly put horse, sheep and camel in one group, explaining that "the ones over here are animals", but when asked why pail or house did not fit into the group, he responded that: "Some of them do. You need a pail to water the animals".[51] Luria argued that this group of barely literate peasants represented a transitional stage in which categorical thinking was already taking root, but in which situational logic was still widely used when the subjects were left to their own premises.

Considered as a pilot project, Luria's study was enormously important and inspiring, but unfortunately it was destined to remain unpublished for over forty years. Soviet critics hastily accused Luria and Vygotsky of being apologetic followers of Durkheim and Lévy-Bruhl, and of portraying national minorities as being devoid of rational reasoning. As a result of those accusations the cultural-historical aspect of Vygotsky's program was seriously undermined. Interest in this problem was renewed in the Soviet Union only in the mid-1970s, largely because of the gradual opening to Western studies in cross-cultural psychology. Thanks to the efforts of Michael Cole, Luria's work became available in English and served as an inspiration for a number of field studies comparing the cognition of illiterate peoples from "primitive" societies to that of educated Westerners. In the process, however, a certain shift in emphasis had occurred. The original idea of Vygotsky and Luria had been to study cognitive processes in "primitive" people as an approximation to studying mental processes in people of a different historical epoch. The cultural-historical approach aimed at discovering the changes in mental processes that occur as a result of changes in the social and cultural organization of society.[52] If implemented, this approach could result in truly historical studies of the cognition of people in ancient, medieval or Renaissance times, with each type of cognition being put in correspondence to a specific form of material production and culture. In more recent Western studies this problem—which has never been fully elaborated—has been narrowed to the problem of the influence of different types of literacy on cognition.

It has become clear that a school-based type of literacy, long perceived as the only natural one because of its predominance in modern Western societies, represents only one facet of the overall phenomenon.[53] Researchers have become aware of different types of literacy—some school-based, some acquired outside school through the learning of an indigenous script of a given group, and some taught in alternative educational settings such as religious schools. There are indications that different types of literacy vary in their relationships to the development of higher mental processes. One possible approach to this phenomenon is to order different types of literacy depending on their contribution to a decontextualized type of sign use. If, for example, a literacy based on a given script can be used only for a very specific type of activity, that would place this literacy into a category of contextual rather than decontextualized means. Such contextual literacy might be of little consequence for overall cognitive development.[54]

Another relevant question is how schooling as such is related to the development of cognitive and behavorial functions. As many authors state, the problem is complicated because it is almost impossible to separate cognitive skills acquired through "pure schooling" from the hypothetical benefits of literacy taken by itself. One might wish however to inquire into special types of schooling such as religious instruction in Judaism in a community whose culture is not based on the Hebrew language. This type of instruction has all the features of systematic schooling, including extensive use and interpretation of a number of texts, problem-solving exercises, logical reasoning, etc. At the same time it remains highly contextual because Hebrew, in this case, is not used outside the religious school and the problems discussed do not transcend the content of sacred texts.

Some authors, such as David Olson, have argued that there is little direct connection between literacy and the development of higher cognitive processes. Olson interpreted Luria's data as reflecting primarily a difference in perspectives between the experimenter and the "primitive" subject, rather than the latter's inability to use the higher forms of cognition: "Members of traditional societies are quite capable of drawing inferences from premises which are regarded as realistic and empirical. . . . In the example mentioned above the inability to solve the syllogism about white bears stems from the fact that the experimenter is talking about the *words*, while the subject is talking about bears".[55] This opinion was also shared by Cole, who questioned the notion of the cultural-historical emergence of a new type of cognitive process: "What Luria interprets as the acquisition of new modes of thought, I am more inclined to interpret as changes in the application of previously available modes to particular problems and contexts of discourse represented by the experimental setting".[56]

One possible answer to Cole's criticism would be to stress the difference between various cognitive *processes* leading to the solution of a test problem. It is true that both "primitive" and educated people are capable of solving certain syllogistic problems, but the point made by the cultural-historical theory was that they do this in different ways. While the "primitive" individual arrived at a correct answer by substituting his or her personal experiences for the terms of the syllogism, the educated individual relied on thinking in verbal, idealized meanings of the words. In both cases the *structure* of syllogism remained the same, but the mechanism of its solution was different. Cole implied that the syllogistic reasoning first applicable to concrete experiences later became applicable to verbal statements as well. The cultural-historical point of view emphasized that such a transition changes the entire system of reasoning, with personal experiences, once at the forefront, later becoming subordinate moments in the predominantly verbal type of thinking. The difference between "primitive" and educated logic resembles the difference between solving a mathematical problem by means of arithmetic operations versus algebraic formula. In both cases the result is the same, but the algebraic solution does not require concrete numbers until the last stage.

One of the central issues of cultural-historical theory was the denaturalization of psychological functions under the influence of psychological tools. Instead of an immediate interaction with problems posed by the environment, the human mind becomes involved in the indirect relationships mediated by more and more sophisticated systems of symbolic tools. Let us examine this transition using as an example the changing system of the measurement of time. The early forms of time measurement were characterized by using natural processes to immediately and perceptually mark equal intervals. In such measurements the comprehension of time duration was not yet detached from the natural processes involved, be it a movement of sand in a sand glass or running water in a clepsydra. No symbolic signifiers were interposed between the process of measurement and its representation to the individual. This original immediacy disappeared with the invention of the mechanical clock in which the actual process of measuring intervals of time is separated from the symbolic representation of the process on the dial. The actual movement of the hands of the clock remained the only link between the "natural time" of the mechanism and the "symbolic time" of the dial. The natural aspect disappeared completely and the chronometer became a purely symbolic tool when electronic digital technology replaced the clockwork mechanism. The process of perceiving time has become highly mediated. In order for an individual to read a watch, the whole system of symbols such as digits, language abbreviations, positions on the screen, etc., have to be learned.

The central object of cultural-historical theory was to show how such supposedly individual psychological phenomena as memorization, decision making and concept formation depend on historically specific extrapersonal systems of mediation. In this capacity cultural-historical theory promised to become a synthetic social theory, a type of theory for which modern social scientists such as Clifford Geertz are still longing. Actually there is a strong consensus of opinion between Vygotsky and Geertz when it comes to defining the fundamentals of a theory of human conduct. Geertz, who approached this problem as an anthropologist, suggested that

> culture is best seen . . . as a set of controlling mechanisms—plans, recipes, instructions . . . for the governing of behavior. . . . Man is precisely the animal most desperately dependent upon such extragenetic, outside-the-skin control mechanisms, such cultural programs, for ordering his behavior. . . . Thinking consists not of "happenings in the head" (though happenings there and elsewhere are necessary for it to occur) but of a traffic of what have been called, by G. H. Mead and others, significant symbols—words for the most part but also gestures, drawings, musical sound, mechanical devices like clocks, or natural objects like jewels—anything, in fact, that is disengaged from its mere actuality and used to impose meaning upon experience.[57]

There is one intriguing question that so far remains unanswered, namely, what was the original source of Vygotsky's concept of psychological tools. In a number of his works he referred to several literary sources, each of which could have served as inspiration. He quoted Richard Turnwald's study of the memory aids used in ancient Peru called *quipu*. He also mentioned the book of Arseniev, a Russian traveler to Siberia and the Far East, who described amulets used by Siberian people that served as attention-getters and memory aids. Vygotsky, however, could have had another reason for being sensitive to the issue of psychological tools; this originated in his early youth, and could have unconsciously influenced the direction of his thought. Certain objects involved in Jewish religious ritual are psychological tools *par excellence*. The major part of the spiritual life of a Jew is to be constantly reminded of his link to the Almighty. Apart from such a permanent artificial reminder of the covenant between the people of Israel and the Almighty as circumcision, there are a number of auxiliary psychological tools. One of them is *tsitses*, the tassels attached to the corners of garments: "You must make tassels like flowers on the corners of your garments, you and your children's children. Into this tassel you shall work a violet thread, and whenever you see this in the tassel, you shall remember all the Lord's commandments and obey them . . ." (Numbers, 15: 38–40). Another conspicuous psychological tool of Jewish life are phylacteries, which consist of two small leather boxes with leather laces attached, one box being tied on the forehead, and one on the left arm. Each box has a piece of parchment on which some passages from the holy text are written: "Bind them on your wrist as a sign, and let them be a pendant on your forehead" (Deuteronomy, 6: 8–9). It seems important that in the Biblical text these "tools" are introduced not as symbols, nor as ritual objects, but as purely psychological aids aimed at affecting the memory of a Jew and regulating his behavior. One possible aspect of the cultural-historical analysis which remains to be studied is an inquiry into the process of the transformation of simple psychological tools into complex, multidimensional symbols of different religions and ideologies.

THE DEVELOPMENT OF HIGHER PSYCHOLOGICAL PROCESSES

A study of the historical change in the mechanisms of human conduct under the influence of the changing systems of psychological tools constituted only one aspect of Vygotsky's project.

The other aspect of the same project was an inquiry into the dynamics of the appropriation of cultural means of behavior by a child.

Methodology

As an alternative to the traditional understanding of child development as a process of natural maturation, Vygotsky suggested a cultural development schema that focused on the child's acquisition and use of psychological tools. Correspondingly, the method of study had been changed from that of evoking a child's natural responses, to that of prompting a child to use artificial sign-mediators. This methodology became known as the principle of "double stimulation". In addition to target stimuli (such as words to be remembered, or items to be noticed) a child was supplied with auxiliary means (such as picture cards, symbols, rehearsal techniques, etc.) that were potentially useful in the organization of the child's performance. The tasks were selected in such a way that the child could make only limited progress without the help of these auxiliary means. Vygotsky argued that such a method not only helped to uncover the dynamics of the child's acquisition of mediated skills, but also "externalized"— that is, brought into the field of observation—some inner mechanisms of cognitive development that would otherwise remain hidden.

To amplify the dynamic aspect of the study Vygotsky and his collaborators did not limit themselves to a study of children of different ages, but also included children with various handicaps, and adults. By providing a child with new auxiliary means, by encouraging or discouraging verbal mediation, and by occasionally withholding mediators from a child or an adult who had already become accustomed to them, Vygotsky sought to get every frame from the picture of mental dynamics.

Memory

One of the early targets of Vygotsky's developmental program was the study of a child's memory. Vygotsky suggested two terms to designate what he considered to be two radically different forms of memory: *mneme*, an organic, natural form of retention of images characteristic of all living organisms; and *mnemo-*

technique, based on a system of artificial devices and techniques aimed at organizing human mnemonic processes.[58] The developmental process was seen as a transition from "immediate" (only organically mediated) mneme to culturally mediated mnemotechnique. A paradigm for the study of this process was developed by Vygotsky and Leontiev, following Janet's idea that what we now call *souvenirs* were an original form of mnemotechnique with an object-souvenir serving as a reminder of a specific place or event.[59]

Children of different ages were presented with a list of fifteen words to be remembered. In the first session they had to do this without any help; in the second session they were offered fifteen picture cards that could be used as memory aids; the third session was identical to the second, but words to be remembered included abstract notions like "meeting", rather than simple names of objects used in the second session. In two series of experiments pictures were either matched with words by the experimenter, or they were simply placed on the table and the child was free to match them as he or she wished. The major quantitative result of this study was what Vygotsky called "parallelogram of development".[60] In preschool children the use of memory aids did not bring any significant differences in memorization. The situation changed dramatically for seven- to eight-year-olds, who recalled about 75 percent of the words with the help of picture cards, against 30 percent without them. In adults the difference narrowed again, with mediated recall yielding 93 versus 60 percent of unmediated. Vygotsky argued that adults even in "unmediated" conditions used certain mnemotechniques that were already internalized and thus they did not depend on external memory aids.

Concerning qualitative changes, Vygotsky remarked that observing the children's use of picture cards he could not escape the feeling of being a witness to an experimentally evoked process of transition from a natural to a cultural type of memory. He argued that the use of memory aids helped a child to abandon simple, associative types of mnemonic connections in favor of a structural system resembling a Gestalt. The mnemotechnique process consisted of three constituent parts: (1) the use of a card as a memory aid; (2) the formation of a new memory structure that included a target word and a picture; and (3) the act of recall during which the target word is identified within the previously formed structure. For example, to the target word "death" a child selected a card with a picture of a camel. This was the first stage—the card was used in connection with a memorization task. Then the child formed a structure: "The camel is in the desert; a traveler dies without water". And finally the child recalled the target word "death", identifying it within the structure of this miniature story he had just created.[61]

From the point of view of natural memorization this procedure is strange and should be counterproductive because, instead of retaining a single target word, the child had to operate with a series of items. Vygotsky's point was that the natural mnemonic function was replaced by a functional system that included imagination, abstraction and discourse. Natural retention became a subordinate element in the new system of higher mental processes. The activity of *mnema*, that is, remembering in an organic sense, is superseded by such operations as composition, abstraction of common features, imagination, etc. All these new functions now serve memory and replace its more primitive forms.

These early studies have had an interesting counterpart in some more recent Western memory research, which developed independently of Vygotsky's tradition and lacked its integrating theoretical framework. For example, J. Meacham and J. Colombo confirmed that sign-mediators are effective in improving the so-called prospective memory in children, that is, the ability to remember an action that should be done in the future.[62] The role of symbolic mediators has been acknowledged in studies of so-called everyday memory, and is now taken into account in the rehabilitation of patients with memory problems.[63] John Flavell reviewed a number of studies of mediated memory in children and concluded that there is indeed a developmental sequence from the stage when a child engages in an activity with a potential mediator to a stage when a child is capable of using this mediator *as a tool* directed at his or her own memory processes. Flavell further indicated that although a majority of studies had been focusing on the mediatory function of verbal rehearsal, this does not mean that specific mnemonic tasks would not require visual imagery or model-building mediation.[64]

Finally, there has recently been a growing awareness among

students of memory that an individual's activity in storing and retrieving information is of principal importance for understanding human remembering. A number of studies in so-called "reality monitoring"—the ability to distinguish between memories of perceived and imagined items—revealed the significant role played by the subject's generative activity. Reality monitoring has been found to be enhanced when the items to be remembered and differentiated are generated by the subject himself or herself.[65] On a more general plane, it seems plausible that successful recollection essentially depends on the markers left by the mnemonic operations made by a subject. Furthermore, these markers could be more or less effective depending on the level of processing, with the semantic level displaying certain advantages. This line of reasoning could eventually contribute to the revival of the discussion initiated by some of Vygotsky's students in the 1930s. Their discussion focused on the relative importance of memory aids as such versus the generative activity of the subject prompted by the presence of memory aids. For example, extending Leontiev's study, one might inquire into the respective contributions of a picture card compared with those of other possible mediators such as pictograms, random dot patterns, numbers, knots, etc. On the other hand, one might also focus on the child's level of verbal proficiency, which allows a structure like "the traveler in the desert" to develop. Some of the relevant problems raised by Vygotsky's followers will be discussed later.

Attention

Another higher mental function investigated by Vygotsky's group was voluntary attention. From the cultural-historical point of view voluntary attention was seen as the separate Master and Slave functions now integrated in one person.[66] Leontiev suggested that in "primitive" societies the majority of people are compelled to do punishingly hard and monotonous work that turns them into little more than "speaking tools". The task of organizing the work of these "tools" contributes to the development of a special system of stimuli and commands aimed at controlling their behavior: "Signals given by a foreman, the rhythmic sounds of a drum, working songs—these created the center around which the labor activities of the primitive man were built up".[67] A system of commands originally intènded for others has the potential of becoming a command for oneself: "The transition from the organization of the attention of others to the creation of stimuli organizing one's own attention—this is the route marked out in the history of the development of voluntary attention".[68]

In ontogenesis voluntary attention appears as a regulatory mechanism for natural, spontaneous attentional processes that are descernible at a very early age. The route from natural to culturally mediated attention is long and it is not until school age that a child is capable of utilizing auxiliary stimuli to direct his or her attention. It takes even longer for this process to "ingrow", that is, to become internalized and thus to attain the status of a true higher mental function.

To get some "cuts" of this process Vygotsky and Leontiev designed a series of experiments in which children of various ages were engaged in a "forbidden colors" game. I will describe these experiments only briefly since they have been discussed in some detail elsewhere.[69] "Forbidden colours" is a popular verbal game in Russia in which one child asks questions concerning the color of things, such as "What color is a cucumber?", and the other must answer while avoiding some colors (such as green or yellow), which are agreed to be forbidden. Additional complexity can be achieved by forbidding the repetition of the name of any color twice. The winner is the child who makes fewer mistakes while giving plausible answers. In Leontiev's experiments children of different ages, from preschoolers to adolescents, as well as adults, answered eighteen questions, of which seven concerned color. In addition to natural, unmediated conditions, children were given nine color cards and told that "they must help you to win". As in the case of the memory study discussed in the previous section, the major qualitative result was that the school-age children, particularly the ten- to thirteen-year-olds, dramatically improved their performance when aided by the card-mediators. In contrast, in many preschoolers the color cards not only failed to improve performance, but actually made it more difficult. For example, the availability of a white card caused some younger children to give the repeated response "white", which was a forbidden color. Leontiev concluded that for preschoolers the color cards competed as a stimuli with the main stimulus questions thus complicating the situation and failing to serve as psychological tools.

Although school-age children used cards in a number of ways, two major patterns could be discerned. A more primitive approach consisted of putting away the color card corresponding to the forbidden color as if to erase these colors from the list of possible responses. Leontiev linked this approach to a "magic attitude" observed in children, but also reported in "primitive" cultures. The second method of operation included keeping all the cards in view until the question was asked, then checking them, and putting the "used" card aside or in a different row. It is also worth mentioning that on one occasion a child who played without cards spontaneously turned to surrounding colored objects with the idea of using them to assist him in his task.[70]

Vygotsky suggested that the use of color cards helped children to differentiate two stages of the game: first, when a possible answer should be checked against the list of forbidden colors, and second, when a plausible answer should be found and given. A child often achieved this by placing cards corresponding to the forbidden colors in the front row and by keeping his or her attention on them. Once the child detected a provocative question, he or she stopped, and gave a modified answer. For example, to a question about the color of grass (with green being a forbidden color) one child responded: "The grass is yellow in the Fall".[71]

Vygotsky's explanation should be kept in mind when considering the recent failure of A. K. Adams *et al.* to replicate the Leontiev-Vygotsky study.[72] The dynamics observed by the American researchers coincided with those reported by Leontiev: the preschoolers' performance did not improve with the availability of color cards, and the difference between natural and card-mediated conditions was maximal in the ten- to thirteen-year-olds. Statistically, however, the differences between the two conditions had been insignificant. Children of all ages above six made many fewer errors under natural conditions than did those in Leontiev's sample. The authors also reported that the overall use of cards was infrequent. One could find certain methodological peculiarities that may account for the differences in the data reported by Adams *et al.* and Leontiev. For example, it seemed that the task was too easy for the American sample: children of school age made no more than two mistakes under natural conditions, and thus there was little room for improvement. I am more interested, however, not in these details but in the line of reasoning advanced by Adams *et al.* They argued that the improvement in performance with age was caused not by the mastery of psychological tools but by gaining access to alternative strategies for answering provocative questions. Older children were able to rely on compounded (e.g. off-white) or related (e.g. beige) color terms and thus escaped the trap. The authors thus focused on the second stage of the game when the child had already noticed the trap and was seeking a plausible answer. The role of card-mediators, as described by Leontiev, is primarily in keeping attention on possible traps and in inhibiting forbidden responses, and thus belongs to the first stage of the game. As for the alternative strategies in answering provocative questions, Adams *et al.* confirmed Vygotsky's idea mentioned above.

Decision Making

The ability of psychological tools to differentiate what originally appears as an immediate response became a focus of the third series of Vygotsky's studies, that of decision making. For the paradigm of decision making Vygotsky took the case of the proverbial ass who allegedly died of hunger being unable to choose between two bundles of hay. One could also add the well known phenomenon of experimental neurosis in dogs discovered by Pavlov. A dog who had been conditioned to respond in different ways to pictures of a square and a circle became neurotic when shown a picture of an ellipse. Both examples reveal the limits of natural behavior when it comes to a choice between equally strong stimuli. To overcome this limitation, even the most primitive of human cultures has developed a number of techniques aimed at providing artificial mediation in the situation of decision making. Whereas the proverbial ass died and the Pavlovian dog became hysterical, people in traditional societies cast lots or interpret dreams. By assigning special trigger functions to external signs (such as dice, coins, etc.) with no natural connection to the subject matter of the decision, the individual becomes capable of regulating his or her own behaviour.

Vygotsky believed that casting lots was one of those psychological "fossils" or rudiments which, together with tying knots and counting fingers, represented the most ancient form of psychological tools. These rudiments are important because they revealed the very essence of culturally mediated behavior. They are the preserved "formulas" of cultural development. Mediation, however, can be more exotic than casting lots. Vygotsky recalled Lévy-Bruhl's study of "primitive" people who widely used the interpretation of dreams as a decision-making tool. When one Kaffir chief faced a particularly tough decision he said: "I will dream about this".[73] Dreams, through the system of socially determined meanings assigned to them, could become tools of decision making. A dream for a Kaffir chief is not a passive natural phenomenon happening to him but an active instrument with the help of which an important choice could be made. This particular mediating mechanism may be primitive and the solution illogical, but the underlying psychological process is cultural rather than natural.

From the ontogenetic perspective the introduction of a psychological tool in the form of a sign-mediator helps to create a functional barrier between the sensory and the motor parts of the behavioral acts of a child. Consider the following simple experiment designed by Vygotsky. Four- and five-year-olds were instructed to press one of five keys on a keyboard responding to a picture-stimulus perceived. In this form the task was too complex for children to accomplish: they displayed considerable uncertainty in choosing a key. What was more important, however, was that this uncertainty revealed itself in an integral, undifferentiated behavior. Instead of choosing a key, the children actually initiated some movement, then slowed down, corrected it, shifted toward another key, etc. The search for the solution involved perception, memory and motor apparatus as an integral, organic whole. The children were then offered a number of symbols mounted on small boards that could be attached to the keys. The availability of these mediators drastically changed the children's performance. They not only improved the accuracy of their responses, but more importantly, they changed their structure. Symbol-mediators created a sort of functional barrier separating the perceptual-memory system responsible for decision making from the motor system, which retained only an executive role. By creating such a barrier the symbolic mediators not only differentiated the decision from its implementation, but also allowed for a delayed action. The inclusion of symbolic operations created an entirely new psychological "field". Operation in this field depends not so much on what is immediately given, but takes into account images of possible future events. This creates the necessary conditions for the emergence of "free" action that is not bound by the present situation.[74]

This differentiation between the decision part and the implementation part of an action had a direct relevance for the understanding of the phenomenon of the human will. Vygotsky criticized attempts to interpret human decision making following the model of competing reflexes in dogs suggested by Sherrington. In the field of reflexes competition occurs between two implementations, not two choices. In human subjects the conflict between motives occurs at the stage of decision making rather than in the execution of an action. In his reasoning Vygotsky followed the argument advanced by Kurt Lewin in his study of will.[75]

Lewin explained his position with the help of the following example. Suppose I should send a letter. To do this I establish an artificial connection between my intention and the image of a mailbox. Only at this stage the decision process takes place, all the rest is an automatic implementation of the previously made decision. Once I am in the street the sight of the first mailbox automatically triggers the "natural" response of depositing the letter. The paradox of will, concluded Vygotsky, is that the willful act is implemented by an automatic action which itself is beyond the will.[76]

Repeating some of Lewin's experiments, Vygotsky observed how a child who found himself in a difficult situation with two equally attractive goals requiring mutually exclusive actions, was making a transition from an unmediated type of choice, full of hesitations, reversals and global responses, to one mediated by arbitrary means such as dice, coins, etc. These mediators helped to separate the decision part, which is conscious and willful, from the implementation part, which is automatic and deterministic. In those experiments and observations Vygotsky saw the psychological equivalent of the fundamental philosophical problem of free will versus determinism. On the one hand, casting lots creates a purely deterministic situation. A child who only a moment ago could not choose between two actions, now responds in a definite, reflex-like way to the sight of, say, the black side of a die. The action itself is therefore purely deterministic. On the other hand, however, neither the black nor the white side of a die has any natural relation to the child's action. It was a child who first created what Lewin called a quasi-need (*quasi-Bedürfnisse*) linking the black side of a die with a certain response. From this second point of view the behavior observed was a clear case of the action of free will. Using an artificial mediator the child willfully created a new situation in which his choice became linked to a deliberately selected stimulus: "Free will, as the experiments show, is exercised not by the freedom from motives, but by the child's comprehension of a situation and by the realization of the necessity of a choice determined by the motive; as the philosophical maxim has it, freedom is in the comprehension of necessity".[77]

NOTES

1. Lev Vygotsky, "Consciousness as a problem of the psychology of behavior". *Soviet Psychology*, vol. 17, 1979, pp. 5–35.
2. See Alexander Luria, *The Making of Mind*. Cambridge, MA: Harvard University Press, 1978.
3. Semion Dobkin, "Ages and days". In K. Levitin, *One is not Born a Personality*. Moscow: Progress, 1982, p. 37.
4. See Lev Vygotsky, *Istoriya Razvitiya Vysshikh Psikhicheskikh Funckcii (The History of the Development of Higher Psychological Functions)*. In L. Vygotsky, *Sobranie Sochinenii (Collected Papers)*, vol. 3. Moscow: Pedagogika, 1983, pp. 5–328.
5. Alexander Luria, "Problems of the cultural behavior of the child". *Journal of Genetic Psychology*, vol. 35, 1928, pp. 493–506.
6. On the issue of periodization, see Norris Minick, "The development of Vygotsky's thought". In L. Vygotsky, *Problems of General Psychology*. New York: Plenum Press, 1987.
7. See Lev Vygotsky, "The problem of the cultural development of

the child". *Journal of Genetic Psychology*, vol. 36, 1929, pp. 414–34; Lev Vygotsky, *Orudie i Znak v Razvitie Rebenka*. In L. Vygotsky, *Collected Papers*, vol. 6, pp. 5–90. See also L. Vygotsky, *Mind in Society*. Cambridge, MA: Harvard University Press, 1978.

8. See Vygotsky, *Orudie i Znak*, p. 56.

9. Ibid, pp. 57–8.

10. Vygotsky, *Istoriya Razvitiya*, p. 24.

11. See Lev Vygotsky, "The geneisis of higher mental functions". In J. Wertsch, ed., *The Concept of Activity in Soviet Psychology*. New York: Sharpe, 1981, p. 161 (original work written in 1931). For modern Western counterparts to this analysis of the child's gesture, see A. Lock, ed., *Action, Gesture and Symbol*. London: Academic Press, 1978.

12. See Vygotsky, *Thought and Language*, ch. 3.

13. See Benjamin Lee, "Origins of Vygotsky's semiotic analysis". In J. Wertsch, ed., *Culture, Communication and Cognition*. Cambridge: Cambridge University Press, 1985. See also V. P. Zinchenko, Vygotsky's "Ideas about units for the analysis of mind", J. Wertsch, ed., *op.cit.*.

14. Lev Vygotsky, "The instrumental method in psychology". In J. Wertsch, ed., *The Concept of Activity in Soviet Psychology*, p. 140 (original work written in 1930).

15. Vygotsky, *Istoriya Razvitiya*, p. 90.

16. Ibid, p. 157. See also R. van der Veer and Jaan Valsiner, "Lev Vygotsky and Pierre Janet". *Developmental Review*, vol. 8, 1988, pp. 52–65.

17. Vygotsky, "Genesis of higher mental functions", p. 163.

18. G. H. Mead. *Mind, Self and Society*. Chicago: University of Chicago Press, 1974, p. 192 (original work published in 1934).

19. Vygotsky, "Genesis of higher mental functions", p. 162. See also James Wertsch and C. A. Stone, "The concept of internalization in Vygotsky's account of the genesis of higher mental functions". In J. Wertsch, ed., *Culture, Communication and Cognition*, pp. 162–79.

20. Vygotsky, *Orudie i Znak*, pp. 15–16.

21. Ibid, pp. 55–6.

22. Ibid, pp. 71–2.

23. Heinz Werner, *Einführung in die Entwicklungspsychologie*. Leipzig, 1926. See also Heinz Werner, *Comparative Psychology of Mental Development*. New York: International Universities Press, 1948, and Heinz Werner and Bernard Kaplan, *Symbol Formation*. New York: Wiley, 1963.

24. Vygotsky, *Istoriya Razvitiya*, p. 89.

25. Ibid, pp. 143.
26. Alexandre Kojeve, *Introduction to the Reading of Hegel*. Ithaca, NY: Cornell University Press, 1980, p. 42.
27. Ibid, p. 52.
28. Herbert Marcuse, *Reason and Revolution*. Boston: Beacon Press, 1960, p. 77.
29. V. V. Davydov and L. A. Radzikhovsky, "Vygotsky's theory and the activity-oriented approach in psychology". In *Culture, Communication and Cognition*, p. 56.
30. Alexei N. Leontiev, *Activity, Consciousness, and Personality*. Englewood Cliffs, NJ: Prentice Hall, 1978.
31. Alexei N. Leontiev, *Problemy Razvitiya Psikhiki* (*Problems of the Development of Mind*). Moscow: MGU, 1981, pp. 318–49 (original work published in 1959).
32. Alexei A. Leontiev, "Sign and activity". In *The Concept of Activity in Soviet Psychology*.
33. Lev Vygotsky, *Istoricheskiy Smysl Psikhologicheskogo Krizisa*. In L. Vygotsky, *Collected Papers*, vol. 1, p. 398.
34. Emile Durkheim, *Selected Writings*. Cambridge: Cambridge University Press, 1972, p. 71 (original work published in 1895).
35. Ibid, p. 265.
36. Maurice Halbwachs, *The Collective Memory*. New York: Harper and Row, 1980, p. 46 (original work published in 1925).
37. Maurice Halbwachs, *La Topographie légendaire des évangiles en terre sainte*. Paris: RUF, 1941.
38. Michael Cole and Silvia Scribner, *Culture and Thought*. New York: Wiley, 1974.
39. Lucien Lévy-Bruhl, *Primitive Mentality*. New York: Macmillan, 1922.
40. An analysis of the phenomenon of totemism is given in A. R. Radcliffe-Brown, *Structure and Function in Primitive Society*. New York: Free Press, 1965, p. 117–32 (original paper published in 1929).
41. Vygotsky, *Thought and Language*, p. 130.
42. Emile Durkheim, *Essays on Sociology and Philosophy*. New York: Harper and Row, 1964, p. 337 (original work published in 1914).
43. Charles Blondel, *Introduction à la psychologie collective*. Paris, 1924.
44. Sergei Rubinshtein, "Problema Individualnogo i Obschestvennogo v Soznanii Cheloveka" ("The problem of individual and social in human consciousness"). In S. Rubinshtein, *Principy i Puti Razvitiya Psikhologii* (*The Paths and Principles in the Development of Psychology*). Moscow: Academy of Sciences Press, 1959.
45. Alexander Luria, "Speech and intellect of rural, urban, and home-

less children." *Selected Writings*. New York: Sharpe, 1978, pp. 49–50. (original work published in 1930).

46. Ibid, p. 60.
47. Ibid, p. 64.
48. Alexander Luria, *Cognitive Development*. Cambridge MA: Harvard University Press, 1977; Michael Cole and Sylvia Scribner, *Culture and Thought*. New York: Wiley, 1974.
49. Luria, *Cognitive Development*, p. 56.
50. Ibid, p. 109.
51. Ibid, p. 73.
52. This overall project was sketched by Vygotsky and Luria in their book *Etudy po Istorii Povedeniia (Essay on the History of Behavior)*. Moscow: Sozekgiz, 1930.
53. See S. de Castell, A. Luke and K. Egan, eds *Literacy, Society, and Schooling*. Cambridge: Cambridge University Press, 1986.
54. For a detailed discussion, see James Wertsch, *Vygotsky and the Social Formation of Mind*. Cambridge, MA: Harvard University Press, 1985, pp. 34–40.
55. David Olson and J. W. Astington, "Talking about texts". Paper presented at Boston Conference on Language Development, October 19–21, 1986.
56. Michael Cole, Foreword, in A. Luria, *Cognitive Development* p. xv.
57. Clifford Geertz, *The Interpretation of Cultures*. New York: Basic Books, 1973, pp. 44–5.
58. Vygotsky, *Istoriya Razvitiya*, p. 240.
59. Pierre Janet, *L'Evolution de la mémoire et de la notion du temps*. Paris: Chahine, 1928, p. 262. Janet's work is quoted by Alexei Leontiev, *Razvitie Pamiati (The Development of Memory)*. Moscow, 1931.
60. Leontiev, *Razvitie Pamiati*.
61. Vygotsky, *Istoriya Razvitiya*, pp. 241–3.
62. J. Meacham and J. Colombo, "External retrieval clues facilitate prospective remembering in children", *Journal of Educational Research*, vol. 73, 1980, pp. 299–301.
63. J. E. Harris and P. E. Morris, eds, *Everyday Memory*. New York: Academic Press, 1984.
64. John Flavell, "Developmental studies of mediated memory". In H. W. Reese and L. P. Lippsitt, eds, *Advances in Child Development and Behavior*. New York Academic Press, 1970.
65. M. Johnson, C. Raye, H. Foley and M. A. Foley. "Cognitive operations and decisions bias in reality monitoring". *American Journal of Psychology*, vol. 94, 1981, pp. 37–64.

66. On the dialectic of Master and Slave, see G. W. F. Hegel, *The Phenomenology of Mind* (J. B. Baillie, trans.). New York: Macmillan, 1931, pp. 230–40; see also p. 119 above.
67. Alexei N. Leontiev, "The development of voluntary attention of the child". *Journal of Genetic Psychology*, vol. 40, 1932, p. 62.
68. Ibid, p. 62.
69. Ibid; see also Vygotsky, *Mind in Society*, pp. 40–5.
70. Leontiev, *op. cit.*, p. 71.
71. Vygotsky, *Istoriya Razvitiya*, p. 211.
72. A. K. Adams, A. Scortino-Brudzynsky, K. Bjorn and R. Tharp, "Forbidden colors: Vygotsky's experiment revisited". Paper presented at the meeting of the Society for Research in Child Development, Baltimore, April 1987.
73. Vygotsky, *Istoriya Razvitiya*, p. 68.
74. Vygotsky, *Orudie i Znak*, p. 50.
75. Vygotsky referred to Kurt Lewin's *Vorsatz, Wille und Bedürfnis*. Berlin: Springer, 1926; see also Kurt Lewin, *Dynamic Theory of Personality*. New York: McGraw-Hill, 1935.
76. Vygotsky, *Istoriya Razvitiya*, p. 280.
77. Ibid, p. 278.

CHAPTER FIVE

Thought and Language

ALTHOUGH Vygotsky's theory embraced all higher psychological processes, he was primarily interested in the development of language in its relation to thought, and, in a more general sense, in the relationship between human language and consciousness. Vygotsky's work on this problem became the basis of his most popular book, *Myshlenie i Rech* (*Thought and Language*).[1]

The problems confronting the translator, that is, the person whose job it is to present what the author (in this case Vygotsky) *means*, while being confined to what the author *says*, are typical in this respect. Consider the following difficulties facing the translator. The dictionary meaning of the Russian *rech* is "speech", but there is a subtle inaccuracy in such a rendition, because the semantic fields of Russian *rech* and English "speech" overlap, but do not coincide. For example, a primary school textbook of Russian language and literature is called *Russkaya Rech*, literally *Russian Speech*, but what is meant is clearly "language" or "discourse" and not "speech". Or consider, for example, Vygotsky's use of *slovo* ("word"); more often than not "word" is used as a synecdoche and stands for any form of verbal discourse. This small example of a "translator's headaches" gives some idea of what kind of problems were at the center of Vygotsky's research. He wanted to understand how a *concept*—an intellectual idea—is related to its *meaning* and the latter to its various *verbal embodiments*.

While pursuing this line of inquiry Vygotsky seemed to formulate many of the problems which in the 1960s became the focus in American research into the psychology of language. Among these problems were the ontogenetically changing relationships between intellectual and verbal processes; the hierarchical organization of concept formation from the syncretic agglomerates of images to the logical structures of scientific concepts; different modes of verbal production such as communicative speech, egocentric speech, inner speech and written discourse; and finally, the issue of reading and writing activity as sovereign psychological processes.

Although thematically Vygotsky's research proved to be directed toward the future of psychology, its immediate inspiration came from the psychological works of his contemporaries such as Karl Bühler, Wolfgang Köhler, Jean Piaget and William Stern. In addition, the practical problems of the Soviet educational system of the 1930s blended easily in Vygotsky's writings with the most abstract of psychological discussions. And finally, Vygotsky seemed to respond to the same undercurrent of humanistic thought that compelled contemporaries such as Mikhail Bakhtin in Russia and Martin Heidegger in Germany to seek new formulas for the relationship between human language and human existence.

ONTO- AND PHYLOGENESIS OF LANGUAGE AND THOUGHT

One of the first targets of Vygotskys critical analysis was the nature of the relationship between thought and language in onto- and phylogenesis. Vygotsky's argument ran roughly as follows.

Intellect and speech have different genetic roots and they have developed along different lines. There is no fixed correlation between their development in phylogenesis. Anthropoid apes display an intellect resembling that of humans in certain respects (such as the use of tools), while their "language" resembles human speech in a quite different respect (such as its function as a means˙ of social communication). Anthropogenesis—the emergence of *Homo sapiens*—is related to the process of the establishment of a dynamic interrelationship between intellect and speech. In ontogenesis one can discern a preintellectual stage in the development of speech, and a prelinguistic stage in the development of thought. At a certain moment these two developmental lines become intertwined, whereupon thought becomes verbal, and speech intellectual. This moment signifies a switch from a natural track of development to a cultural one.

The inspiration for Vygotsky's analysis of the relationship between thought and language in phylogenesis came from Köhler's study of intelligence in chimpanzees.[2] Köhler's study, which has since become a classic, revealed a highly developed practical intelligence in chimpanzees, who proved to be capable of using primitive tools to achieve their goals. Köhler's critics, who challenged his explanation of the ape's intelligence based on the principles of Gestalt psychology, seemed to agree with him when it came to the assessment of the ape's speech. For example, Bühler wrote that: "The achievements of the chimpanzee are quite independent of language", further elaborating that in the case of man, "technical thinking, or thinking in terms of tools [*Werkzeugdenken*] is far less closely bound up with language and concepts than other forms of thinking".[3]

It is not that Köhler's chimpanzees were "autistic"; on the contrary, they displayed a vast repertoire of affective gestures and vocalizations, as well as expressive movements that served as a means of social contact. The peculiarity of chimpanzee "language" was that it seemed to contain the functions of emotional release and social contact, but not those of representation or signification. What seemed to be lacking in Köhler's chimpanzees was the use of language as a tool of thought. Their ability to solve problems by "insight" rather than trial-and-error was limited to situations in which all the elements required for solution were present in the visual field. The chimpanzees' behavior suggested that they were capable of performing certain mental operations resembling imagination and combinatorial activity, but they needed constant returns to the home base in the form of the actual perception of their situation. Language, which in human beings serves precisely this role—that of mental representation and communication of the virtual situation—seemed to be used by chimpanzees only for the release of emotions and for social contact. All attempts to teach chimpanzees some elements of human speech had been unsuccessful.

Vygotsky interpreted Köhler's observations as a confirmation of his own thesis about the separate lines in the development of intellect and speech in phylogenesis. Vygotsky was not categorical in his pronouncements, citing an apparent lack of proper methodology for the study of ape language. He made the truly prophetic suggestion that the issue of vocalization should be excluded, and that communication with apes could be studied with the help of the sign language of the deaf.[4] It is not a phonetic quality that makes human language a language, but the functional use of signs.

Vygotsky absolutely correctly foresaw the direction that would be taken by research into ape language in the 1960s. In a number of celebrated studies chimpanzees were taught to communicate with their human teachers using either American Sign Language (ASL) or an artificial language in which plastic tokens of different shapes and colors were used to represent different words.[5] These studies, in the beginning, generated extremely high expectations regarding the chimpanzees' ability to use signs functionally and even to display some grammatical competence. At certain times it even seemed that the question posed by Vygotsky about the apes' ability to integrate tool-assisted problem solving with communication could be answered in the positive. For example, two chimpanzees, Austin and Sherman, were taught to communicate with each other with the help of a computer. The chimpanzees lived in two separate adjacent rooms and could not see each other. Each had access to a computer keyboard with symbols attached to the keys. By pressing a key Austin could communicate a chosen symbol to Sherman, who would see it on his screen. The integration of the tool action with communication was achieved in the following way. Sherman was shown a place in his room where a small portion of food was hidden, but to access the food he needed a tool from the toolbox in Austin's room. Sherman was successfully taught how to request the desired tool from Austin using an appropriate symbol on the computer keyboard. The cooperation between chimpanzees was achieved by training them to share food after it was found.[6]

Although this seemed to be the best possible confirmation of the functional use of communication in apes, the leader of the project, Savage-Rumbaugh, as well as some other researchers like H. S. Terrace, had a number of reservations.

First, careful analysis revealed that data from some of the earlier projects using ASL or tokens did not allow one to distinguish "true" communication from the imitation of the teacher's signs and from certain differentially reinforced behavioral sequences that are not necessarily "linguistic" in nature. It must be mentioned in passing that in the 1960s when these projects were initiated, many American psychologists continued to subscribe to the idea that even human language is best described as a behavioral rather than cognitive phenomenon. In that intellectual atmosphere it was easy to identify linguistic capacity in apes with their ability to retain and reproduce sequences of gestures or actions with tokens. But by the time Savage-Rumbaugh started her study of the chimpanzees Austin and Sherman, the intellectual climate had changed. As a result her prime concern was not with assessing the proximity of the apes' language to that of humans, but in learning about the type of communicative processes that could be developed in chimpanzees. In so doing she was as interested in what distinguishes chimpanzee communication from the language of a child as in what seems to be common. One important observation was that whereas in human families adults interpret even the nonsymbolic behavior of a child, like a grasping gesture, as a communicative act and treat the child accordingly, the chimpanzee mother seems to be incapable of doing this: "For those who wonder why the chimpanzee does not develop language in the wild, the answer lies, then, in the absence of a caretaker who is able to attribute communicative intent before its true onset".[7]

Another important difference is that children quite early in their development begin to realize the value of words, whereas even after they had learned to use symbols to request objects and actions Austin and Sherman still showed no inclination to rely on this new mediator unless prompted by their teachers. This observation led Savage-Rumbaugh to a more general discussion of the role of human teachers and their task in the development of chimpanzee communication. Human teachers not only trained chimpanzees to recognize and use symbols, they also created a social situation which alone made the communicative behavior valuable for the apes: "The simple giving of an item in response to a symbolic request requires that the ape move beyond the ritualized performance of executing given symbols for particular goals. . . . This means not only a conceptual orientation alien to the ape's natural level of communication, but an alien social orientation as well".[8] The question at this stage of research, therefore, was not of the apes' individual capacity for language, but whether humans could create conditions for interspecific communication. The conclusions reached by Savage-Rumbaugh were compatible with Vygotsky's understanding of the experimental procedure as a *formative* process out of which a new psychological function emerges. One thus cannot pass judgment on the relationship between language and thought in phylogenesis without inquiring into those concrete generative situations within which such a relationship does or does not occur.

Ontogenetically, the relationship between thought and speech is even more intricate and obscure, but here, too, Vygotsky proposed to distinguish between preintellectual speech and preverbal thought. Köhler and Bühler showed early on that a child is capable of goal-directed action long before speech assumes a regulative and planning role. These observations were brilliantly confirmed by Piaget in a series of studies of so-called sensory-motor intelligence in children.[9] These studies revealed that during the first two years of life a child passes through a number of stages, from that of simple reflexes and perceptual images to that of fully coordinated sensory-motor behavior. Sensory-motor intelligence thus consists of those internalized sensory-motor schemas that allow a child to coordinate his or her perception and habits and to achieve, at this practical level, the constancy of objects and the constancy of the child's own body as one of these objects.

Vygotsky suggested, however, that while intelligence has its preverbal forms, speech also has its preintellectual manifestations. He was particularly impressed by the studies of Charlotte Bühler in which it was shown that children under one year of age use vocal activity as a means of social contact.[10] The most important event occurs at about the age of two when the developments in thought and in speech, until then separate, come into contact and engender new mental processes—verbal thought and intelligent speech. This pronouncement by Vygotsky should not be taken simplistically as a claim that there exists one specific developmental moment when verbal and intellectual lines merge. One of Vygotsky's major contributions to the field of child language research was the discovery of a dynamic pattern of "engagements" and "separations" between verbal and intellectual functions. Rather than a merger of two "strings", the relationship between language and thought looks more like a nodical line with some threads from one string being interwoven into those of the other after each node.

Vygotsky suggested that the sequence of engagement between thought and speech has four major stages. The first is a "primitive" stage when speech is still largely preintellectual and intelligence operates without the help of the verbal function. Next comes the stage of practical intelligence, at which a child masters the logic of problem-solving activity at the sensory-motor level. Speech at this stage is characterized by the appearance of grammatical forms and structures which, however, are still divorced from their corresponding logical operations. For example, a child may use such forms as *because, if, when* and *but,* being still unaware of the causal, conditional or temporal relations. The syntax of speech, as Vygotsky said, comes before the syntax of thought. The syntax of thought at this stage is still embedded in concrete operations, whereas the syntax of speech is embedded in concrete communicative tasks. During the third stage the child starts using external symbolic means for internal problem solving. The child counts on fingers, uses primitive mnemonic aids, etc. Verbal production at this stage is characterized by large quantities of so-called egocentric speech. This type of speech, according to Vygotsky, serves as a transitory form between primitive communicative speech and the more mature verbal forms aimed at the control of one's own behavior and thinking. (The phenomenon of egocentric speech will be discussed at some length later in this chapter.) Finally comes the fourth stage, of which the processes of internalization are characteristic. Operations with external symbolic means "go inside"; the child is now able, for example, to solve arithmetic and logical problems in his head, without resorting to manipulation with actual mediators. Speech also undergoes internalization, becoming silent inner speech, which is indispensable for planning intellectual as well as verbal actions.

The leading idea of Vygotsky's inquiry into the development of language and thought in childhood was that child concepts, far from being set up once and forever, do evolve. It would be erroneous, therefore, to talk about some unitary "child logic" as opposed to "adult logic". It would also be wrong to imagine that once a child starts using correct names for certain objects and processes, that he or she has actually learned the same concepts that adults use. These pitfalls had already been identified by Vygotsky's contemporary, Georgian psychologist Dmitri Uznadze: "Words take over the function of concepts and may serve as means of communication long before they reach the level of concepts characteristic of fully developed thought".[11] Uznadze suggested that a special study should be undertaken of what he called "functional equivalents" of concepts. The methodological difficulty in designing such a study stems from the fact that, as their name suggests, the child's preconceptual representations are often functionally equivalent to concepts. The functional aspect, therefore, cannot serve as a basis for discrimination between preconceptual and conceptual forms of thinking. Vygotsky decided that he had found the required methodological approach when his colleague, Lev Sakharov, developed a modification of Ach's sorting test.[12]

The material used in this sorting test consisted of twenty-two wooden blocks varying in color, shape, height and size. On the underside of each block was written one of four nonsense words: *lag*, *bik*, *mur* and *sev*. Regardless of color or shape, *lag* was written on all tall large blocks, *bik* on all flat large figures, *mur* on the tall small ones, and *sev* on the flat small ones. At the beginning of the experiment all blocks were scattered in the center of a special board with four corner areas. The experimenter picked up a sample block, showed it to the subject and read its "name", after which the subject was asked to select all blocks that might belong to the same kind and place them into one of the corner areas. After the subject finished sorting the experimenter picked one of the wrongly selected blocks, read its name, and encouraged the subject to continue trying. After each new sorting attempt another of the wrongly selected blocks was turned up and its name revealed. Gradually the subject would discover to which characteristics of the blocks the nonsense words referred.[13]

This method was originally known as the "method of double stimulation" and subsequently became known in the West as "Vygotsky's blocks test".[14] The original name reflected Vygotsky's idea of the two interacting sets of "stimulation" present in this test. One set consisted of the physical properties of the blocks, the other of the nonsense words which, in the course of the experiment, became the real names of a given group of blocks. The subject's handling of the task, according to Vygotsky, would show how the two functions, verbal and nonverbal, come into contact forming a functional system. The design of the test allowed for the dynamics of problem solving to be "unfolded" from the first approach to the task to its ultimate solution. The subject's manipulation of the blocks at different stages of problem solving and his or her responses to corrections would serve as indicators of the level of conceptual thinking.

The major qualitative result of the study of concept formation in children was that the level of truly conceptual problem solving is achieved only by adolescents. Younger children employ functional equivalents of concepts, which differ from real concepts in the type of generalization involved and the way words are used to designate it. Vygotsky concluded that "the central moment in concept formation, and its generative course, is a special use of words as functional tools".[15] The study revealed three major types of preconceptual representations: syncretic grouping, "complexes" and potential concepts. These types should not be mistaken for natural "stages" in a child's cognitive development; rather, they are methodological devices for distinguishing what seems to be the most pronounced form of concept formation at any given age. It is also important to remember that preconceptual types of representation are retained by older children and adults, who quite often revert to these more "primitive" forms depending on their interpretation of a given task and on their chosen strategy for solution.

The first type of preconceptual representation is characterized by syncretic problem solving. Blocks are grouped together on the basis of a diffuse and labile *feeling* by the child that they belong together. The basis for this type of grouping is highly subjective and can easily be changed. The artificial word which is supposed to designate a selected group is perceived as little more than a name for this vague feeling of belonging. Very close to this syncretic type is the so-called "physiognomic grouping" observed by Hanfmann and Kasanin.[16] A subject could, for example, assign some particular anthropomorphic meaning to a number of blocks claiming that all of them are "policemen" or "hard-working people".

The next major type of representation is the so-called "complex". Unlike the syncretic grouping, complexes are capable of serving as functional equivalents of concepts because they reflect certain features actually shared by some blocks. Within the complex, bonds between its components are concrete and factual, rather than abstract and logical. One of the most typical of the complex selection of blocks is "collection". In a group selected in this way each block complements another; for example, a round block is complemented by a triangular one, red by blue, tall by flat, and so on. Another form is the "chain complex" in which two subsequently selected blocks share some common feature; for example, if the first block is red and round, the second one could be red and triangular, the third one triangular and green, etc. In the chain complex the difference between preconceptual and conceptual groupings becomes particularly clear. In a complex there is no hierarchical organization of the relations between different attributes of the selected blocks. All attributes are functionally equal, and each of them can become the basis for selection. In the chain complex, for example, there could be no central feature at all, with only adjacent elements sharing one common feature.

It is important to remember that there is nothing inherently immature in the complex type of grouping. In our everyday experience with household items we constantly employ the principle of complex grouping by complementing cups with saucers and spoons, or a table with chairs and a couch. By calling all members of a given family the Joneses or the Ivanovs we also practice the complex type of grouping. Moreover, a simple etymological study would reveal the complex character of many of our words and terms. For example, the term for the political crisis during the Nixon Administration, Watergate, was derived from the name of the hotel and apartment complex in which the original break-in into the Democratic Party offices took place. Later "Watergate" became cannibalized into "Water" and "gate", with the newly invented suffix "gate" standing for any political scandal. In due time this kind of creative linguistics allowed "Irangate" to appear as the name for the political scandal triggered by the arms-for-hostages trade with Iran. The term "Irangate" is a pure complex because there is absolutely no logical connection between the apartment complex on the Potomac and trading in arms.

The third main type of representation is "potential concepts". If thinking in complexes is the preconceptual form of generalization, then potential concepts carry the elementary function of abstraction. For a child to be able to form a generalized representation of a group of blocks, it is necessary for him or her to distinguish between essential and nonessential attributes. Potential concepts making this operation possible develop out of the isolating abstraction that can be learned even by very young children. In its most primitive form isolating abstraction is little more than a product of habit formation. Simple association is sufficient for selecting a specific attribute, such as color, when such a choice is consistently reinforced. Isolating abstraction, however, is absolutely insufficient for conceptual problem solving. For a solution to become a conceptual abstraction it should be complemented by a generalization, and this can be achieved only after a child masters the most advanced form of complex reasoning.

This most advanced form of complex reasoning was designated by Vygotsky as a pseudoconcept. A pseudoconcept occupies a special place within the range of preconceptual forms of representation because it is a functional equivalent of the concept *par excellence*. A pseudoconcept, while retaining its "complex" substructure, functions very much like a concept, and thus marks the borderline between prelogical and logical thought. Pseudoconceptual type of thinking is of particular interest here because its interpretation touches upon some deeper theoretical issues of twentieth-century psychology. These issues, as I have attempted to show earlier, became apparent only for post-classical psychological and philosophical thought (they were sketched out at the end of Chapter Three). Vygotsky's discussion of the pseudoconcept thus leads far beyond the mere issue of child development and has a bearing on the interpretation of human self and consciousness as they have become understood in twentieth-century culture.

The major feature of the pseudoconcept is that phenotypically it is often indistinguishable from the concept. For example, during the sorting test a child may start selecting all objects sharing some common feature, like color, which appears as an attempt at conceptual solution. The preconceptual nature of the child's selection becomes apparent only with the experimenter turns one of the selected blocks and reveals its "wrong" name. A child guided by truly conceptual reasoning responds by removing all selected blocks and starting anew. Pseudoconceptual reasoning, on the contrary, allows a child to remove only one, "wrong" block and to continue insisting on the appropriateness of all the others. It is significant, however, that functionally the selection based on pseudoconceptual reasoning could be quite indistinguishable from the conceptual one. If, for example, the experimenter selects colors as the sorting principle, it would be impossible to tell from the child's selections alone whether the child is operating conceptually or preconceptually.

The phenotypical similarity between conceptual and pseudo-conceptual generalizations in real life serves as a powerful force in the development of the child's concepts. It helps a child to arrive at final cognitive products that coincide with the concepts of adults. In this way a child begins to practice conceptual generalizations before he or she is aware of the operations involved. In Vygotsky's terms the "concept-in-itself" and the "concept-for-others" is developed in a child before the "concept-for-myself".[17] This state of affairs becomes possible because in his or her interaction with adults a child often receives a positive response to a pseudoconceptual generalization. This phenomenon has a clear bearing on the fundamental issue of the "constructive" nature of human consciousness. The awareness of one's own cognitive operations comes only after the *practice* of phenotypically similar operations, and their "endorsement" by others. A child is not "endowed" with a conceptual type of reasoning, but develops it out of the forms which appear as conceptual for others, but which are not understood as such by the child him or herself. The child's reasoning is constructed from the "outside" through the necessary coincidence in the child's and the adult's representations. Human consciousness thus appears as a social construction, rather than as an obedient instrument of its self-conscious master, as was envisaged by classical Rationalism.

The operation of pseudoconceptual thought suggests that the principle "from action to thought" should be applied not only to the development of intelligence, but also to its functioning. There seems to be a certain priority of intellectual *action* over the reflective self-awareness of one's own intellectual operations. This double-faceted nature of thought suggests that the interpretative or metacognitive function of consciousness may have a certain autonomy from regulative and controlling functions. In simple terms, it means that there is a great difference between an intelligent-looking action, and an adequate knowledge of one's own intellectual operations. A person may solve problems in a way suggestive of conceptual reasoning, but his or her own interpretation of this solution may still be carried out at the preconceptual level. With respect to educational practices this implies that there is a considerable difference between learning how to operate with concepts and becoming aware of the conceptual structure involved. One example, often invoked by Vygotsky, is the difference between the functional use of one's native language versus the understanding of the conceptual structure of a foreign one. Even with the native language conceptual awareness is neither primary nor spontaneous, but is a result of a particular learning process. These observations reinforce the twentieth-century idea of the heterogeneity of human consciousness and its origin in the sedimentation of action.

Another important feature of the pseudoconcept is that functionally it looks so like true concepts that adults often do not notice the difference. This observation indicates how deceptive functional appearance can be. "Thought-complexes" can appear as if they are concepts, thus concealing their actual substructure. The use of one and the same words and the understanding they bring about may correspond to only a superficial level of functional communication, while the underlying intellectual substructures of the communicants may remain alien to each other. This phenomenon identified in child–adult communication has a much broader significance. It poses the question of what kind of understanding is achieved when the participants in a dialogue belong to different social or cultural groups. Since the appearance of understanding often hinges on the shared referential similarity of the words used, it may obscure profound differences in the communicants' representational substructures. The most obvious illustration is that of an intercultural dialogue conducted almost exclusively in European languages with all their presumed cognitive substructures; the "understanding" achieved in such a dialogue could easily be of a pseudoconceptual quality. A non-Western communicant may employ the terms offered only in a functional sense, that is, only as far as it does not disrupt the dialogue, but the substructure of his or her reasoning may remain absolutely culture-specific. Moreover, the Western communicant, being satisfied with the understanding achieved, may start rationalizing and interpreting the reasoning of the other party along the lines of the Western substructure of thought. The same issue could be raised in the context of dialogues between genders, different generations, and different socioeconomic groups. The underlying problem is that different types of thinking may lead to one and the same cognitive product, which could be mistakenly perceived as a sign of similar reasoning.

At the center of this problem lies the relationship between symbol, concept and the nonverbal referent. The success of pseudoconceptual reasoning hinges on the coincidence between symbol and referent, with the concept out of picture. Another interesting possibility has been discussed by the French philosopher Henri Lefebvre, who pointed out the domination of symbols over referents in twentieth-century everyday life.[18] With the breakdown of traditional life in which referents were rather rigidly tied to symbols and concepts, and with the proliferation of mediated and the decline of first-hand experience, in the life of a modern man symbols have assumed the role of ultimate reality. Communication and understanding depends more and more on a shared symbolic code, rather than on shared experiences with the referents themselves.

Finally, Vygotsky's study of pseudoconcepts in children brought to light the phenomenon of the "readiness of language". He observed that in real-life situations complexes corresponding to word meanings are not spontaneously developed by a child, but they are predetermined by the meaning a given word already has in the language of adults. After all, a child learns to use words by relying on the contextual meanings he or she extracts from the speech of adults. Only in an experimental study like the sorting test is one able to distinguish between the "complex" process of the formation of meaning and its final embodiment, which often coincides with the words of adults. The phenomenon of the readiness of language returns us to the philosophical issue of the "ownership" of individual language and cognition. It is probably more correct to use the apt expression of the Spanish philosopher Ortega-y-Gasset that "we are possessed by our ideas" rather than that "we have ideas". Our reasoning often moves along the track laid down by the contextual usage of the words without any genuine "ownership" of these words. The complex reasoning of a child cast in words supplied by adults provides us with a paradigmatic example of what happens when someone enters an unfamiliar cultural or linguistic system. The adaptation of the newcomer is hardly spontaneous and independent; most probably it requires the development of pseudoconcepts coinciding functionally with the predominant conceptual structure of this system. Since the needs of the newcomer are predominantly functional and communicative, he or she seeks understanding and responses based on coincidences in the words used. This functional achievement, however, does not prevent the newcomer from continuing to reason in categories that may differ substantially from those accepted in the host system. Ready-made meanings embodied in commercials, political slogans and ideological cliché easily penetrate the consciousness of the newcomer and remain there as substitutes for more conceptual understanding. Moreover, meanings which probably constituted some conceptual system in their original form, easily become preconceptual when assimilated by an ideological apprentice. The phenomenon of the readiness of language thus reveals an important psychological mechanism underlying the functioning of ideological and other preconceptual forms of reasoning in modern society.

Neither Vygotsky's original work, nor its possible theoretical ramifications outlined above, had any significant influence on Western psychology at the time. The only group that adopted Vygotsky's version of the sorting test were American psychiatrists working in the tradition of Kurt Goldstein and Gestalt psychology (the relevance of Vygotsky's theory to their work will be discussed in Chapter Six). This does not mean, however, that Vygotsky's research vanished without a trace. Heinz Werner, while working on his own and quite original theory of human development, confronted the same problems as Vygotsky did, and, unlike others, did acquaint himself and his students with the results of Vygotsky's research. Although this is not my task here, it is tempting to present Vygotsky's and Werner's theories as two sociocultural variations of one and the same psychological theme. The lists of references in their respective works overlap remarkably. And, of course, the issue of Development, with a capital "D" and extending beyond ontogenesis, was the focus of their theories, yet ultimately only their shared intellectual background united them. Werner's theory, possibly as a result of his transformation from a German into an American psychologist, developed in the direction of the structural and systemic interpretation of the differentiation of psychological processes, while Vygotsky's remained closely tied to issues of cultural and social development. On occasions, however, Werner's works seem to be a direct amplification of Vygotsky's position. The study in question had been undertaken in the late 1940s by Edith Kaplan under Werner's direction and was aimed at understanding the development of word meaning in children.[19] The experimental design was not unlike that of Vygotsky. Children were given sets of sentences, each set containing an artificial, nonexistent word. The task of the children was to discover the meanings of these artificial words. The authors believed that the child would reveal in this test the same method which he or she ordinarily used while learning new words in everyday contexts. It turned out that the method used by younger children was not unlike the thinking in complexes described by Vygotsky. For example, the children revealed the fusion of the word meaning with the meaning of the whole sentence, and carried this sentence context into future applications. The children also showed a proclivity to be influenced by the first context in which the artificial word appeared, and to be unable to abstract the meaning from this context. As in Vygotsky's experiments, the most difficult task for the children proved to be the identification of the tentative word meaning in a number of sentences (abstraction) *and* then their integration in one final meaning (generalization). These peculiarities of the child's verbal intelligence became apparent, however, only in specially designed experiments. In ordinary life, including primary school instruction, children often do not need to operate with the decontextualized meanings, their context-dependent answers being quite satisfactory from the adult point of view.

The next step in Vygotsky's program was to investigate the development of concepts actually learned by a child in school and to compare them with those spontaneously acquired through everyday activity.[20] The shift in the focus of the investigation was determined by two requirements, first to make the study of concept formation relevant to the problems of education, and second, to fill scientific gaps left by the experimental study of artificial concepts. Vygotsky was convinced that only by complementing the study of artificial concepts by an inquiry into the acquisition of real ones would he be able to pass judgment on the underlying processes of cognitive development. Vygotsky was fully aware that for all its importance the study of artificial concepts had some built-in limitations. The very nature of the sorting test did not allow for the formation of hierarchical conceptual systems. In addition, each time a child made a mistake he or she had to disassemble the unsatisfactory group and to start anew. Both of these moments—the hierarchization of the conceptual structure and the building of new concepts on the foundation of the previous, sometimes very approximate representations—turned out to be essential in the development of real concepts.[21]

The empirical material for the analysis of real concepts was provided by Vygotsky's student and collaborator Zhozephina Shif, who studied the understanding of causal (*because*) and adversative (*but, although*) relations by seven- and ten-year-old children. The children were asked to complete sentences the content of which either pertained to an everyday situation (such as "the boy fell off his bicycle because . . ."), or was derived from the social science topics learned in school. In addition, Piagetian-type clinical interviews were used to appraise the children's comprehension of the material.

Theoretically this study was based on the distinction between so-called "scientific" concepts and spontaneous, "everyday" concepts. "Scientific" concepts originate in the highly structured and specialized activity of classroom instruction and are characterized by hierarchical, logical organization. The concepts themselves do not necessarily relate to scientific issues—they may represent historical, linguistic, or practical knowledge—but their organization is "scientific" in the sense of formal, logical and decontextualized structures. Everyday concepts, on the other hand, emerge spontaneously from the child's own reflections on immediate, everyday experiences; they are experientially rich but unsystematic and highly contextual. In this sense they are not concepts, but rather "complexes". By asking children questions pertaining to these two different conceptual realms Vygotsky hoped to establish their interrelationship.

The major qualitative result of the study was that scientific concepts develop more rapidly, outpacing everyday concepts. Children produced more correct answers when responding to questions relating to concepts learned in school, than to those spontaneously acquired in everyday life. The fundamental conclusion drawn by Vygotsky was that if "scientific" concepts represent education and everyday concepts represent development, then education runs ahead of and supports development. The phrasing of this conclusion was suggested by Vygotsky's argument with Piaget regarding the relationships between child development and education. Vygotsky, who was acquainted only with the early works of Piaget, was far-sighted enough to distinguish in them the future doctrine of the natural stages of mental development. This doctrine essentially put the level of classroom instruction dependent upon the level of the natural cognitive development achieved by the child. Everyday concepts were supposed to serve as a gauge of the child's cognitive progress. Vygotsky disagreed with Piaget and argued that "scientific" concepts are no less natural for a child than everyday ones, because the former reflect an important aspect of the child's life—systematic education and interaction with adults. Moreover, "scientific" and everyday concepts, far from being unrelated, actually interact with each other. In order to start acquiring "scientific" concepts a child should have some experience with generalizations which usually take the form of spontaneous, everyday concepts. But once the learning of "scientific" concepts gains momentum it begins to exercise a reciprocal influence on everyday concepts.

Scientific concepts themselves appear in Vygotsky's theory as changeable, dynamic structures. They are not assimilated by the child in a ready-made form but require a special process of adaptation in which already present everyday representations play an important role. At any given developmental moment there seems to exist a "proportion" between "scientific" and everyday concepts. "Scientific" concepts bring systematicity, consciousness and hierarchical organization into the child's thinking. But these concepts lack the richness of everyday connections characteristic of everyday concepts. "Scientific" concepts run the risk of remaining empty verbal formulas applicable to a rather narrow range of topics learned in school. School practice is full of situations in which a child becomes helpless when required to apply the concepts learned in the classroom to phenomena outside the school curriculum. Everyday concepts, in contrast, are rich in experiential connotations, but they lack a system and are bound by concrete life contexts. For example, a child learns quite early what it means to be a brother or a sister, but it takes a long time to place this everyday experience into a formal structure of familial relationships. A child's inability to solve a popular puzzle like "who is my father's son who is not my brother?" attests to this limitation of everyday concepts. It takes the interaction of "scientific" concepts, which progress downward from empty generalizations to greater concreteness, with everyday concepts, which move upward toward greater systematicity, to make up the development of a child's thought: "In working its slow way upwards, an everyday concept clears the path for a scientific concept in its downward development. It creates a series of structures necessary for the evolution of a concept's more primitive, elementary aspects, which give it body and vitality. Scientific concepts, in turn, supply structures for the upward development of the child's spontaneous concepts toward consciousness and deliberate use".[22]

If one accepts the importance of "scientific" concepts in a child's development, the entire system of intelligence testing based on the assessment of a child's spontaneous concepts becomes problematic. There is no basis for considering the development of spontaneous concepts as a model for the development of "scientific" concepts. Moreover, if the essence of mental development is in the socialization of the child's mind—and this assumption seems to have been shared by Piaget and Vygotsky—then it could be misleading to focus the assessment on the spontaneous forms of child intelligence. It is much more appropriate, reasoned Vygotsky, to focus on the collaborative forms of thinking in which the child's everyday concepts come into contact with the "scientific" concepts introduced by adults. Then a true advance in the child's reasoning could be operationalized as the difference between the child's independent performance and his or her performance in cooperaion with an adult. The developmental potential reflected in this difference was called the zone of proximal development (*zo-ped*). Zo-ped taps those psychological functions which are in the process of development and which are likely to be overlooked if the focus is exclusively on the unassisted child's performance.

As with Vygotsky's other ideas, the notion of zo-ped attracted the attention of Western psychologists only recently, in the 1970s. Its acceptance, although delayed, was enthusiastic.[23] Western psychologists not only assimilated Vygotsky's ideas into their studies but also broadened and enriched the notion of zo-ped. For Vygotsky, zo-ped was specifically related to the process of the interaction between "scientific" and everyday concepts, while in later interpretations it became a catchword to indicate a dialogical, intersubjective element in the child's learning. The focus correspondingly shifted toward subjects such as the establishment of a shared social world, or the intersubjectivity between a child and an adult through the process of the negotiation of meanings.[24]

Beyond zo-ped the importance of "scientific" concepts in child development led Vygotsky to the reassessment of the centuries-old doctrine of "formal discipline". The gist of this doctrine is that systematic instruction in certain subjects is beneficial to the development of students' mental faculties in general. This doctrine served as a theoretical rationale for the classical curriculum with its emphasis on Latin, Greek and mathematics. It was believed that by learning these subjects students would automatically acquire formal intellectual skills that would be transferable to any other problem. Vygotsky was quite aware of the educational excesses that came out of the rigid adherence to the classical curriculum and which early on had become a target of criticism by more enlightened teachers. He was not ready, however, to dismiss the ideas of formal discipline as such. Vygotsky was also dissatisfied with the psychological critique of formal discipline provided by Edward Thorndike.[25] In a series of systematic experiments Thorndike showed that there is little transference of training across tasks and concluded that the notion of formal discipline had no empirical foundation. After reexamining Thorndike's data Vygotsky concluded that Thorndike's critique was mostly misleading in that it failed to distinguish between elementary skills and higher mental processes. The original doctrine of formal discipline focused on higher-order learning involving what Vygotsky called "scientific" concepts, yet Thorndike attempted to discredit this doctrine by experimenting with highly specialized elementary skills which, predictably, showed no sign of transfer. Vygotsky suggested that the recognition of the effect of "scientific" concept learning on mental development may revive the original spirit of formal discipline: the systematic learning of scientific concepts in one field translates into developmental changes in the direction of greater abstraction of thought and greater awareness of and control over one's own actions.[26] These changes, in their turn, support learning in other fields.

Such processes, however, do not occur automatically. Classroom learning and mental development have different "rhythms". For example, a student's learning of a specific grammatical rule does not translate immediately into a greater awareness of his or her own language. There is also no uniform pattern in the relationship between learning and mental development. For each discipline and each student the interacting curves of learning and development need to be plotted individually. Special attention should be paid to so-called sensitive periods during which even a limited investment in learning produces an abundant return in mental development. One example would be the "explosion" of verbal awareness in children who are taught to write between four and a half and five years of age.

Although the doctrine of formal discipline has not been mentioned by Soviet educators since Vygotsky, the actual pedagogical practice in the Soviet Union often upholds its major tenets. Instruction in the formal principles of grammar, syntax and composition still plays an important role in the primary and secondary school curricula, as does mathematics, which starts rather early and continues as a required subject until the final year. In the United Stated, in contrast, different attitudes, often associated with the "progressive education" model, have been prevalent among educationalists. As with many other problems once discussed by Vygotsky, formal discipline seems to be about to make a comeback. Focusing on the transfer of general intellectual skills in graduate training, a group of American psychologists has demonstrated that specialized training in medicine, law and psychology seems to have an effect on real-life problem solving requiring statistical and logical reasoning. The authors observed that "twentieth-century psychologists have been too quick to conclude that formal discipline is not possible and that rule training has little generalized educational potential".[27]

Another relevant development in American psychology is represented by the recent rediscovery of the problem of scientific versus everyday concepts, appearing now as the problem of restructuring the child's knowledge from that of "novice" to that of "expert". The author of a detailed monograph on this problem, Susan Carey, apparently was not influenced by Vygotsky's work (his name does not appear in her bibliography[28]); her points of departure are Piagetian stage theory on the one hand, and the philosophy of science notion of theory change on the other. At the heart of Carey's work lies the same old problem of the peculiarity of children's concepts and the transition from them to adult-type reasoning. By asking children questions about different animals and plants, and by teaching children about certain organs and physiological functions, Carey attempted to discover whether there is a substantial change in a child's definition of what is alive, or what is animal, between the ages of four and ten. She concluded that older children seem to develop a special explanatory system that could be called "naive biology", involving the processes of abstracting certain physiological functions and then reintegrating them under the superordinate concept of animal or living thing. For younger children the questions pertaining to biology are still fused with "naive psychology", that is, they define an animal as a *behaving thing*. Behavior, in turn, is comprehended through the prototypical identification and comparison with human behavior. A person is considered by younger children as a prototypical behaving thing and by implication as a prototypical living thing. Questions about other living things are answered by comparing them to a human prototype. The discovered importance of "comparison-to-exemplar" type of reasoning is interesting in two respects. First, it may contribute to the refinement of the Vygotskian typology of preconceptual thought (syncrets, complexes, etc.) developed through the study of artificial concepts. Second, it touches on the important question of childhood animism. If, as Carey's research suggests, the child's animism is related to the use of a human person as a referential prototype, then the question arises whether this is a natural or a culturally conditioned stage in the child's development. Some modern Vygotskians suggest that the child's animism is a direct product of specific cultural influences exercised by adults.[29] If this is correct then some of the most typical features of a child's spontaneous, everyday concepts should be considered the products of cultural, rather than natural development.

SPEECH MODES AND SPEECH GENRES

In the previous section the major emphasis was on conceptual development; now it is time to explore the Vygotskian perspective in the study of various modes and genres of speech. Vygotsky's inquiry into the phenomenon of so-called egocentric speech in children remains the best known of his studies in terms of international recognition.[30] To place this study in its proper context one should first be aware, however, of Vygotsky's general idea of language development. From his point of view a child''s earliest speech is "already social"; he recognized that such speech is very immature and preintellectual, but he refused to accept Piaget's notion that it is a mere verbal accompaniment to autistic thought. For Vygotsky the early speech of a child is an attempt at primitive communication, rather than a reflection of autism. Vygotsky also disagreed with the schema of mental development advanced in Piaget's early works, according to which autism is the original, earliest form of a child's thought, with logic and socialized speech appearing rather later, and the egocentric thought and speech that accompany it being the genetic link between autism and logic.[31] Vygotsky argued that although egocentric speech indeed represents a transitory stage, this is not a transition from autistic to socialized speech, but rather from the primitive communicative speech-for-others to the inner speech-for-oneself. Egocentric speech thus stands at a crossroads from which one "road" leads to mature communicative speech while the other leads to internalized and abbreviated inner speech. The history of speech development does not end here, however. Vygotsky found it necessary to point out that written speech, far from being a simple "transcription" of oral speech, has a developmental history of its own, and enters into specific relationships with the development of intelligence. Moreover, vignettes provided by Vygotsky in Chapter Seven of *Thought and Language* allowed one to extend this development even further to include different genres of literary discourse.

Let us start with the phenomenon of egocentric speech. According to Piaget's definition, which Vygotsky accepted, this speech is not addressed or adapted to a listener and is carried on by a child with apparent satisfaction in the absence of any response from others. This speech includes collective monologues, echolalia and repetition, and comments on his or her own thoughts or actions. The importance of egocentric speech lies in its apparent childhood specificity: it seems to be quite representative of the verbal production of children between the ages of three and five. In addition, Vygotsky suggested, this speech might provide an experimental "window" into the processes occurring in the silent speech-for-oneself, which in its turn plays an important role in the verbal thinking of older children and adults. In the development of speech styles, egocentric speech is an undifferentiated, polymorphous entity out of which separate speech genres are later differentiated.

Egocentric speech is a transitory phenomenon; its roots are to be found in the primitive communicative speech-for-others, but its "fate" is to become internalized as inner speech-for-oneself. To prove this point Vygotsky designed a series of experiments in which these two "facets" of egocentric speech were addressed. I will describe these experiments only briefly, because they are well known and have generated numerous replications.[32] In the first series of experiments Vygotsky attempted to prove that egocentric speech, far from being a simple accompaniment to egocentric thought, is involved in realistic problem solving. To do this Vygotsky arranged for some child activity, such as drawing, playing or problem solving, to be impeded in some way. The coefficient of egocentric speech was measured while the activity was uninterrupted, and again after the emergence of an obstacle. These experiments showed the coefficient of egocentric speech rising dramatically once the child confronted the obstacle to his or her activity. Vygotsky concluded, and his conclusion since then has been confirmed, that the difficulties confronting children stimulate them to "think aloud". Such "thinking aloud" in response to a problematic situation indicates that egocentric speech is indeed involved in realistic problem solving.

In the second series of experiments Vygotsky's goal was to prove that egocentric speech remains connected to the sphere of social communication from which it originated. A child who produces egocentric utterances does this with an unconscious assumption that he or she is actually understood by others. To prove this point, after measuring the child's coefficient of egocentric speech, Vygotsky placed the child in a situation that undermined the illusion of understanding. In one experiment the child was placed in a room with deaf-mute or foreign-speaking children, in another experiment a child was physically separated from peers sitting at the far end of the room. Finally, in one of the experiments conditions were created to impede the result of vocalization—a window was opened onto a noisy street or loud music was played in an adjacent room. Under each of these conditions the coefficient of egocentric speech was considerably lower than in the control situation. Vygotsky concluded that although egocentric speech had already acquired some functions of self-regulation, it remained intimately connected with the function of social communication and that presupposition of understanding is necessary for egocentric speech to occur. Recent replications of Vygotskys experiments have revealed that children's production of egocentric utterances is sensitive not only to the possibility of understanding, but also to the presumed attitudes of others. Children produce more egocentric utterances in the presence of an adult perceived as willing to assist them in the problem-solving task, than in the presence of an adult who is not.[33]

Beyond the replication of Vygotsky's experiments, recent

studies have greatly enhanced our knowledge about the child's acommunicative speech. The range of accommunicative speech has turned out to be rather wide: from simple repetition to elaborate dialogues with an absent interlocutor. Accordingly, the term "egocentric speech" has been retained to designate Piagetian interpretation, rather than the phenomenon itself. One of the ramifications of the phenomenon of "private" or "acommunicative" speech is so-called "crib speech", that is, solitary language play by two- to three-year-olds. Stan Kuczaj, who recorded the crib speech of a number of children, came to the conclusion that this speech plays an important role as language practice.[34] Through imitation, repetition and modification of utterances, children seem to practice grammatical constructions and to compare old and new information. My own recordings of a two and a half year-old boy indicate that crib speech also plays a significant role in organizing, verbally, the daily experiences of the child and developing his narrative thinking. The boy in question regularly produced crib speech very much like that reported by Kuczaj, but the objects and events mentioned pertained almost exclusively to recent experiences and were gradually organized into a number of stories.

The current broadening of the concept of private speech makes it even more difficult to evaluate the original clash of opinions between Piaget and Vygotsky. For one thing a sustained dialogue between these two thinkers never took place. Vygotsky based his arguments exclusively on the two books Piaget published in the 1920s, and because of Vygotsky's early death his writings could not reflect the later changes in Piaget's position. Piaget, in turn, seemed to be rather indifferent to Vygotsky's work. He did not become acquainted with Vygotsky's position until 1962 when the editors of the first English translation of *Thought and Language* solicited his comments. This indifference is a historical-psychological phenomenon in itself. Consider the following simple facts: Piaget's *The Language and Thought of the Child* was published in Russian in 1932 with an introduction written by Vygotsky, while the French translation of Vygotsky's *Thought and Language* was not made for another fifty(!) years. Even without paying much attention to these historical peculiarities some critics maintain that Vygotsky's focus on the *functional* importance of egocentric speech is largely irrelevant for the

Piagetian *structural* approach to the development of the mind.[35] Anyway, in his comments Piaget acknowledged that "When Vygotsky concluded that the early function of language must be that of global communication and that later speech becomes differentiated into egocentric and communicative proper, I believe I agree with him. But when he maintains that these two linguistic forms are equally socialized and differ only in function, I cannot go along with him because the word *socialized* becomes ambiguous in this context".[36] To this Vygotsky would most probably have replied that the term "socialized" is ambiguous indeed, and that egocentric speech is not socialized, but rather social in the sense that it develops out of the earlier global speech which is essentially social, and not autistic. In general it seems that Piaget was primarily interested in proving what he saw as the undifferentiated character of egocentric speech, while Vygotsky focused instead on the future "fate" of this speech. Vygotsky also volunteered the following explanation of his disagreement with Piaget:

> The social forms of behavior are more complex and more advanced in a child, and when individualized, they first acquire a simpler modus of operation. For example, egocentric speech is more primitive in its structure than communicative speech, yet as a stage in the development of thought it is higher than the social speech of the child of the same age. Perhaps this is the reason why Piaget considered egocentric speech to be a predecessor, rather than a consequence of socialized speech.[37]

The phenomenon of egocentric speech is accorded such importance not only because of its crucial position in a child's development but also because it provides a "window" into the inner world of silent speech-for-oneself. The phenomenon of inner speech is as elusive as it is persistent. Our ordinary introspection informs us that certain verbal processes are involved in the inner formation of our thoughts and feelings. At the same time, because of their very nature, these processes elude direct empirical inquiry. Vygotsky suggested that audible egocentric speech does not disappear around the age of seven, but instead goes inside and becomes inner speech. By studying gradually disappearing features of egocentric speech and by provoking their temporary return under special experimental conditions it was possible to sketch a portrait of the otherwise elusive inner speech.

One of the major determinants of inner speech is its *predicative* character. This conclusion is based on the observation of the gradual disappearance of a subject from the child's egocentric utterances. A child "already knows" what he or she is talking about and therefore there is no need for naming the subject. In the language of contemporary psycholinguistics this means that only "new information" or "rheme" is retained in inner speech, while "old information" or "theme" is simply presumed. The predicative character of inner speech seems to be a direct result of the shrinkage of the distance between addresser and addressee.[38] In other words, the closer the position of the speaker to that of the listener, the closer their apperception, the more abbreviated and more predicative will be the speech. According to this position inner speech is just the ultimate point in the continuum of communicative conditions judged by the degree of "intimacy" between addresser and addressee. In the case of inner speech they are one and the same person, and thus their apperception coincides. To approach this phenomenon Vygotsky suggested studying situations in which interlocutors share apperception to an extraordinary degree.[39] One of the vignettes provided by Vygotsky is excerpted from Leo Tolstoy's *Anna Karenina*:

> "I have long wished to ask you something."
> "Please do."
> "This", he said, and wrote the intial letters: W y a: i c n b, d y m t o n. These letters meant: "When you answered: it can not be, did you mean then or never?" It seemed impossible that she would be able to understand the complicated sentence.
> "I understand", she said, blushing.
> "What word is that?", he asked, pointing to the *n* which stood for "never".
> "The word is 'never' ", she said. . . . [40]

This understanding based on a highly abbreviated text is possible because of the extreme intimacy of thoughts and speech between Levin and Kitty, because of the coincidence in their apperception. Tolstoy, according to his memoirs, used an actual episode from his own life in this scene.

It would be simplistic, however, to think that inner speech is an absolutely homogeneous phenomenon. First of all, there is a fundamental contradiction between the genetic roots of inner speech, which are social and therefore "dialogical", and the functional mode of inner speech, which Vygotsky believed to be monological. Second, there is the intriguing problem of the relationship between inner and/or egocentric speech and the integration of a child's personality. My own observations suggest that a child passes in his or her speech through the stage of "heteroglossia", with a number of voices of important figures coexisting in the child's language. A somewhat similar observation was reported by Daniel Stern, based on the crib talk of a two-year-old girl who regularly had dialogues with her father before going to bed. When left alone the girl started a monologue in which she practiced her speech and word usage. But beyond this language practice she seemed to be using her father's voice to control herself emotionally: "Sometimes she seemed to intone in his voice or to recreate something like the previous dialogue with him, in order to reactivate his presence and carry it with her toward the abyss of sleep".[41] Finally, there is the problem of genres in inner speech. Certainly, inner speech is not just an abbreviated version of the child's egocentric utterances. All speech forms develop, and inner speech is no exception. Beyond its role as a problem-solving tool and a blueprint for an oral or written narrative, inner speech can certainly become a recap of the past and a rehearsal for future *dialogic* conversations. Moreover, in speech-for-oneself, such as in inner dialogue, no limits are imposed on different "voices". Of course, all these voices are remembered or invented by *the* speaker, the self, and in this sense any inner dialogue is only conditionally dialogical. This limitation notwithstanding, the voices of others are indispensable in the "theater" of our inner speech. This feature of inner speech has an obvious similarity to a work of literature which on the one hand is encompassed by the language of its author, while on the other contains a multitude of separate voices from different characters. To pursue this analogy we must digress from the topic of language development and inquire into the problem of speech genres as such.

Although a typology of speech genres is possible and necessary, this does not mean that one is capable of composing an exhaustive list of all genres. Beyond such general categories as oral and written speech, one can distinguish between monologues and dialogues, prose and poetry, greetings, commands, requests, comments, historical narratives, love-letters, etc., *ad infinitum*. A pioneering role in the study of speech genres was played by Vygotsky's contemporary, philologist and philosopher Mikhail Bakhtin (1895–1975).[42] Although there is no hard evidence that Vygotsky and Bakhtin were acquainted or influenced each other, their positions in the realm of twentieth-century thought bear intriguing signs of similarity. First, there is a considerable overlap in Vygotsky's and Bakhtin's linguistic sources, including Potebnya and other followers of Humboldt. Moreover, in the 1920s Bakhtin belonged to the same intellectual circle in Leningrad as Vygotsky's cousin David. And it is from David that Vygotsky most probably learned about the new developments in linguistics and literary theory.[43] Second, there is an interesting parallel between Vygotsky's and Bakhtin's rediscovery in the West. Both of them seem to offer some insights into human language and thought, which became relevant only in the 1970s and 1980s.[44]

Bakhtin believed that language is the primary reality of human consciousness and that literary discourse, as a rather late product of language development, expresses those forms and mechanisms of speech that only start developing in ordinary oral speech. But since the development of speech plays an important role in the formation of human consciousness, the analysis of literary discourse may become a methodological tool in the study of not only everyday language, but also of consciousness itself. The naturalistic approach, which is shared by many psychologists, attempts to derive even the most complex forms of verbal behavior from elementary preverbal cognitive and behavioral processes, with respect to which language is a more or less passive system of labeling. Bakhtin, in contrast, suggested that the superior processes of writing and interpreting culturally meaningful texts provide an adequate perspective for the assessment of even an elementary form of conduct. Language for Bakhtin was not a label for extralinguistic reality but rather it was a tool for turning this from a "given" into a developing reality. Language, as it is revealed in literary discourse, thus offers a paradigm for any action, to the extent that this action is addressed and interpreted. The boundary between "artificial" (literature) and "natural" (individual speech) is removed; literary discourse becomes a model for the reconstruction of individual consciousness.[45]

Concerning the relationship between linguistics and literary theory, Bakhtin's position seems to be a complementary opposite to that of Roman Jakobson and other Formalists. The Formalists worked their way from the bottom up, claiming for linguistics a certain role in the analysis of works of literature. Bakhtin suggested starting from the top down, such as from speech genres as they are identified in literary theory to their precursors and/or counterparts in individual speech.[46]

According to Bakhtin the study of speech genres traditionally suffered from two misconceptions, one concerning the differences between oral and written discourse, the other regarding the unit of speech analysis.[47] The first misconception was based on the idea that the obvious difference between everyday oral speech on the one hand, and literary discourse on the other, warranted their total separation and their treatment within two largely unrelated frameworks of linguistics (and psycholinguistics) in the first case, and the theory of literature in the second. The other misconception was that a sentence is a "natural" unit of speech analysis. Bakhtin convincingly argued (and more recent studies have supported this) that both oral and written language is realized in the form of individual *utterances*. The boundaries of each utterance are determined by actual or imagined changes of speakers. The very problem of similarities and differences between oral and written discourse could be properly formulated only when these misconceptions are overcome.

A study of speech genres built on the foundation of utterance as a speech unit may also help to unravel the core mystery of human language—its individual uniqueness coexisting with its essential commonality: "Utterances and their types, that is speech genres, are the drive belts from the history of society to the history of language. There is not a single new phenomenon (phonetic, logical, or grammatical) that can enter the system of language without having traversed the long and complicated path of generic-stylistic testing and modification".[48]

The utterance has been selected as a unit of speech because it reflects the very essence of verbal communication, its direction toward the other. The utterance, from a single-word rejoinder to a large novel, has an absolute beginning and absolute end: in the beginning it is preceded by the speech of others, and it ends in anticipation of a response. The utterance, therefore, is always an implicit (or explicit) response to something that has been said or written before and, at the same time, an implicit projection into an anticipated rejoinder in the future. The "speaker", even when he or she is a writer, does not produce monologues intended for no one, but, unconsciously, expects some responsive understanding with delayed action.[49]

Human speech is always cast in definite speech genres. We use them confidently and skillfully, and when hearing others' speech we guess its genre almost immediately. At the same time, just as we are ordinarily oblivious of our lexicon and syntax, neither do we consciously register speech genres. Some speech genres are more standardized than others. For example, the genre of greetings and salutations is highly formalized, while those of social conversation or artistic discourse are open to free creative reformulations. A considerable proportion of the traditional social education of children from higher classes consisted of teaching them how to select the proper speech genre depending on the circumstances.[50] But the importance of speech genres goes beyond "good table manners", and into the sphere of the self-realization of human individuality. Bakhtin believed that the better our command of genres and the more freely we employ them, the more fully we reveal our own individuality. This position suggests that a superior literary discourse which skillfully combines a multitude of different genres could be the model for a fully developed individual language. Psychologists thus may wish to approach the problem of verbal functions from the position of this model, rather than from generalizations based on empirical samples of everyday oral speech.

The flexibility in the individual use of different speech genres belongs to the macro-level of verbal analysis. On the micro-level, each word and each utterance is filled with *dialogical overtones*. These overtones appear as a natural result of the dialogic nature of verbal activity: "After all, our thought itself—philosophical, scientific, artistic—is born and shaped in the process of interaction and struggle with others' thought, and this cannot but be reflected in the forms that verbally express our thought as well".[51] On the micro-level each utterance contains a number of imaginary changes of subjects with words, intonations and speech constructions of others being incorporated within it. The principle of dialogue thus penetrates even apparently monological speech: "The utterance appears to be furrowed with distant and barely audible echoes of changes of speech subjects and dialogic overtones".[52]

In his analysis of Dostoevsky's novels Bakhtin convincingly showed that in these novels the main "characters" are different consciousnesses reflecting and quoting each other.[53] Special discourse analysis reveals a profound heteroglossia, that is, an intertwining of different social, cultural and idiosyncratic voices in the speech of the nominal characters of Dostoevsky's novels. The novelistic discourse, therefore, is a special form of language that "permits readers to see things that are obscured by the restraints on expression in other applications of language".[54] Literature does not invent life, nor does it provide a written copy of life events; rather, it reveals such capacities of human consciousness and communication which remain underdeveloped or invisible in other media of expression.

It is time now to return to Vygotsky's analysis of various modes of speech. Just as inner speech is not "talking minus sound", writing is not a "transciption" of oral speech. Unlike that of oral exchanges, the potential addressee of the written message is often unknown, which imposes very special requirements on writing. Ordinarily we are more elaborate in our writing than in oral dialogue. The ideas must be fully deployed because the reader has little or no circumstantial information from which to reconstruct the author's intentions. Written speech also lacks those expressive and prosodic means that make oral exchanges so natural. This speech is not triggered by immediate responses, as in a dialogue where need always leads to request, question to answer, and puzzlement to explanation. In oral dialogue the dynamics of turn-taking takes care of the direction of speech; in writing the unfolding of a plot or argument is based on a much more abstractive foundation. Vygotsky believed that in the beginning a child has little natural motivation to learn this abstractive skill. Moreover, the psychological processes upon which writing depends have not yet been developed at the time instruction in writing usually begins.

This conclusion returns us to the notion of the zone of proximal development and the relationships between development and education. Psychological development, according to Vygotsky, does not precede instruction, but essentially depends on it. Psychologically, writing is not a paper-and-pencil application of verbal functions already developed through oral speech, but a creation of new psychological systems which do not emerge spontaneously but become possible only because of systematic instruction. In a broader sense, the mastery of reading and writing is the road to a higher form of consciousness. Symbolization, which in oral speech occurs spontaneously and unconsciously, is mastered anew on a conscious and purposeful level in written speech. That is why, for example, the study of grammar in school leads not only to the acquisition of a useful social skill, but also to a new phase in the development of the child's mind.

The transition from natural to cultural psychological functions is associated in Vygotsky's theory with the transition from oral speech to writing. This thesis, which in itself may not be controversial at all, attains a special meaning in the framework of the current discussion regarding the educational implications of orality versus writing, and contextual talk versus autonomous text. Let us briefly attend to these issues now. First, one may claim that there is a certain contradiction between Vygotsky's emphasis on the dialogical character of human thought and language, and his belief in the superior status of monological written speech. Second, there is an uncertainty with respect to what kind of verbal thinking should be considered as developmentally superior: decontextualized conceptual reasoning or intertextually rich narrative thinking?

The current controversy over the issue of orality versus writing sprang from two sources: from the scientific argument regarding the influence of writing on cognition, and from the public debate about illiteracy in American society and its social consequences.[55] On the scientific side of the discussion, David Olson's thesis on the cultural and developmental superiority of the written "autonomous text" over oral contextual speech has become a standard point of reference. "My argument", Olson wrote, "will be that there is a transition from utterance to text both culturally and developmentally and that this transition can be described as one of increasing explicitness, with language increasingly able to stand as an unambiguous or autonomous representation of meaning".[56] Olson proceeded to show that the development of writing had led to the scientific essay, which is a pure example of decontextualized autonomous text. Such text represents, in Olson's words, the "truth of correspondence" between statements and observations, which should be distinguished from the "truth of wisdom" perpetuated in the oral and poetic tradition.

Although there is much truth in what Olson said about the cognitive consequences of writing, his choice of the scientific essay as the the teleos of language development and the paradigm of autonomous text seems inappropriate. Scientific statements about processes in nature are indifferent to the mode of expression. They could be made in the form of graphs, formulas, cartoons, films or oral presentation. The truth of correspondence ultimately depends on the replication of the experimental procedure and not on the conformity to the original text. The text of the scientific essay becomes important only when we are interested in the scientist's position or theory, but in this perspective the text becomes clearly contextual.[57]

The above discussion has a direct bearing on the Vygotskian interpretation of the place of writing in the overall development of language and thought. In his pursuit of the issue of decontextualization of speech Vygotsky focused on the transition from sign–object relations to sign–sign relations characteristic of "scientific" concepts. There are, however, some other types of sign–sign relations beyond those captured by "scientific" concepts, and these relations were not explored by Vygotsky in any detail.[58] The simplest of these relations is reported speech, that is, an utterance of one person imbedded in the speech of another; for example, "And she said, 'I have nothing to forget and forgive' ". It has been shown that the mastery of reported speech is a rather late product of child development, and that younger children are incapable of properly framing another person's speech.[59] Even such a simple case as reported speech immediately suggests that the literary text is a treasure trove of sign–sign relations unavailable in "scientific" concepts. Not only is reported speech a norm in a work of literature, but the lexicon and style of one character is embedded in or projected onto the speech of another. The "heteroglossia" (the coexistence of conflicting individual styles in the speech of a nominal character) observed by Bakhtin in Dostoevsky's novels, is the paradigmatic case of the higher-order sign–sign relations.

One step farther along this line of inquiry is the phenomenon of intertextuality. The notion of intertextuality has been introduced, not without Bakhtin's influence, to overcome the limitations of the structuralist approach in linguistics and literary theory.[60] Intertextuality denotes, in a general sense, the transposition of one or several sign systems into another, and more specifically the presence of anticedent texts in the consequent literary text. The phenomenon of intertextuality is important because, upon close observation, it seems to be pervasive in all humanistic texts. These texts always appear as a response, reply, amplification or clarification of some other text, which cannot but continue to "live" in the consequent text.

The intertextuality of literary texts provides a suggestive model for the study of sign–sign relationships in individual speech. The developmental superiority of decontextualized "scientific" concepts can be challenged by *narrative thinking*, which is on the contrary highly contextual, but whose context is provided not by deictic, extralinguistic stimuli, but by intralinguistic relations rooted in the literate tradition.[61] The connection between narrative thinking and literacy is determined not only by the fact that literary intertextuality is taken here as a model, but also by the empirical fact that the success of an oral exchange between literate adults often depends on shared cultural texts. The elements of these shared texts serve as mediators for communication providing the necessary intersubjectivity. Intersubjectivity in this case, however, is achieved by the "participation" of two or more persons in one original text. The participation becomes possible because each communicant recognises the echo of the original text in the other's speech. This echo provides the communicant with a base from which the individual development of a theme in the speech of the other can be observed. Reading and writing, therefore, exercise a powerful reciprocal influence on the oral speech of a literate person. Writing is monological only in the sense that its context is mental, rather than physical. To keep the context in mind and to plan the whole text in the absence of the immediate stimulation certainly requires a higher development of cognitive functions, which cannot but influence oral speech as well.

SENSE AND MEANING

The final issue to be addressed in this chapter is the Vygotskian analysis of the relationships between thought, verbal meaning and words themselves. Vygotsky succinctly presented his position as follows: "Word meaning is a phenomenon of thought only insofar as thought is embodied in speech, and of speech only insofar as speech is connected with thought and illuminated by it. It is a phenomenon of verbal thought, or meaningful speech—a union of word and thought".[62] The generative sequence which ultimately leads to the word (utterance) starts with motivation or intention. Motivation engenders thought, which at that stage is devoid of specific linguistic form. Next comes the realization of thought in the form of verbal meanings, which takes place in inner speech. The relationship between verbal meanings and actual words is still ambivalent. Only at the final stage are the concrete words of oral or written speech chosen.

A number of psychological vignettes drawn by Vygotsky from works of literature and the arts were intended as illustrations of the different relationships mentioned in the above sequence. For example, in his work with actors the famous stage director and theoretician Konstantin Stanislavsky used extensive "motivation lists" in which each utterance or passage in the text of a play was "transcribed" in terms of the underlying motivation of a character.[63] From the same work of Stanislavsky Vygotsky also borrowed an elaboration on the theme of ambiguity in the relationship between the surface utterance and the underlying thought. Stanislavsky's idea of the "subtext" in acting is based on the recognition of this ambiguity. Keeping in mind the subtext of the role, that is, the thoughts behind the words, the actor shows "what is meant" by the character rather than "what is said". The same problem of the difficulty in matching thoughts with words found its expression in the traditional lamentation of poets about the inexpressibility of thought. "If only thought might speak without words", exclaimed the nineteenth-century poet Alexander Fet. It is not only that thought and words do not coincide; thought unexpressed remains immature and eventually dies out. Language, therefore, is not just an *expression* of otherwise independent and fully formed thought, but rather is a necessary form of the thought's realization. This idea has been poetically rendered by Vygotsky's favorite author, Osip Mandelstam:

> The word I forgot
> Which once I wished to say
> And voiceless thought
> Returns to shadow's chamber.[64]

The most enigmatic processes occur, however, in inner speech where the interaction between the not-yet-verbal thought and word meanings takes place. Following the French linguist Frédéric Paulhan, Vygotsky made a potent distinction between word meaning in a general sense, and in the more restrictive terms "sense" (*smysl*) and "meaning" (*znachenie*).[65] The dictionary meaning of a word, according to Vygotsky, represents a stable zone, the core of the otherwise ever-changing meaning of the word. These meanings which change depending on the context are the senses of the word. A word in a context means both more and less than the same word taken as its meaning; it means more because it is enriched by each new context, and it means less because it becomes a prisoner of specific contexts. This contextuality of the sense of the word is reflected in the unlimited flexibility of the sense-word relations when one and the same meaning can be carried by different words, while one and the same word can acquire diametrically opposite meanings depending on the context. In an oral dialogue one starts with the core meaning and moves, depending on the context, to the soft fringes sometimes reaching an idiosyncratic sense of the word. In inner speech the process starts at the opposite end, from the idiosyncratic sense dominated by the not-yet-verbal thought. In inner speech the word meaning is dominated by the sense. In developing the same issue, Bakhtin pointed out that the neutral dictionary meanings of words ensure mutual understanding between communicants, but that real-life communication is always individual and contextual in nature: "Any word exists for the speaker in three aspects: as a neutral word of a language, belonging to nobody; as an *other's* word, which belongs to another person and is filled with echoes of the other's utterance, and, finally, *my* word, for, since I am dealing with it in a particular situation, with a particular speech plan, it is already imbued with my expression".[66]

The processes in inner speech, as described by Vygotsky, bear a striking similarity to the phenomena of condensation and displacement defined by Freud. One of these processes is what Vygotsky called the "influx of sense".[67] The senses of different words flow into each other and literally influence each other. Thus one word recurring in a poem or a book gradually absorbs all different "senses" contained in the book and becomes, in psychoanalytic parlance, "overdetermined"; it stands for the book as a whole. Freud seemed to refer to the same phenomenon when he wrote: "The process may go so far that a single word, if it is specially suitable on account of its numerous connections, takes over the representation of a whole train of thought".[68] For Freud, however, overdetermination is the result of a "primary process" representing primitive or regressive psychological activity. Vygotsky viewed the "influx of sense" as a stage in the normal unfolding of speech, which could be best analyzed in creative, artistic language. In the inner speech of the author "nobody's words" are personalized becoming an idiosyncratic sense of the author's idea. At this stage certain words or rhymes become a nucleus, a monad of the future creative text. Next comes a long and tortuous process of matching idiosyncratic sense with actual linguistic forms. At this stage an intense inner dialogue is taking place: the author realizes his or her, "sense" through the language of others. This is a dialogue of the author-as-a-reader with the author-as-a-creator. The result of this dialogue is a miracle of literary text that is open to all and at the same time uniquely individual.

What lies beyond the unfolding of speech from the motivation to the overt word is the ultimate frontier of Vygotskian psychology: the problem of human consciousness. Vygotsky left no coherent text discussing this issue, just a number of notes, remarks and formulaic two-liners, essentially his own inner speech put on paper.[69] The following insights emerge from this inner speech. It is incorrect to consider language as a correlative of thought, language is a correlative of consciousness. The mode of language correlative to consciousness is meanings. The work of consciousness with meanings leads to the generation of sense, and in the process consciousness acquires a sensible (meaningful) structure. To study human consciousness means to study this sensible structure, and verbal meaning is the methodological unit of this study. Such a study can be carried out at the abstractive as well as the concrete level. At the level of abstract psychology we can study general rules of signification; at the concrete level we should be concerned with specific "sense-generating" activity that changes the consciousness of a person. Intersubjectivity and interpersonal communication are the driving belts of the sensible structure of consciousness:

> Consciousness is reflected in a word as the sun in a drop of water. A word relates to consciousness as a living cell relates to an organism, as an atom relates to the universe. A word is the microcosm of human consciousness.[70]

NOTES

1. Lev Vygotsky, *Thought and Language* (revised edn). Cambridge, MA: MIT Press, 1986 (original work published as *Myshlenie i Rech*. Moscow and Leningrad: Sotzekgiz, 1934).
2. Wolfgang Köhler, *The Mentality of Apes*. London: Routledge and Kegan Paul, 1973 (original work published in 1917).
3. Karl Bühler, *The Mental Development of the Child*. New York: Harcourt Brace, 1930, pp. 50–1.
4. Vygotsky, *Thought and Language*, pp. 75–6.
5. For the review of these works, see Thomas Sebeok and Jean Umiker-Sebeok, eds, *Speaking of Apes*. New York: Plenum, 1980.
6. E. Sue Savage-Rumbaugh, *Ape Language*. New York: Columbia University Press, 1986.
7. Ibid, p. 21.
8. Ibid, p. 29.
9. Jean Piaget, *The Psychology of Intelligence*. New York: Humanities Press, 1969 (original work published in 1947).

10. Charlotte Bühler, H. Hetzer and B. Tudor-Hart, *The First Year of Life*. New York: Day, 1930.
11. Dmitri Uznadze, *Psikhologicheskie Issledovaniya (Psychological Investigations)*. Moscow: Nauka, 1966, p. 77 (original paper published in German in 1929).
12. Lev Sakharov, "O metodakh issledovaniya ponyatii" ("Methods of studying concepts"). *Psikhologiya*, vol. 3, No. 1, 1930.
13. See Vygotsky, *Thought and Language*, pp. 103–4.
14. Eugenia Hanfmann and Jacob Kasanin, *Conceptual Thinking in Schizophrenia*. New York: NMDP, 1942.
15. Vygotsky, *Thought and Language*, p. 107.
16. Hanfmann and Kasanin, *op. cit.*, pp. 23–5.
17. Vygotsky, *Thought and Language*, p. 124.
18. Henri Levebvre, *Everyday Life in the Modern World*. New Brunswick, NJ: Transaction Books, 1984, ch. 3.
19. Heinz Werner and Edith Kaplan, "The acquisition of word meanings: A developmental study". *Monographs of the Society for Research in Child Development*, vol. XV, No. 1, 1950.
20. See Vygotsky, *Thought and Language*, ch. 6.
21. Ibid, p. 202.
22. Ibid, p. 194.
23. Barbara Rogoff and James Wertsch, *Children's Learning in the Zone of Proximal Development*. San Francisco: Jossey-Bass, 1984; Denis Newman, Peg Griffin and Michael Cole, *The Construction Zone*. New York: Cambridge University Press, 1989.
24. See James Wertsch, *L. S. Vygotsky and the Social Formation of Mind*. Cambridge, MA: Harvard University Press, 1985, pp. 158–66.
25. Edward Thorndike, *The Psychology of Learning*. New York: Mason-Henry, 1913.
26. See Vygotsky, *Thought and Language*, pp. 180–90.
27. Darrin Lehman, R. O. Lempert and R. E. Nisbett, "The effects of graduate training on reasoning". *American Psychologist*, vol. 43, 1988, pp. 431–42.
28. Susan Carey, *Conceptual Change in Childhood*. Cambridge, MA: MIT Press, 1985.
29. Peter Tulviste, "Is there a form of verbal thought specific to childhood?". *Soviet Psychology*, vol. 21, 1982, pp. 3–17.
30. Vygotsky, *Thought and Language*, chs 2 and 7.
31. Jean Piaget, *The Language and Thought of the Child*. London: Routledge and Kegan Paul, 1959. See also Piaget's Comments in Vygotsky, *Thought and Language*, pp. 262–76.
32. Vygotsky, *Thought and Language*, pp. 29–31; 232–5. For

replications of Vygotsky's study see Lawrence Kohlberg, J. Yaeger, and E. Hjertholm, "Private speech". *Child Development*, vol. 39, 1968, pp. 691–736; and Gail Zivin, *The Development of Self-regulation Through Private Speech*. New York: Wiley, 1979.

33. See Wertsch, *Vygotsky and the Social Construction*, pp. 116–20.
34. Stan Kuczaj, *Crib Speech and Language Play*. New York: Springer, 1983.
35. Zivin, *The Development of Self-regulation*, pp. 16–28.
36. Piaget in Vygotsky, *Thought and Language*, p. 275.
37. Lev Vygotsky, *Orudie i Znak*. In *Collected Papers*, vol. 6. Moscow: Pedagogika, 1984, p. 71–2.
38. The subject of the shrinkage of distance between addresser and addressee has been explored in Heinz Werner and Bernard Kaplan, *Symbol Formation*. New York: Wiley, 1963.
39. The concept of shared apperception was borrowed by Vygotsky from Lev Jakubinsky, "O dialogicheskoi rechi" ("On verbal dialogue"). In L. Scherba, ed., *Russkaya Rech (Russian Speech)*. Petrograd, 1923. See an abridged English translation in *Dispositio*, vol. 4, 1979, pp. 321–36.
40. Vygotsky, *Thought and Language*, p. 273.
41. Daniel Stern, *The Interpersonal World of the Infant*. New York: Basic Books, 1985, p. 172–3.
42. Bakhtin's life and work is comprehensively discussed in Katerina Clark and Michael Holquist, *Mikhail Bakhtin*. Cambridge, MA: Harvard University Press, 1984.
43. The closeness of this circle is underscored by the fact that during the Stalin purges David Vygodsky found himself in the same Gulag camp where one of Bakhtin's principal co-authors, Pavel Medvedev, was imprisoned.
44. See James Wertsch, "The semiotic mediation of mental life: Vygotsky and Bakhtin". In E. Mertz and R. J. Parmentier, eds, *Semiotic Mediation*. Orlando, FL: Academic Press, 1986. Caryl Emerson, "The outer word and inner speech: Bakhtin, Vygotsky and the internalization of language", *Critical Inquiry*, vol. 10, 1983, pp. 245–64.
45. There seems to be an interesting and still unexplored similarity in Bakhtin's and Heidegger's theories of language, as well as in the *language* of their theories; cf. "Poetry proper is never merely a higher mode (*melos*) of everyday language. It is rather the reverse: everyday language is a forgotten and therefore used up poem, from which there hardly resounds a call any longer" (Martin Heidegger, *Poetry, Language, Thought*. New York: Harper and Row, 1971, p. 208).

46. About the relevance of Bakhtin for post-structuralist linguistics, see Julia Kristeva. "Word, dialogue and novel". In *Julia Kristeva Reader*. New York: Columbia University Press, 1986.

47. Mikhail Bakhtin, *Speech Genres and Other Late Essays*. Austin, TX: University of Texas Press, 1986.

48. Ibid, p. 65.

49. The issue of response and anticipation in writing has been recently explored by Martin Nystrand, *The Structure of Written Communication*. New York: Academic Press, 1986. See David Olson's critical review in *Contemporary Psychology*, vol. 34(2), 1989, pp. 119–21.

50. It is only recently that psycholinguists have realized that learning how to use proper speech genre is as important for a child as a proper lexicon and syntax. See J. Berko Gleason, R. Y. Perlmann and E. B. Greif, "What's the magic word: Learning language through politeness routines". *Discourse Processes*, vol. 7, 1984, pp. 495–503.

51. Bakhtin, *Speech Genres*, p. 92.

52. Ibid, p. 93.

53. Mikhail Bakhtin, *Problems of Dostoevsky's Poetics*. Minneapolis: University of Minnesota Press, 1984 (original work published in 1929).

54. Clark and Holquist, *Mikhail Bakhtin*, p. 243.

55. James Gee, "Orality and literature". *TESOL Quarterly*, vol. 20, 1986, pp. 719–46.

56. David Olson, "From utterance to text". *Harvard Educational Review*, vol. 47, 1977, p. 258.

57. See Courtney Cazden, "The myth of autonomous text". In D. M. Topping, ed., *A Study of Thinking*. New York: Erlbaum, in press.

58. See Wertsch, *Vygotsky and the Social Formation*, pp. 150–7.

59. Maya Hickmann, "Metapragmatics in child language". In E. Mertz and R. J. Parmentier, eds, *Semiotic Mediation*. Orlando, FL: Academic Press, 1985.

60. See Kristeva, *Word, Dialogue and Novel*, pp. 36–7.

61. A somewhat different approach to narrative thinking has been proposed by Jerome Bruner, *Actual Minds, Possible Worlds*. Cambridge, MA: Harvard University Press, 1986.

62. Vygotsky, *Thought and Language*, p. 212.

63. See Konstantin Stanislavsky, *Creating a Role*. New York: Theater Art Books, 1961.

64. Vygotsky used these lines from the early version of Mandelstam's poem "The Swallow" as an epigraph to Chapter 7 of *Thought and Language* (p. 210). Mandelstam's influence on Vygotsky appar-

ently extended beyond poetry and included some ideas developed by Mandelstam in his essays:

> Old psychology knew only how to objectify the representation. . . . According to this view the decisive factor was that of givenness. The givenness of the products of our consciousness makes them like objects of the external world, thus permitting us to regard representations as something objective. However, the extremely rapid humanization of science, including the category of knowledge, forces us to move in another direction. We can consider representations not only as objective data of consciousness, but also as human organs. . . . (Osip Mandelstam, "On the nature of the word". In *The Complete Critical Prose and Letters of Osip Mandelstam*. Ann Arbor, MI: Ardis, 1979, p. 130)

Word meanings, therefore, can be conceived of not as the inner doubles of external objects, but as active organs of human consciousness.

65. Frédéric Paulhan, "Qu'est-ce que le sens des mots?". *Journal de Psychologie*, vol. 25, 1928, pp. 289–329.
66. Bakhtin, *Speech Genres*, p. 88.
67. Vygotsky, *Thought and Language*, pp. 246–7.
68. Sigmund Freud, *The Unconscious*. In James Strachey, ed., *The Standard Edition of the Complete Psychological Works*, vol. 14. 1953–74, p. 199, London: Hogarth Press (original work published in 1915).
69. Lev Vygotsky, *Problema Soznaniya (The Problem of Consciousness)*. In *Collected Papers*, vol. 1. Moscow: Pedagogika, 1982. Vygotsky's position regarding the social origins of consciousness is expressed in "Consciousness as a problem of the psychology of behavior", *Soviet Psychology*, vol. 17, 1979, pp. 5–35.
70. Vygotsky, *Thought and Language*, p. 256.

CHAPTER SIX

Mind in Trouble

V̲YGOTSKY'S interest in the deviant forms of psychological development, with the troubles of the mind, began at the very beginning of his psychological career and lasted to its very end. As early as 1924 he wrote the paper "Defect and compensation", while the last talk he delivered in 1934 was about clinical neuropsychology. The psychology of handicapped children, together with the neuro- and psychopathology of adults, were seen by Vygotsky as an indispensable aspect of the general theory of human development.

He did not believe in meaningless defect or retrogression: since the construction of the human mind follows a certain pattern, its destruction also cannot be arbitrary and therefore reveals specific rupture lines characteristic of the formation of the human psyche. That is why observations of the acquisition of language in the deaf-mute, concept formation in schizophrenics, and the rehabilitation of aphasics were for Vygotsky no less a part of developmental psychology than the sensory-motor behavior of the two-year-old. In general it seems fair to say that Vygotsky's views on the relationship between development and regression had been formed under the influence of the "organicist" tradition. This tradition originated in the works of British neurologists John Hughlings Jackson and Henry Head, and was continued by German-American Kurt Goldstein. The essence of their position, which had already been formulated by Jackson, lay in the rejection of the idea of negative impairment. What we perceive as symptoms of impairment are usually mani-festations of the process of compensation. The higher function is not simply "switched off", but is substituted for by the lower, developmentally more archaic function, which then finds itself without the higher control and produces deviant forms of behavior and cognition.[1]

Such were the theoretical premises of Vygotsky's interest. There was also a more practical reason for Vygotsky's concern with abnormal behavior and handicapped development. In the 1920s many thousands of children of all ages roamed the streets of Russian cities and towns. All of them were direct or indirect victims of the Revolution and the Civil War: some were orphans, some had simply lost track of their families, and others had been sent away from famine-stricken areas. This mass of young vagrants, and some of their only slightly luckier peers who stayed with what remained of their families, represented an enormous medical, social and psychological problem. These were children who had suffered abandonment and deprivation for a period of four to five years and whose development was consequently often severely disturbed. The complexity of the conditions made it extremely difficult to distinguish between purely medical con-ditions, such as malnutrition, birth defects and complications following illness, and the sociopsychological problems related to homelessness and lack of education. The first task was therefore to identify those in need of serious medical-pedagogical inter-vention, primarily the cases of severe physical and mental dis-ability. Those cases were handled in the framework of the so-called "defectological" service. As early as 1925 Vygotsky was active in establishing a laboratory for the study of abnormal child development, which in 1929 was upgraded to become the Institute of Defectology. During the last years of his life Vygot-sky served as the scientific director of this institute, which now-adays remains the leading research center for the study of handi-capped children in the Soviet Union.[2]

In addition to the task of identifying and rehabilitating severely disabled children, the problem arose of how to stream-line children of different backgrounds, abilities and psychological profiles into the system of compulsory education set up in the 1920s by the Soviet government. As a response to this challenge a special scientific and practical field started to emerge under the name of "pedology". The subject of pedology, according to Vygotsky, is the child as a total human being. This field was conceived of as a scientific counterpart to pedagogy. In reality it was often reduced to the development and administration of simple batteries of psychological tests and the provision of certain guidelines for teachers concerning desirable courses of educational intervention. Pedology was not a homogeneous field and Vygotsky openly disagreed with some pedological ideas and practices. Still he probably had no inkling that in 1936 the Communist Party would condemn pedology as a "bourgeois deviation", disband all pedological research groups, and put all former pedologists, including Vygotsky (posthumously) on the blacklist.[3]

PSYCHOLOGY OF THE HANDICAPPED

Although the consequences of the Civil War created very special circumstances for the study and treatment of handicapped children, the subject itself certainly was not new. In Moscow the first sanatorium school for anomalous children had been organized in 1908 by V. P. Kaschenko, who thus ventured into the field which in the West is called "special education". In St Petersburg, A. S. Griboedov founded the institute for training special education teachers. After the Revolution the field received the name "defectology" and specialists in anomalous development and special education became known as defectologists (the term "defectology" possibly carried some technological associations, but no sense of prejudice).[4]

The special circumstances of the 1920s seemed to warrant an holistic approach to the study and treatment of a wide variety of disabilities, from blindness to mental retardation, under one roof. At that time all handicaps, both physical and mental, were seen in one social perspective. The very name of the first national meeting dedicated to child welfare underscored this point, for it was called the Congress for the Struggle with Child Defectiveness, Delinquency and Homelessness (1920). The Soviet government was then designing a comprehensive welfare system, closing down private hospitals and schools, and even questioning the role of the family. Under those circumstances one could not rely on the traditional taxonomy of disabilities. All forms of deviancy and disability were viewed primarily in terms of their social consequences and requirements for the welfare system. The problem was considered serious enough for the People's Commissar of Health, N. A. Semashko himself, to produce a study on the social and physical factors contributing to child disability and delinquency.

Historically, the issue of the special education of handicapped children had first become a subject of special discussion in the early nineteenth century. There were two basic reasons for the emergence of this issue. One of them was a gradual "medicalization" of disability, which ceased to be viewed as a mystical curse and became aligned with other medical conditions. The second contributing factor was the proliferation of schools and consequently the necessity to decide about the educational status of the handicapped. Both factors contributed to the establishment of special schools for handicapped children. This process took different forms in Britain and in Central Europe. In Britain separate special education schools were established for various categories of disabled children, or at least separate classes were created in state schools. In Central Europe, in contrast, the holistic tradition prevailed, with different types of disability being treated together within the framework of the so-called "curative pedagogy" (*Heilpädagogik*).

One may argue that this difference in approaches stemmed from purely sociological factors. After all, the school systems in Britain and in Central Europe were different, and even the target groups of disabled children were not identical. It is important, however, not to forget the different philosophies behind these systems of special education. The British system not only separated disabilities, but made the physical type of disability into a criterion of differentiation, which meant that an original sensory or motor defect was chosen as a decisive identifying factor. The process of rehabilitation within this system took the form of training what remained of an impaired organ and its vicarious compensation through the development of complementary organs or senses. It is hard to avoid the impression that the tradition of British empiricism (versus continental rationalism) played a major intellectual role in the formation of this philosophy of special education. British empiricism always insisted on the priority of the sense data over categories of thought. To get proper knowledge one first had to have a proper sensory input. The rehabilitation of the handicapped within this philosophical tradition could mean nothing but a vicarious rehabilitation of sensory abilities.

German rationalist philosophy, in contrast, emphasized the priority of categories of thought over raw sense data. The essence of any disability, for this tradition, is in the child's failure to reach the proper level of rational reasoning. Rehabilitation, therefore, should be aimed at attaining the higher level of abstractive, conceptual reasoning that would compensate for the failure of the sensory-motor sphere. This philosophy stimulated a holistic approach to the handicapped child as an "underdeveloped rational human being", rather than a "normal child minus sensory organ". It also established a particular hierarchy of mental representations and a corresponding hierarchy of rehabilitation techniques. For example, the "oralist" method in the education of the deaf—based on lip reading—reigned supreme in Central Europe in the late nineteenth century. It was argued that lip reading facilitates the acquisition of a real, cultured language, thus allowing for the development of abstract reasoning. The sign language of the deaf, it was alleged, corresponds to the lower level of thinking in images and blocks the higher development of a deaf person.

These divergent philosophies of special education had a direct connection to the problems facing Vygotsky in his attempt to set up a program for Soviet defectology. It seems appropriate now to recap those elements of Vygotsky's developmental theory that are relevant to the study of handicapped children.

The fundamental distinction between higher, culturally developed functions and natural psychological processes finds its counterpart in the distinction between a physical defect and its psychological consequences. Although congenital deafness, blindness or cerebral paralysis are undoubtedly organic in nature, their consequences for a child are mediated by the social and psychological factors of handicapped development. A physical defect creates certain natural limitations for a child, but it is the secondary, socially and psychologically mediated limitations that form the particular profile of a handicapped person.[5] Such an understanding of disability set Vygotsky in opposition to the British tradition, which viewed rehabilitation primarily as the vicarious compensation of sensory apparatus. Vygotsky argued that what is impaired is the natural process of vision, hearing, motor or intellectual activity, while what should be rehabilitated and developed are the higher, culturally informed processes of selective attention, verbal intelligence, logical memory, etc. That is why, argued Vygotsky, there is not much sense in the attempts to compensate for lost sight by training, for example, the physical acuteness of hearing. More in line with the German tradition, Vygotsky argued that true rehabilitation could be achieved only via the compensatory development of the higher forms of intellectual activity, which in a roundabout way substitute for the lost functions. The input of sensory data can be achieved in an alternative way: what is important is to develop the higher processes that are capable of utilizing these data: "The range of development in the sphere of higher forms of knowledge is much farther ahead than the limit that could be reached through sensory-motor training. The concept is a higher form of compensation for the insufficiency of [sensory] representations".[6]

This assertion brings us to another of Vygotsky's major notions, that of the systemic organization of higher mental processes. Higher mental function is not just an extension of the natural one, and thus a deaf child is not just a normal child minus hearing. The "weight" of the disability essentially depends on the place a given function occupies in the overall system of higher processes. For example, the impairment of sight, which biologically is a more severe disability than the loss of hearing, turns out to be more amenable to psychological compensation. Since hearing contributes to the functional systems of verbal communication and verbal intelligence, deafness, primarily because of the difficulty in the acquisition of speech, leads to the disruption of all functions dependent on the verbal factor. At the same time the systemic, interfunctional organization of higher mental processes could become a guideline for the development of rehabilitation techniques. For example, if a blind person is taught to read using the tactile Braille alphabet, and is encouraged to use his or her ability to engage in oral communication, this will lead to an advanced development of verbal intelligence, which in turn will compensate for the lost visual input. The flexibility of once-established functional systems allows for the substitution of a purely intellectual operation for the impaired sensory process. What a child with intact vision grasps in an immediate perceptual act, a blind child understands through imagination and combinatorial activity of the mind. The concept of functional systems achieved its full development in Luria's work on the rehabilitation of patients with brain lesions.[7]

Because normal development, according to Vygotsky, essentially depends on the internalization of psychological tools, the latter notion was also adopted in defectological studies. In the process of its adoption it became clear that the concept of psychological tools has a number of aspects. Such tools could be viewed as artificial sign-stimuli influencing human behavior "from the outside"; they could also be understood as signs carrying a specific meaning; and finally the signs themselves could became nonessential "carriers" with meaning coming to the forefront and making "semantics" the major object of internalization. For the rehabilitation of the handicapped the possibility of substituting one semiotic system for another while retaining its semantics is of paramount importance. Vygotsky suggested that: "Different symbolic systems correspond to one and the same content of education. . . . Meaning rather than a sign is important. Let us change signs but retain meaning".[8]

The anomalous course of handicapped development requires modified educational methods and alternative symbolic systems, but the goal of the development should be the same as for a normal child. The coincidence of normal and handicapped development occurs in their common semantic structure. This structure, therefore, should become the only gauge of a child's psychological achievements. That is why educators and psychologists must be very cautious when they assess the progress made by a handicapped child with the help of standard test instruments. For example, the oral speech of a deaf child could seem seriously retarded leading to the belief that his or her verbal sphere is impoverished. If, however, the same child is assessed with the help of tests adjusted to sign language and written speech, we may find that the child's verbal functions, taken in their semantic, meaningful aspect, are not poor at all. This semantic orientation rules out a behavioristic approach to rehabilitating the handicapped, because what should be acquired is not a particular behavioral act, but a meaning that could have a variety of behavioral concomitants.

Another theoretical construct relevant for the study of the handicapped is the notion of spontaneous and "scientific" representations. In normal development mental representations acquired by a child spontaneously in the course of his or her everyday activity provide rich psychological material. This material later comes into contact with the systematic, scientific concepts learned in school. In *Thought and Language* Vygotsky elaborated on the issue of the interaction between these two types of representations. In a handicapped child the balance between spontaneous and "scientific" representations tips in favor of the latter. Being insulated from ordinary life, such a child is forced to learn in a systematic, "scientific" way the simplest things that his or her peers acquire spontaneously. This became dramatically evident in the case of some highly talented and severely disabled-deaf blind children who succeeded in mastering abstract scientific and logical notions, but found themselves much less prepared for interpersonal and moral issues which for their peers posed no problem.[9] In less successful cases, it is everyday routines and self-care which pose a major problem, because they need to be learned in a systematic, "scientific" way unknown to children without disability.

Finally, an important concept for the theory of handicapped development is that of the zone of proximal development, in which the encounter between child's and adult's behavior and thinking takes place. Operationally this zone is defined as the difference between the mental age of a child derived from the child's solitary performance and his or her performance when assisted by an adult. The identification of this zone for a handicapped child seems to be particularly important because his or her actualized behavior is so limited. In practice this means that any activity of a handicapped child must first take the form of an activity shared with an adult educator. The educator diagnoses the depth of the zone and constructs a sequence of activities with the gradually diminishing contribution of an adult and the growing contribution of the disabled child.

Vygotsky's approach to the rehabilitation of the handicapped was influenced by the principles developed by Austrian psychotherapist and educator Alfred Adler. Adler, a one-time colleague of Freud, had left his mentor to establish an independent school of so-called individual psychology. The central concept of Adlerian psychology is the inferiority complex (*Mindenwentigke-itsgefühl*). According to Adler any disability carries within itself the potential for psychological compensation and even over-compensation. The psychological feeling of inferiority caused by the social consequences of a handicap triggers compensatory mechanisms, leading to overcoming the natural defect via the development of higher functions. The original defect thus becomes the starting point of and the driving force behind the mental development of a handicapped person.[10] Vygotsky was particularly enthusiastic about Adler's idea of the mediated structure of compensatory processes. Instead of a traditional defect-compensation schema, Adler suggested defect-inferiority complex-compensation. In the traditional schema both defect and compensation could be conceived of as natural processes, whereas in Adler's formula the social consequences of disability and the psychological reflection upon them become integral elements of the compensatory process. Defects, therefore, do not affect psychological development immediately, but only through the mediation of the relationship with the social environment.

Vygotsky's enthusiasm did not prevent him from detecting the weak points of Adler's system, however. Two issues seemed to be particularly problematic. One is the differentiation between genuinely overcoming the defect and the illusion of overcoming it. The feeling of psychological inferiority could lead to the mobilization of resources and ultimately to overcoming the disability, but in another handicapped individual the same feeling could lead him or her into an illusory world in which the defect is "compensated for" only in fantasy. The latter path of development engenders a whole array of new pathological symptoms.[11] The second problematic issue concerns the level at which the feeling of inferiority works. Adler's position implied that the successful overcoming of the defect presupposes a conscious comprehension of inferiority. But how then would one explain the compensatory process in children who because of their age or mental status are unable to experience their inferiority consciously? Vygotsky suggested paying closer attention to the social life of a handicapped child: the collective experience provides material for a compensatory process even when this experience does not reach a conscious level.

According to Vygotsky the most promising line of rehabilitation lies in the development of alternative routes toward higher mental functions. Because the defect in both the negative and positive sense acts not so much by itself but rather through its social and psychological consequences, the rehabilitation should also aim at these secondary formations. Deafness as a natural disability is not very severe, but through the secondary impairment of speech and social communication it affects the entire psychological structure of a child. Since we cannot always restore hearing itself, we must focus on alternative routes toward developing higher forms of communication and social interaction. That is why a special school cannot be just a scaled-down version of an ordinary school, but an entirely original institution where the same educational goals are achieved through entirely different means. The task of rehabilitation is not in creating a comfortable yet secluded environment for the handicapped, but in developing the handicapped into fully functional human beings. That is why Vygotsky cautioned against excessive reliance on sign language in the rehabilitation of the deaf. This language provides a limited system of communication, which helps a deaf person to obtain information and to express his or her desires, but at the same time confines such a person to the world of deaf people and their instructors.[12]

The idea of the development of higher psychological processes in the handicapped is based on the observation of the uneven character of retardation of different functions. Certain elementary processes may remain severely underdeveloped, while others provide a fertile ground for the development of higher functions. Two conclusions could be drawn from this observation: first, that the standard system of testing which lumps together elementary and higher processes is largely inadequate, and second, that the focus of pedagogical intervention should be on the secondary disability, on the development of those higher processes that are more amenable to compensation.

This schema could be applicable not only to children with physical defects but also to the mentally retarded. A major role here is played by the collective experience that mediates psychological development. The general theory of development states that psychological processes originate in interpersonal relations. The future inner process starts as an actual interaction between children. The composition of child collective is thus one of the leading factors in child development; this holds true for the development of the mentally retarded. All too often, for example, mentally retarded children are grouped according to the severity of their handicap. This is a convenient practice for educators who thus create groups with relatively uniform levels of intelligence. But this composition turns out to be less than ideal for the children themselves. Just as normal children tend to form groups in which some members are several years older than others, the same is true for the mentally retarded if mental rather than chronological age is taken into account. In a heterogeneous group the more advanced among the retarded are able to show their social activity towards the less advanced, while the latter find their ideal of realistic achievement in the performance of the more advanced children. It was observed that spontaneously formed groups consisting of both more and less retarded children had a larger number of members and existed for longer periods of time than homogeneous groups.[13]

In his study of mentally retarded children, Vygotsky realized a revision of the approach that had originated in the work of Kurt Lewin.[14] Lewin was one of the first to pay attention to the fact that it is not defective intellect alone that is responsible for the mental disability of a retarded child. He demonstrated that the immaturity of motivation is a dominant component of mental retardation. The immature character of the affective processes in retarded children was revealed in a number of experiments to assess such processes as psychological satiation, the effect of unfinished action, and the value of a substitute action. Lewin concluded that the dynamic structures of the retarded mind are less differentiated and more rigid than in the normal psyche. Retarded children often behave in an "either-or" fashion, being unable to produce measured adjustments.[15] Lewin also mentioned an extraordinary concreteness of thinking in retarded children, who found it particularly difficult to abstract an object or event from the situation here and now.

Vygotsky further developed Lewin's theory, emphasizing that

the rigidity of behavior is directly connected to the excessive concreteness of retarded thinking. While the rigidity in the affective sphere confines thought to a concrete situation, thinking that attains greater abstraction allows behavior to become more flexible.[16] Vygotsky and his colleagues replicated some of Lewin's experiments with modifications aimed at exploring the reciprocal influence of intelligence on affective processes. In a study of psychological satiation children were asked to perform certain tasks, like drawing lines, again and again. Eventually each child would refuse to continue, thus signalling that a state of satiation had been reached. At this moment the situation was modified in such a way as to prompt the child to continue his or her activity. Vygotsky discovered that in order to prompt a retarded child to continue, the conditions had to be changed *physically*; for example, a black pencil should be replaced by a colored one, then the colored pencil by a paint brush, and so on. For the normal child it was enough to change the *meaning* of the situation without changing it physically. For example, it was sufficient to tell the child that he is now an "instructor" who shows another child "how it should be done". With retarded children this method of changing meaning did not work. Vygotsky concluded that the flexibility of motivation essentially depends on the development of abstraction and imagination.

In another series of experiments Vygotsky inquired into the phenomenon of the substitution of one activity by another. Children were given clay and asked to sculpt a toy dog. Then this activity was interrupted and children were asked to do one of two things: either to draw an outline of a dog, or to use clay and sculpt rails for a toy train. The value of the substitute activity was measured by the ratio of the children's return to the first task. The behavior of normal and retarded children turned out to be almost diametrically opposite. For normal children the drawing of a dog had a much greater substitute value than sculpting rails, while for retarded children the greater substitute value was associated with the same material—clay, and the same type of action—sculpting. So again, as in the first series, the motivation of normal children essentially depended on the meaning of situations, while for retarded children the motivation was limited by the concrete circumstances.

Vygotsky concluded that Lewin's thesis about the influence of motivation on cognition should be complemented by the thesis of a reciprocal influence of intelligence on affective processes. The comparative analysis of mentally retarded and normal children showed that it is neither intelligence nor motivation in and by itself that distinguishes the normal mind from the retarded one; rather, it is the particular form of *interfunctional relationship* between these two spheres.[17]

A few words should be said now about the developments in Soviet defectology after Vygotsky. Vygotsky's theory, which had been purged from Moscow University and the Institute of Psychology in the late 1930s, managed to survive in a subliminal form at the Institute of Defectology. One contributing factor was that the Institute of Defectology became a haven where some of Vygotsky's students such as Roza Levina, Natalya Morozova and Zhozephina Shif weathered the stormy years of the 1930s and 1940s. Another explanation lies in the fact that one of the leading figures of Soviet defectology, Ivan Sokolyansky, who was not a member of Vygotsky's group, put into practice the same methods of rehabilitation that Vygotsky had outlined in theory. The founder of the Kharkov School for the Deaf-Blind, Sokolyansky developed the principle of shared activity in the rehabilitation of disabled children. Following this principle, first the educator carried out an entire action holding the child's hands, then the child stepped in, and at the final stage the educator merely provided the signal for the action. In this way, Sokolyansky introduced the zone of proximal development in an almost pure form. Sokolyansky's school became well known for its many successful students, notably Olga Skorokhodova, a deaf-blind girl who became a writer and a researcher into defectology. In the 1940s Sokolyansky continued his work in Moscow at the Institute of Defectology.

The next celebrated case of the rehabilitation of the deaf-blind is associated with the name of Alexander Mescheryakov, a student of Luria and Sokolyansky,[18] who effectively combined practical methods developed by Sokolyansky with the theoretical principles of Vygotsky and his school. Mescheryakov succeeded in establishing a special school for severely handicapped children in Zagorsk, near Moscow, and developed a comprehensive method for their rehabilitation. Four of Mescheryakov's deaf-blind students were so successful that after graduating from the school they continued their studies in the psychology program at Moscow University. Their case triggered rather heated discussions between psychologists, educators and philosophers, reviving the centuries-old problem of the influence of nature versus nurture. Some philosophers, notably Evald Ilyenkov, claimed that the successful rehabilitation of the deaf-blind provided conclusive proof in favor of the nurture hypothesis. Even the most severe of handicaps failed to determine the course of the psychological development of the individual. The higher psychological processes were successfully "planted" from the outside with the help of an elaborate educational technique. That is why, continued Ilyenkov, there is little sense in labeling some normal students as "gifted" and others as "slow learners", and there is even less sense in talking about natural giftedness for mathematics or the humanities or the arts; each of these fields requires the development of higher psychological processes that cannot be inherited.

Ilyenkov's views were not universally accepted. Some psychologists and educators legitimately feared that the prevalence of the nurture hypothesis would hinder the study of human psychogenetics. In addition, the thesis "everyone is gifted, we only need proper education" in the reality of the Soviet educational system could easily mean fewer opportunities for children with special talents. The nature versus nurture debate thus helped to bring the problems of special education, which otherwise rarely crossed professional borders, to the attention of the general educated public.[19]

Finally, it seems appropriate to elaborate on those of Vygotsky's ideas which continue to be controversial in Soviet defectology. One of these issues is the place and role of sign language in the education of the deaf. As mentioned earlier, Vygotsky believed that the goal of the rehabilitation of a deaf child should be to allow him or her to function in the normal human environment and to be able to use all those categories of thought available for a normal person. The teaching of speech, therefore, should focus on the acquisition of meaningful oral communication. Ontogenetic studies of normal children have shown that the process of acquisition starts with an integral form of speech: the development proceeds from the phrase to word, from the word to syllable, and from the syllable to sound. In the deaf, therefore, the imperfect acquisition of a meaningful statement is always preferable to the precise articulation of meaningless sounds which then do not easily combine together. But since communication is only one aspect of verbal activity, special means should be found for the development of language as an element of verbal thought.

In the spirit of Vygotsky's studies, in 1978 the Soviet Ministry of Education suggested the following guidelines for the rehabilitation of the deaf: (1) the development of spoken language with a strong emphasis on the development of residual hearing supported by lip reading, (2) finger-spelling (handwriting in the air); and (3) written language.[20] The suggestion that all these forms of communication should be used fitted well with Vygotsky's thesis: "let us change sign, but retain meaning". The technique of oral speech instruction also essentially followed Vygotsky's suggestion to start with the whole and only later rectify details. The acquisition of spoken language by the deaf is carried out in stages: in the beginning only eighteen sounds are introduced to help them form meaningful messages, which only later will be perfected phonetically. The oral training is accompanied by learning finger-spelling; a person spelling with fingers represents item by item what appears on the printed page. Oral speech in the form of reading aloud, combined with finger-spelling of the same text, leads to the synthesis of a number of functional systems connected to one another through the *meaning* of the text.

One form of communication conspicuously omitted from the Ministry of Education guidelines is sign language. This is a peculiar fact if one takes into account that in the United States, for example, sign language has become a major form of communication for the deaf. As has been mentioned earlier in this chapter, Vygotsky warned against the excessive use of sign language. There are basically two arguments against the use of sign language as a predominant form of communication by the deaf. First, that this artificial system confines a deaf person to the world of the deaf and their teachers, and second, that the very structure of sign language leads to primitive, undifferentiated forms of verbal thinking. Critics have argued that in sign language many generic terms are absent, while one and the same sign often has a number of different meanings.

Vygotsky, however, did not object to the use of sign language as one of the elements of the overall system of verbal training. He suggested that the most productive path of language development in a deaf child lies in "polyglossia"—the concurrent acquisition of language by different semiotic means.[21] Sign language could become a valuable component of this polyglossia, and this seems to be confirmed by recent studies conducted by Soviet champions of sign language. The importance of verbal and nonverbal contexts, which is already apparent in the case of ordinary oral communication, becomes even clearer in the case of sign language. In ordinary speech the proper meaning is selected from the total content of a semantic field evoked by a given word depending on context. The same principle of contextual differentiation can be acquired in sign language, thus reducing its polysemy. It has been shown that deaf students who use sign language in addition to reading are facilitated in their understanding and retention of such abstractive literary notions as "artistic image", "character", "plot", etc.[22] It seems, therefore, that a more careful reading of Vygotsky's works would be helpful to overcome the parochialism of Soviet defectology, without abandoning its specific character.

PSYCHOPATHOLOGY AND REGRESSION

Next to the study of handicapped development, the problems of psychopathology and the concept of psychological regression loomed large on Vygotsky's research agenda. The concept of regression—together with its counterpart, the concept of development—aims at providing a *dynamic* interpretation of behavioral and cognitive functions. In spite of their complementary nature the notions of development and regression rarely find themselves comfortably integrated in one and the same psychological system. This state of affairs was historically conditioned by the fact that the psychoanalytic model of regression revealed a clear tendency to encroach on what a study of normal development would consider its own domain.[23] The notion of regression, which brought with itself the interpretative methodology of psychoanalysis, was not immediately acceptable to "mainstream" developmentalists for a number of well founded reasons.[24] At the same time this mainstream developmental psychology itself paid remarkably little attention to the problem of regression. One may suspect that behaviorists and cognitivists alike were generally lacking a theoretical framework that would allow for an incorporation of regressive phenomena. That is why Vygotsky's attempts to make regressive phenomena legitimate components of the study of human psychological development deserve closer scrutiny. It seems also important to identify the points of correspondence and disagreement between the Vygotskian and psychoanalytic interpretations of regression.

Let us start with the idea of regression as it appeared in Freud's works. In the Freudian schema of the dynamic process, wishes or impulses are moving in a progressive direction to become manifested as thoughts or motor acts. Regression is conceived of as a movement backward until wishes or impulses become transformed from thoughts back into images, and further to hallucinations and dreams. This type of regression occurs both topographically and temporally. Infantile wish fulfillment provides a paradigmatic example. An infant's need, and subsequent satisfaction of that need, lays down a memory trace. Subsequent experience of this need brings about a situation in which the regressive movement of excitation is halted at the memory image and efforts are then made to re-establish the reality, which involves previously experienced satisfaction. This retrogressive movement not only arouses memory images associated with satisfaction, but re-evokes the perception itself to constitute an hallucinatory wish fulfillment.

Freud considered this hallucinatory wish fulfillment as "the psychical apparatus's primary method of working" which includes such mechanisms as condensation and displacement.[25] Retrogressive movement from thought to hallucinatory perception provides an example of topographic regression, but the same movement viewed as a return to a "primary method" — which in healthy adults is developmentally superseded — provides an example of temporal regression.[26] Psychological processes characteristic of progressive and retrogressive modes are correspondingly secondary and primary processes.

The concept of regression in psychoanalysis essentially depends on the "energy" model of the mind. It is assumed that nervous or psychical energy exists in two forms, one freely movable and the other, by contrast, bound. The quanta of this energy are invested in mental representations; this investment (*Besetzung*) is called *cathexis*. The distribution of energy and its balance is called the economy of mind:

> Economically, the primary process is characterized by large amounts and freedom of cathexis, and the secondary process by small amounts, the use of hypercathexis, and binding and/or neutralization. . . . Genetically, the primary process becomes progressively overlain by secondary, but roots of the secondary are present from the beginning. An appreciation of time and the relative placing and integration of events in time is characteristic of the secondary process. . . . Structurally, the primary process in its macrostructural aspect takes place on the lower level of the psychic hierarchy, and the secondary on more advanced levels, while microstructurally the mechanisms of displacement and condensation or more specific "techniques" like indirect representation or faulty reasoning likewise range on the primary- to secondary-process continuum. . . . And adaptively, there is the primary- to secondary-process range from a complete ignoring of the external world to a veridical evaluation and control of thought and behavior in accord with the nature of the external world.[27]

Now let us turn to Vygotsky's understanding of human psychodynamics in its advancement and regression. Vygotsky singled out two major misunderstandings that limit the progress of developmental studies: one is a reductionist position that seeks to explain the higher forms of behavior and cognition by means of principles established for elementary functions. American behaviorism and Russian reflexology paid a heavy tribute to this type of reductionism. The other position, which historically appeared as a response to this reductionist program, simply transfers the explanatory principles found in the study of higher forms of behavior to the analysis of the lower forms. Vygotsky saw this type of misperception in the works of the Gestaltists, but it could be generalized to include all the attempts to present the child's psychological functions as merely "weak" versions of those of adults.

According to Vygotsky, dynamic psychology has a double task: to distinguish the lower forms imbedded in the higher, but also to reveal how the higher forms mature out of the lower ones. This double task could be accomplished only if one accepts that not only the individual him- or herself, but each one of the psychological formations (such as concepts, actions, affects, etc.) could become a subject of developmental analysis. Each and every psychological formation contains a number of developmental layers. Primitive forms of concept formation, for example, do not disappear in a mature concept; they are *aufgehöben*, that is, "superseded" and "saved" at one and the same time. On a number of occasions Vygotsky returned to this Hegelian term, *aufheben*, which has a fairly accurate Russian equivalent, *snyatie*, but no precise equivalent in English. For example, in a handicapped child the primary, organic disability does not disappear in the higher forms of development, but it is supplanted by and incorporated into these higher forms. Depending on the concrete situation and form of human activity involved, different layers of a given psychological formation may be activated. To study development and regression thus means to study those specific conditions that provide for the structural establishment of different layers and for their functional activation depending on changing types of activity. This broader understanding of development and regression rests upon material drawn from a number of domains: phylogenetic (the comparison of animal and human problem solving); historical (psychological functioning in traditional versus modern cultures); ontogenetic (the comparison of child and adult language and psychological functions); microgenetic (such as the dynamics of individual concept formation from the level of trial-and-error to that of logical-conceptual apperception); and pathological (such as concept formation in handicapped children, in aphasic and schizophrenic subjects).

In each of these domains Vygotsky inquired into the characteristic changes that occur when (*a*) psychological processes advance from unmediated to mediated forms or retreat in the opposite direction; and (*b*) a psychological function joins others, thus forming a functional system or when the formation of such a system is retarded or breaks down.

The first tentative definition of regression is that immature or regressive forms are characterized by the weakness or primitivity of the mediated structure. Leontiev's study of memory in normal and retarded children underscores this approach.[28] Children were asked to remember words read by the experimenter and then to reproduce them. Memorization was carried out either "naturally" or with the help of picture cards which were unrelated to the meaning of words. It was found that normal ten- to twelve-year-old children memorized twice as many words with the help of card-mediators than without them. At the same time, mentally retarded children (aged nine to fourteen) whose immediate memorization was almost as good as that of normal children, failed to benefit from the use of cards and actually reproduced *fewer* words than they did without mediation. It is significant that retarded children proved to be capable of establishing associations between words and picture cards, which means that their elementary psychological processes were not impaired. What they were unable to do was to organize the process of memorization and retrieval with the help of cards as *tools*. Words and pictures existed side by side in a natural way, thus merely doubling the amount of material instead of restructuring it along the lines of semiotic mediation.

The other example of regression from the level of psychological tool action to the level of unmediated behavior has been provided by Luria.[29] In one of his neuropsychological studies of frontal lobe functions, Luria asked a patient suffering from a frontal lesion to take a memory test similar to that used by Leontiev discussed above. Before the operation the patient's abilities to use sign-mediators were so diminished that he could not use picture cards at all. Three weeks after the operation the patient recovered enough to be able to understand instructions and to perform the memory task. His handling of card-mediators, however, remained purely associative. For example, as a pair to the word "moon" a picture of rubber boots was offered. The patient formed an associative structure: "We see the moon after the rain . . . which means that rubber boots can be useful". But when asked to recall the original word using the card, the patient was able to produce only an obvious association "rubber-boots"—"rain"; the original structure leading to the word "moon" was not recovered. Luria concluded that this case illustrated the general tendency of frontal lobe patients to be deficient in the ability to turn signs and other objects into means of cognitive mediation. In this particular subject the function of mediated memory was restored only two months after the operation.

Luria's study is important for a number of reasons. First, it gives an example of the *dynamics* of recovery from total regression to the level of unmediated activity. Second, it provides an insight into the special role played by the frontal lobes in mediatory activity (this issue will resurface later in the context of a study of schizophrenic language and thought). And finally, the studies in mediated memory initiated by Leontiev and Luria in many respects presaged contemporary interest in the "levels of processing" in memory. Psychological tools provide memory markers that can be used later for the retrieval of the material. The reliance of our memory on such markers explains the original "paradox" of mediated memory, that is, better memory for *more* rather than less complex material (such as words *and* cards).

Although Vygotsky was primarily interested in the cognitive aspect of development and regression, he eventually extended his model of psychological tools toward the issues of affect as well. Psychological tools, according to Vygotsky, help to create a functional barrier between the sphere of motives and decision making on the one hand, and the sphere of the practical realization of the decision, on the other. In simple experiments (described in Chapter Four) Vygotsky showed how the availability of sign-mediators helped to differentiate previously "integral", impulsive behavior into the decision-making part and the executive part. Whereas in the original task the search for a solution involved perception, memory and motor apparatus as an integral, organic whole, a mediated solution presupposed a sort of functional barrier erected between the perception-memory system, which is responsible for decision making, and the motor system, which retains only an executive role. Symbolic mediation, in creating such a barrier, allows for the delayed actions to be projected into some kind of future situation.

Regression would then mean a surrender of this symbolic mediation and return to the only remaining "mediation" through individual organic "hardware". German psychiatrist Ernst Kretschmer's study of the so-called hypobulic psychological response provided an example of such a regression.[30] Kretschmer and Vygotsky observed that hypobulia is not a diminished power of will but rather an underdevelopment of mediated, goal-directed behavior. The hypobulic response is a direct reaction of an organism to environmental stimuli, rather than a mediated response, which normally involves a complex system of motives. Underdevelopment of motives results in a regression to unmediated integral reactions. Kretschmer suggested distinguishing between primitive responses and personality responses. The primitive response is an affective discharge that is not relayed through the higher levels of personality structure. Vygotsky observed that the primitive response is not pathological in itself, but is simply a developmentally inferior type of functioning which, because of specific circumstances, temporarily acquires a dominant position.[31] For example, frequent affective discharges observed in adolescents point to personality structure instabilities that allow primitive reactions to realize themselves. Primitive responses could be a part of normal as well as pathological development. It would be erroneous to think of them as of a "psychological neoplasma", as something abnormal; they are a normal element of the psychological response hierarchy that may "forget" its proper place. An interesting feature of primitive responses is their lack of personal specificity; they are compatible with any type of personality. In contrast, the personality response is as specific as the handwriting of a given person.

The presence of primitive responses in diagnostically different psychological and psychopathological conditions confirms the thesis of the unity between development and regression: "Development is a key to the understanding of the dissolution, and dissolution is a key to the understanding of development".[32]

At this moment it seems appropriate to compare the Vygotskian notion of the primitive response and the Freudian notion of the primary process. Although Vygotsky never used "economic" metaphors to account for the development of mediated forms of affect, his remarks concerning the "functional barrier" between the sensory-memory and motor parts of human action allows for certain parallels between unmediated and primary processes. There is also close agreement between Vygotsky and Freud with respect to the microstructural level of psychodynamics. Vygotsky's notion of the multilayer character of psychological formulations fits fairly well with the psychoanalytic idea of displacement and condensation as belonging not only to primary but to secondary processes as well. Vygotsky's study of concept formation revealed that one and the same object could be "conceptualized" by an immediate perceptual operation resembling condensation as well as by a highly mediated logical process. The act of *generalization* thus ranges on a continuum of immediate to mediated processes. For example, a number of different meanings could become concentrated in one word, a phenomenon that attracted both Freud and Vygotsky. Freud invoked it in his discussion of the properties of a dreamword: "The process may go so far that a single word, if it is specially suitable on account of its numerous connections, takes over the representation of a whole train of thought".[33] Vygotsky addressed the same issue in his analysis of inner speech and its role in the creative process: "The senses of different words flow into one another—literally 'influence' one another—so that the earlier ones are contained in and modify the later ones. Thus, a word that keeps recurring in a book or a poem sometimes absorbs all the variety of sense contained in it and becomes, in a way, equivalent to the work itself".[34]

The principal difference between the Vygotskian and psychoanalytic positions lies in the evaluation of the above-mentioned processes *vis-à-vis* the principles of reality and pleasure. Vygotsky insisted that unmediated behavior is still realistic, although its realism is primitive, which means that in terms of adaptivity there is a growing sophistication from unmediated to mediated processes, yet both are reality-oriented. The moment of "unreality" is perceived as one of the elements of the mediatory process when imagination, supported by verbal thought, becomes capable of extracting situations for their "here and now" contexts and freely projects them into a virtual time, space and system of relations. This opposition to the unrealistic interpretation of the pleasure principle was articulated by Vygotsky in the context of his debate with Piaget concerning the status of egocentric speech in children.[35]

According to Piaget, egocentric speech reveals the immature, egocentric character of the thinking of young children. Such thinking prefers dreams to reality and is poorly adapted to realistic tasks. All of these features of egocentric thinking are inherited from a yet earlier stage in the child's cognitive development, that of autistic thinking. Original child autism 'is not adopted to reality, but creates for itself a dream world of imagination; it tends, not to establish truth, but to satisfy desires".[36] Child egocentrism appears to be a "compromise" between the original autism and the nascent realistic thinking, a "compromise" which for an outside observer still appears as "autistic". Eventually outward egocentric speech dies out and is replaced by fully socialized adult speech.

Vygotsky's disagreement with this interpretation was twofold: he demonstrated empirically that egocentric speech is far from being a mere verbal accompaniment to unrealistic thinking and does actually play an important realistic role in directing a child's actions. Theoretically Vygotsky objected to linking the "pleasure principle" with the autistic aspect of a child's reasoning and speech.[37] In his critique, Vygotsky found support in the work of the Swiss psychiatrist Eugen Bleuler, the author of the concept of autism. Bleuler suggested that: "The autistic function is not as primitive as the simple forms of reality function, but—in a certain sense—more primitive than the highest forms of the latter. . . . At a certain level of development, the autistic function is added to the reality function and develops with it from there on".[38] This means that regression is not a mere step back from the realistic to the unrealistic level. "The autistic thinking of the imbecile", explained Bleuler, "is just as simplified as his realistic thinking".[39] Both realistic and autistic functions undergo development, and both of them could potentially regress from the higher to the lower level. Later Piaget himself admitted that to link autism to the pleasure principle and logical thought to the reality principle would be to oversimplify the developmental process: "Adaptation to reality goes hand in hand with need and pleasure, because even when assimilation predominates it is always accompanied by some accommodation".[40]

Just as realistic thinking is an original, primitive form of a child's adaptation, the same is true of a child's speech. The primitive speech of the child is intended for communication, not merely as an accompaniment of actions. This primitive communicative function undergoes an interesting transformation when from addressing others the child turns to addressing him or herself. This transformation creates a developmental paradox which, in a certain sense, is an example of "functional regression". At first, the transition from an other-oriented to a self-oriented form of behavior lowers the level of performance: "For example, egocentric speech in comparison with [original] social speech is less advanced as *speech*, but is more advanced as a step in the development of [verbal] *intelligence*".[41]

The transformation of predominantly communicative speech into an instrument of verbal thought indicates the other major form of development: the formation of functional systems. In studying the development of thought and speech in children, Vygotsky observed that the process of their development depends not so much on the changes within these two functions, but rather on changes in the relations between them.[42] Mediation through psychological tools is thus superseded by mediation through another psychological function. Perception, memory, communicative speech and nonverbal intelligence join together bringing about *systems* of functions such as verbal intelligence, logical memory, selective attention, etc. The progressive movement will then be from separate functions to functional systems, regression, a breakdown of interfunctional relations, and a return to isolated functions.

The functional systems model was further developed by Luria,[43] who demonstrated that there exists a developmental patern of transition from isolated functions of speech, memory and motor activity to an integrated functional system which allows children to perform delayed motor actions based on verbal stimulation.[44] The ability to form functional systems could be used as a diagnostic criterion to distinguish between pathological conditions of different nature. Luria reported that two groups of neuropsychologically problematic children demonstrated remarkably different attitudes toward functional system formation. The first group included children with so-called cerebral asthenic syndrome. Their intellectual functions seemed to be largely intact, but the neurodynamic processes were disrupted because of the intoxication or head trauma. The second group comprised children with mental retardation, whose neurodynamics could be disturbed, but could also be largely intact, and whose disabilities expressed themselves in the underdevelopment of the higher intellectual processes. Children from both groups were tested on motor reactions: they were instructed to press a button in response to a red signal, and to refrain from pressing it when a blue signal was on. Then the children were instructed to substitute verbal responses, "shall do" — "shall not do" for the motor reactions. At the final stage of the experiment it was suggested that the children combine verbal and motor responses, first giving a verbal command to him or herself and then executing it. It turned out that only the children with cerebral asthenic syndrome benefited from the formation of the verbal-motor system, and the accuracy of their responses improved considerably. The mentally retarded children, in contrast, proved to be unable to form such a system. The verbal component failed to acquire a signal function in their behavior.[45]

The pattern of the disintegration of functional systems was also observed by Luria in patients with frontal lobe lesions. These patients do not lose their ability to speak or to understand language (that is, the communicative function of speech remains relatively intact), but they cannot use language as an instrument for the regulation of behavior: "Language fails in its role as a mediator between other psychological functions".[46]

Now we are approaching the core question of any theory of regression: to what extent can the parallelist approach be justified? Regressive or primitive phenomena were sought by Vygotsky and others not only in the behavior of children but also in "primitive" people and in cases of neuro- and psychopathology. The observed similarities between primitive forms of functioning in different classes of subjects could be conceptualized in a variety of ways depending on the chosen theoretical perspective.

First, one may simply record empirically similar behavioral and cognitive patterns and present them as a mere collection. This had actually been done by Alfred Storch, a pioneer of comparative studies of regression who was often quoted by Vygotsky.[47] Another possibility is to conceptualize the discovered parallels in the spirit of the doctrine of recapitulation.[48] The notion of recapitulation helps to tie individual development to the development of race: "ontogeny recapitulates phylogeny". From its origin in comparative embryology, where the immature forms of evolutionary more advanced classes of animals were compared with the mature forms of the less advanced classes, the principle of recapitulation developed in the early twentieth century into an all-embracing philosophy. The American developmentalist G. S. Hall claimed that the behavior of children is best explained as a recapitulation of the experiences of "primitive" people. Education, on the other hand, was often seen as a recapitulation of the progress made by civilization. Children were believed to have specific sensitive periods attuned to the acquisition of knowledge characteristic of a particular stage in the historical development of human knowledge. Piaget's stage theory of mental development implicitly contains some elements of this historical version of the recapitulation doctrine.[49]

Regressive forms of mental life, such as dreams, were also believed to repeat the historically preceding stages of human civilization. "In sleep and in dreams we pass through the whole thought of earlier humanity", wrote Friedrich Nietzsche. From this one needs to make just one step toward viewing pathological cases as a regression to ontogenetically or phylogenetically preceding stages of human development. This line of reasoning had been also supported by the neuropsychological studies of John Hughlings Jackson and Henry Head. For Jackson neural evolution is a passage from the most to the least organized, from the most simple to the most complex, and from the most automatic to the most voluntary nervous centers. The dissolution of a function that occurs as the result of a nervous or mental disorder is essentially a return to functioning at the lower evolutionary level. Linking pathological cases with such normal "regressive" states as sleep, Jackson suggested an overall schema of the normal and pathological dissolution of functions.[50]

Freud, who was well acquainted with Jackson's work, made use of exactly this type of recapitulation hypothesis:

> Dreams and neuroses seem to have preserved more mental antiquities than we have imagined possible. . . . Dreaming is on the whole an example of regression to the dreamer's earliest condition, a revival of his childhood, of the instinctual impulses which dominated it and of the methods of expression which were then available to him. Beyond this childhood of the individual we are promised a picture of a phylogenetic childhood—a picture of the development of the human race, of which the individual's development is in fact an abbreviated recapitulation.[51]

Beyond dreams and neuroses the regressive forms of psychic life could be found "among savages or children".[52]

In due time the principle of recapitulation ran into serious trouble from the point of view of biology and embryology, from which it had originated. It is not strange, therefore, that psychiatrists who had not been bound by psychoanalytic dogma preferred to speak of "paleologic" thinking observed in children, "primitive" people and schizophrenics without direct reference to the principle of recapitulation.[53] Apart from theoretical difficulties with the biological theory of recapitulation as such, it became more and more obvious that there is no precise *empirical* coincidence between immature forms of behavior in childen and "primitives" and the regressive behavior of mental patients.[54] In a theoretically sophisticated form this problem has been addressed by the German-American psychologist, Heinz Werner. He pointed out that parallelism does not imply coincidence. Moreover, the developmental approach is not an evolutionistic approach. It does not "place" concrete forms of behavior as "early" or "late" on the historical or ontogenetic scale, but rather considers their position on a *formal* scale of primitivity to advancement.[55] Werner also warned about attempts to draw the sign of equivalence between different regressive forms, reminding us that regression observed in children, "primitives" and mental patients occurs in quite different contexts:

> The child is a growing, labile organism. Primitive man's behavior is completely developed. . . . The child grows out of his child's world into an alien world of adults. His behavior is the result of an interaction between these worlds. . . . The primitive man lives in a world to which he is admirably adjusted. The pathological individual tries to adjust himself by means of primitive behavior to a world for him inadequate and non-primitive. . . . Any degeneration bears signs of the higher level from which it retrogressed.[56]

The question remains as to what Vygotsky's position was *vis-à-vis* the principle of recapitulation.[57] It is clear that he rejected the idea of the recapitulation of phylogenetic stages in ontogenesis, if only because of his belief in the cultural-historical character of higher mental processes. This does not eliminate, however, the possibility of a historical recapitulation. After all, on a number of occasions Vygotsky drew parallels between the behavior of children and that of "primitive" people. The whole of Luria's study of cognition in the illiterate people of Central Asia is based on certain parallels with the cognition of young children.[58] Vygotsky saw the potential danger of interpreting these similarities in the spirit of the recapitulation doctrine. He emphasized that the natural and the cultural lines of the development of the human race are represented but they are not repeated in the child's development: "By this we certainly do not wish to claim that ontogenesis in any form or degree repeats or reproduces phylogenesis or presents a parallel to it . . . Only superficial thinking might see this as a return to the argument of a biogenetic law. . . . While speaking about the similarity between the two lines in the child's development and the two lines in phylogenesis we do not extend this analogy toward the structure and the content of the processes involved".[59] The only basis for comparison is the essential fact of the existence and interaction of the natural path and the cultural path of development. Similarly, comparisons between pathological forms and immature forms should also be made with caution: "The comparison of disordered thinking with phylogenetically earlier forms of thought is usually made on the basis of negative rather than positive criteria. . . . This comparison, based on a negative criterion, is wrong because it treats as approximately equivalent such forms of thinking which from the positive side have nothing in common with each other".[60]

Focusing on the dichotomy between natural and cultural processes in different classes of subjects seemed to be a good first step, but it carried within itself the danger of oversimplification. Vygotsky was well aware of this problem. In one of his last lectures, summing up the achievements and discussing the perspectives of the cultural-historical approach, he observed: "Previously we conducted our analysis in the plane of behavior, rather than the plane of consciousness, and thus the abstractness of our conclusions. . . . For example [we observed] the similarity in the structure of symbolic operations in aphasics, schizophrenics, the mentally disabled, and primitive people. But semantic analysis reveals that the inner structure [of these operations] is different".[61]

Thus the distinction between the formation of higher psychological processes in the history of the human race and the appropriation of the cultural forms of behavior and cognition by a child remained poorly articulated. There seems to be a certain theoretical reason for this lack of articulation. The closest thing to a detailed analysis of different types of cognition offered by the cultural-historical theory was the study of experimental concept formation (see Chapter Five). This study yielded a sequence of types of generalization from syncretic "heaps" to genuine scientific concepts. But the mechanisms underlying the acquisition of the different types of generalization turned out to be sublated (*aufgehöben*) in that study. Vygotsky declared that word meaning is a vital center of generalization and communication—their common denominator. However, while the typology of the structure of generalization had been explored in the above-mentioned study, the corresponding structure of communication had not been elaborated beyond a general counterposition of systematic classroom instruction and spontaneous everyday learning. What was lacking in Vygotsky's theory was a typology of interpersonal communicative situations. In particular, no distinction was made between those "dialogues" which contributed to the development of human verbal cognition in the historical (i.e. diachronic) perspective, and those which are conducted each time a new member of a given group, such as a child, is acquiring its culture (synchronically). Only by complementing the typology of the structures of generalization by the typology of dialogues could a complete version of the cultural-historical theory be achieved. One may wish to consider the following steps in this direction.

First, rather than starting with *empirical* behavioral and mental patterns and searching for a precise coincidence between these patterns in children, "primitives" and mental patients, one could focus on constructing a *formal* scale of development and regression. Such a scale would provide a framework for comparison without requiring a total identification of one form of psychic life (such as a child's reasoning) with another (such as the reasoning of a mental patient). The achievement of symbolic mediation and the establishment of interfunctional systems may tentatively be suggested as guidelines for the construction of such a scale. Specific measures to be used must at the same time reflect essential differences in the type of activity that is characteristic for a child, a person living in a traditional society, or a mental patient.

Second, the mere identification of "regressive" forms is not enough. These forms should be viewed in at least two different perspectives: negative and positive. The negative dimension may, for example, indicate the retrogression from a conceptual to a preconceptual level of reasoning. The positive dimension, in contrast, places this alleged retrogression in the overall developmental or functional context and indicates a particular role played by a given "regressive" form in the total activity of the individual. This sort of analysis may help, for example, to distinguish between some elements of poetic imagery which, although formally regressive, do not indicate a malfunction, and an apparently similar pathological language that is truly regressive.

Third, an important indicator of the advanced psychological form is not so much its conceptual form as such, but rather the ability of the individual to control his or her behavior on different developmental levels, to integrate them and to activate an appropriate level depending on the required type of activity.

THOUGHT AND LANGUAGE IN SCHIZOPHRENIA

All of the above problems related to the issue of regression found their concrete test in a study of thought and language in schizophrenia.[62] This was one of the last projects accomplished by Vygotsky and as such it reflected the evolution of his views. The additional significance of this project lies in the fact that it turned out to be the only work of Vygotsky that exercised a modicum of influence on Western psychology and psychiatry between the 1930s and the 1960s. Vygotsky's goal was to show that whereas the development of thinking in adolescents is characterized by the transition from a preconceptual to conceptual type of reasoning, the peculiarity in the thinking of schizophrenic patients can be characterized as a regression to preconceptual types of generalization. From the beginning Vygotsky warned against confusing the similarity in types of generalization with the identity of psychological organization in general. The reasoning of an adolescent may become a laboratory for the study of certain regressive forms of thought, and vice versa, but this does not mean that the immature psychological attitude is identical to the pathologically disturbed one. It is also important to remember that there are a great many developmental steps between conceptual reasoning and the truly primitive, unmediated psychological attitude. Thus it is not legitimate, according to Vygotsky, to lump together all preconceptual forms: "It is not admissible to make genetic comparison of thought as it occurs in dreams with thought as it occurs in primitive people or in spiders, simply because such forms of thought are all below the stage of conceptual thought".[63] A true analogue for a mechanism of schizophrenic thought should be sought in the forms that immediately precede conceptual reasoning.

The experimental testing of his hypothesis was based on a sorting test first developed by German psychologist Narciss Ach, and perfected by Vygotsky's collaborator Lev Sakharov. In the late 1930s the Ach–Sakharov method was used in the United States by Eugenia Hanfmann and Jakob Kasanin in their systematic study of schizophrenic reasoning.[64] In this test subjects were required to sort blocks which differed in two ways—in their physical properties (size, height, form and color), and by their "names" (triplets of letters attached to the bases of the blocks). Proper classification could be achieved only through the formation of a functional system that includes what could be a nonverbal hypothesis, like "large and tall objects belong together", *mediated* by an artificial concept, such as the triplet of letters "BIK", representing the class of "large and tall" blocks.[65] The advantage of this experimental procedure lay in the fact that every step in the subject's reasoning was reflected in his or her manipulation of the blocks, including the interpretation of the task, the handling of the objects, the response to corrections and the finding of the solution. The analysis of these problem-solving steps in children, adolescents, schizophrenics and brain-damaged patients led to the discovery of a number of levels of concept formation. Possible forms of conceptualization ranged from perceptual-impulsive to logical, and from unmediated to mediated by a functional system of verbal concepts.

In terms of the interpretation of the task some schizophrenic subjects revealed a peculiar attitude: they refused to accept triplets of letters as names or conceptual labels and were unable to use them as instruments to organize their behavior. As Hanfmann and Kasanin remarked, for such people the word is not the name of the block, it is a mere "lettering", one among many attributes that the blocks happen to have.[66]

With regard to the type of grouping, a number of levels of conceptualization were discovered, from so-called "complexes" to genuine concepts. The term "complex" stands for a form of grouping that is oblivious to the superordinate concept and in which connections are made immediately from one individual object to another. Mediation through the superordinate concept (such as "all tall and large blocks") is substituted by a "family" or "collection" type of grouping with blocks being related to each other in various individual ways (such as one block to another on the ground of color, a second one to a third because of size, etc.). Apart from thinking in complexes, schizophrenic subjects revealed a strange form of "physiognomic" mediation. In this case one grouping principle was maintained throughout the task but the principle itself was not conceptual but physiognomic; for example, certain blocks were grouped together because they were perceived as "policemen"—"They beat you up, put you in prison".[67]

One of the most important forms of regression observed is pseudoconceptual reasoning. The pseudoconceptual grouping superficially resembles the conceptual one. For example, one subject put together all blocks of one colour or one shape. The difference between conceptual and pseudoconceptual grouping becomes apparent only at the moment of correction: when the experimenter turned one of the wrongly selected blocks and showed that its name did not match that of a sample block. The subject, working on the conceptual level, reacted immediately: "Oh, this is not a color", and disassembled the group and started afresh. Pseudoconceptual reasoning, being insensitive to contradiction, does not take correction as a signal for a change of hypothesis: this subject obediently removed the wrong block but kept the rest of the group intact.

(A similar phenomenon has been reported in my unpublished experiments with the Wisconsin card-sorting test. A dramatic difference in the behavior of an educated normal subject and a poorly educated schizophrenic patient occurred when the correctly chosen category (color) was suddenly changed. The normal subject paused, uttered something to the effect that "something has been changed" and then proceeded with an exploratory placement in search of a new correct category. The schizophrenic subject, in contrast, continued in a persevering manner for some time and then reverted to a trial-and-error approach. It is also revealing that the schizophrenic subjects were easily distracted from categorically correct responses by the appearance of a card that matched the sample one in two categories. The pressure of purely perceptive affinity was enough to distract the subject from his pseudoconceptual conviction.)

The principle of pseudoconceptual grouping, although phenotypically resembling conceptual classification, actually lacks hierarchical organization. The principle of grouping appears to be a common feature *shared* by different objects but not as a concept superordinate to them. If hierarchical organization is a "trademark" of functional systems, the lack of it may indicate a regressive trend. Such a regression may split a functional system of verbal thought into communicative speech and nonverbal thinking. A psychotic subject may retain his or her ability to communicate and will use the same words as a normal subject in terms of their *objective referent*, but these words exist in different systems of *meanings*. This phenomenon of objective coincidence and conceptual difference was observed in children as well as schizophrenic patients who took a proverbs test. Orientation toward an objective referent in this case produced a literal interpretation, while conceptual symbolism allowed for a figurative meaning.[68] The true difference between advanced and regressive/immature functioning lies in the fact that in an advanced functioning mode the individual is capable of controlling the level of performance, that is, he or she is able to activate an objective reference or a conceptual attitude depending on the situation. In a regressive mode such control is lacking and the individual often responds to a conceptual "question" with an objective referent "answer".

Vygotsky's hypothesis about the regression to preconceptual thought in schizophrenics became well accepted by a small circle of scholars and psychiatrists who shared the "organicist" approach of Kurt Goldstein. This group was responsible for posing the problem of regressive thought beyond the dogmatic frameworks of either behaviorism or psychoanalysis. In 1939

Jacob Kasanin organized a meeting, which resulted in the publication of the volume *Language and Thought in Schizophrenia* in which the Goldstein-Vygotsky model of regression was elaborated.[69] Goldstein's leading idea was that there are several levels on which behavior and cognition operate. The higher the level the greater the capacity for what he called an "abstract" attitude, the lower the level the more "concrete" is the attitude. Examples of the abstract and concrete attitudes provided by Goldstein coincide with what Vygotsky would have called mediated and unmediated attitudes. Since the attitudes mentioned by Goldstein correspond to the level of functioning, rather than to a particular condition, it is not surprising that similar regressive attitudes have been observed in brain-damaged patients and in schizophrenics.[70]

Another related approach was developed by the German psychiatrist von Domarus.[71] The essence of the von Domarus principle is the following: whereas the normal individual identifies only on the basis of identical subjects, the schizophrenic accepts identity based upon identical predicates. When a schizophrenic girl says that she is the Virgin Mary, it is assumed that her logic is: "The Virgin Mary was a virgin; I am a virgin; therefore, I am the Virgin Mary". The same mechanism of identification based on predicates could be observed in a child who called a briefcase "papa", because it belonged to his father.

The next major step in the direction charted by Vygotsky and Goldstein's group was made by Heinz Werner and Bernard Kaplan, who undertook a comparative developmental-psychopathological study of symbolically mediated behavior.[72] Of interest here is the section of the Werner-Kaplan study in which they inquired into the peculiarity of communication in schizophrenic subjects. The subjects were asked to describe visual stimuli under different conditions, such as an immediate response, a description for him or herself, a description for a hypothetical other and a description for a real other person. The lexicon used by the subjects was scored for the presence of idiomatic referents that could be understood by no one except the subject him or herself. It turned out that while describing stimuli to themselves schizophrenic subjects used almost as many idiosyncratic referents as in the immediate response condition, and that was more than twice the amount used by normal subjects. Werner and

Kaplan concluded that in schizophrenic subjects there is a lack of differentiation between the idiosyncratic, inner speech-for-oneself and the social speech-for-others.

The tradition of the study of schizophrenic thought and language outlined above was neglected in the United States in the 1970s and the 1980s. Instead the emphasis shifted toward the study of attentional processes, and toward purely biological and neuro-anatomical foundations of schizophrenia. Vygotsky's maxim that "the disintegration of personality follows certain psychological laws, even though the direct causes of this process may not be psychological in nature" has somehow been lost on the current generation of researchers.[73] In some studies of schizophrenic language methodological "purity" has taken precedence over theoretical meaningfulness.[74] This could easily lead to methodological fetishism when the direction of research is dictated neither by theory nor by the subject of inquiry, but by the methods that guarantee the reliable reproduction of data.

Occasionally, however, a confirmation of the insights of Vygotsky, Goldstein, Werner and Kaplan has appeared. D. R. Rutter, for example, recently confirmed an old Vygotskian observation that communication between two schizophrenic patients is more difficult than between a patient and a caretaker.[75] Using the so-called Cloze technique for determining the communicative value of messages, Rutter assessed the quality of dialogues between patients, nurses and doctors. It turned out that the task of reconstructing a dialogue between two schizophrenics was the most difficult, and the communicative value of messages was minimal. Vygotsky observed a similar phenomenon and explained it as a consequence of the confrontation of two preconceptual systems of thought belonging to two schizophrenic patients, each of whom ignored the task of taking the position of the other into account: "As might be expected, the experiments indicated a better mutual understanding between patients with schizophrenia and normal persons than between schizophrenic persons. An analogous situation is seen in children, who understand adults better than they do each other".[76]

My belief in the theoretical potential of the Vygotsky-Goldstein-Werner interpretation of regressive phenomena does not exclude the possibility of revision. For example, it is clear that a scale of development and/or regression must include not only a formal measure of cognitive advancement but also some kind of typology for those communicative contexts in which immature or regressive trends are displayed. Just as regressive or "paleologic" thinking does not determine the *whole* of the child's or the schizophrenic's reasoning, the conscious life of normal adults is not *all* conceptual. Many episodes of everyday reasoning obey the laws of paleologic thinking and conform to the von Domarus principle of identification on the basis of predicates, which some have perceived as a distinctive feature of schizophrenic thought disorder.[77]

Vygotsky observed that this type of reasoning is not paralogical in any absolute sense, but only when it is misplaced. For example, identification on the basis of a family name is not paralogical in itself, but it becomes so when a conceptual problem is approached with this family name logic. One of the contexts where identification based on predicates is a norm is advertising. Consider the following example from my collection of "paleological" TV commercials:

First we see an attractive young woman playing the piano with great absorption and strength. The voice-over comments that the woman's performance is "without compromise". Suddenly we see a container of yogurt and we are told that this yogurt is also made "without compromise". In complete accord with the von Domarus principle, music and yogurt are identified on the basis of their common predicate, "without compromise". By consuming this particular brand of yogurt the viewer "participates" in piano playing and possibly in the attractive young woman herself. It is important, however, that the viewers clearly understand that what they are viewing is a commercial, i.e. that they are aware of the specific context in which the act of "participation" is carried out and realize that this context is very special.

Another criterion helpful in distinguishing "primitive" and advanced logic could be gleaned from the discussion on Luria's study of nonliterate members of traditional societies. Recent commentators have pointed out that the inability to solve the simple syllogisms reported by Luria does not necessarily indicate a more primitive level of reasoning but rather the inability to switch from the logic of things to the logic of words.[78] Members of traditional societies seem to be quite capable of drawing inferences from premises which they regard as realistic and empirical, but they have difficulty in doing the same when premises are purely hypothetical. What distinguishes illiterate members of traditional societies from their educated contemporaries is not logic itself, but the flexibility to switch from the context of things to the context of speech itself. The "primitive" mentality failed precisely on this point of identifying the communicative context and adjusting the level of reasoning depending on it.

In the psychoanalytic literature this same problem of the contextuality of regression was addressed by Ernst Kris.[79] Although the metaphor of cathexis and mental "economy" used by Kris hardly fits into the present discussion, the gist of his argument is still valid. Kris demonstrated that it would be incorrect to present the primary process type of mentation as exclusively pathological or indicative of a totally "regressive" mental state such as sleep. Kris further suggested that introspective analysis of the creative process indicates that "ego may use the primary process and not to be only overwhelmed by it".[80] As long as the ego is "in charge" it may alternate between an "inspirational" phase characterized by an influx of primary process imagery, and an "elaborational" phase based on secondary process techniques.

It is of considerable interest that Vygotsky seemed to have the same alteration in mind when he spoke of the "influx of sense" in egocentric speech.[81] An important addition made by Vygotsky is that thought should not necessarily leave the verbal domain in order to plug into the primary process resources. The other important issue is the emphasis on context. Similar verbal forms may appear as incomprehensible egocentric utterances when the communicative context is not clear, and as an artistic device when the entire artistic text elaborates and justifies the original condensed meaning. The artistic text as a whole corresponds here to the product of what Kris called an elaborative phase. The social meanings of words are thus deconstructed during the inspirational stage, turned into idiosyncratic senses, only to be reassembled with the help of social principles of artistic form carried by the total text.

The elaboration of the typology of communicative situations seems thus to be a necessary prerequisite for the development of the formal scale of regression. It seems that the notion of regression may regain its heuristic value and narrow the gap between psychoanalytic and cognitive developmental theory if it is reconsidered along the lines suggested by Vygotsky. One of the obstacles to be removed is the pervasive metaphor of mental "economy" which, as Philip Holzman pointedly mentioned, "allegedly explains clinical psychoanalytic *theory* but does not explain the clinical *phenomena* themselves".[82]

As has been admitted in psychoanalytic literature for quite a long time now, psychodynamic theory can not claim wide application before it addresses the "conflict-free ego sphere" in general and the issues of *cognitive* development in particular. In order to broaden its theoretical base the underlying model or paradigm must first be reviewed, since neither purely "economic" nor "regression as recapitulation" paradigms are satisfactory at the present stage of research. As the problems of socially meaningful interpersonal communication come more and more to the forefront of psychological theory, Vygotsky's ideas concerning the developmental role of symbolic mediation offer a promising paradigm for a new approach to regression. The integration of psychopathological, child developmental and cross-cultural findings may become a reality if a *formal* scale of advancement/regression is elaborated and if a typology of the communicative situations involved is taken into account.

NOTES

1. See Kurt Goldstein, *The Organism*. New York: American Book Co., 1939.
2. Some of the papers about handicapped development written by Vygotsky between 1924 and 1935 were reprinted in his *Collected Papers*, vol. 5. Moscow: Pedagogika, 1983.
3. Vygotsky's views on pedology are expressed in *Pedologiya Shkolnogo Vozrasta (The Pedology of School Age)*, 1928; *Pedologiya Yunosti (The Pedology of Youth)*, 1929; *Pedologiya Podrostka (The Pedology of Adolescence)*, 1931. Several chapters from the latter volume were reprinted in Vygotsky's *Collected Papers*, vol. 4. Moscow: Pedagogika, 1984. The history of Soviet pedology is discussed in Raymond Bauer, *The New Man in Soviet Psychology*. Cambridge, MA: Harvard University Press, 1968.

4. The history of defectology is reviewed in William McCagg, *The Origins of Defectology.* In W. McCagg and L. Siegelbaum, eds, *The Disabled in the Soviet Union.* Pittsburgh, PA: University of Pittsburgh Press, 1989.

5. A somewhat similar approach to handicapped development has been formulated, without Vygotsky's influence, by Reuven Feuerstein, *Instrumental Enrichment: An Intervention Program for Cognitive Modifiability.* Baltimore, MD: University Park Press, 1980.

6. Lev Vygotsky, *Kollektiv kak Faktor Razvitiya Defektivnogo rebenka* (*The Collective as a Factor in the Development of a Disabled Child*). In Vygotsky, *Collected Papers*, vol. 5, p. 212 (original work published in 1931).

7. For a review of Luria's work, see Donna Vocate, *The Theory of A. R. Luria.* New York: Erlbaum, 1986. See also Alexander Luria, *The Making of Mind.* Cambridge, MA: Harvard University Press, 1978.

8. Lev Vygotsky, *Psikhologiya i Pedagogika Detskoi Defektivnosti* (*Psychology and Pedagogy of a Child's Disability*). In Vygotsky, *Collected Papers*, vol. 5, p. 54 (original paper published in 1924). Vygotsky's emphasis on the role of meaning in this early paper should put to rest any attempts to divide his views on psychological tools into "earlier" (more behavioristic) and "later" (more semiotic).

9. Their case is described in Karl Levitin, *One is not Born a Personality.* Moscow: Progress, 1982, pp. 213–30.

10. See Alfred Adler, *Study of Organ Inferiority and its Psychical Compensation.* New York: NMDP, 1917.

11. Lev Vygotsky, *K Voprosu o Kompensatornykh Processakh v Razvitii* (*On the Compensatory Processes in Development*). In Vygotsky, *Collected Papers*, vol. 5, p. 122 (original paper presented in 1931).

12. Lev Vygotsky, *Psikhologiya i pedagogika*, p. 78.

13. Vygotsky, *Kollektiv*, p. 208.

14. Kurt Lewin, *The Dynamic Theory of Personality.* New York: McGraw Hill, 1935.

15. There is an interesting parallel to Lewin's findings in Piaget's notion of the "either–or" type of decentration in younger children; see Jean Piaget, *The Psychology of Intelligence.* New York: Humanities Press, 1959.

16. Lev Vygotsky, *Problema Umstvennoi Otstalosti* (*The Problem of Mental Disability*). In Vygotsky, *Collected Papers*, vol. 5, pp. 250–1 (original paper published in 1935).

17. Ibid, p. 255.

18. See Alexander Mescheryakov, *Awakening to Life*. Moscow: Progress, 1980.

19. The works of Sokolyansky, Mescheryakov and Ilyenkov are reviewed in Levitin, *One is not Born a Personality*, pp. 213–300.

20. See Jane Knox and Alex Kozulin, "The Vygotskian tradition in Soviet psychological studies of deaf children". In McCagg and Sigelbaum, eds, *The Disabled in the Soviet Union*. Pittsburg, PA: University of Pittsburgh Press, 1989.

21. Vygotsky, *Kollektiv*, p. 217.

22. See Knox and Kozulin, *op. cit.*

23. H. Hartmann and E. Kris, "The genetic approach to psychoanalysis". *Psychoanalytic Study of the Child*, vol. 1, 1945, pp. 11–29.

24. Peter Wolf, "Psychoanalytic formulations regarding the acquisition of language". In R. Holt, ed., *Motives and Thought*. New York: International Universities Press, 1967.

25. Sigmund Freud, *The Interpretation of Dreams*. In James Strachey, ed., *The Standard Edition of the Complete Psychological Works*. London: Hogarth Press, 1953–4, vol. 5, p. 567 (original paper published in 1900).

26. See Stanley Jackson, "The history of Freud's concept of regression". *Journal of the American Psychoanalytic Association*, vol. 17(3), 1969, pp. 743–84.

27. Morton Gill, "The primary process". In R. Holt, ed., *Motives and Thought*. New York: International Universities Press, 1967, pp. 297–8.

28. Alexei N. Leontiev, "Razvitie Vysshikh Form Zaponimaniia" ("The development of higher forms of memory") In A. Leontiev, *Izbrannye Psikhologicheskie Trudi (Selected Psychological Works)*. Moscow: Pedagogika, 1983, vol. 1 (original paper published in 1931).

29. Alexander Luria, *Mozg Cheloveka i Psikhicheski Processy (The Human Brain and Mental Processes)*. Moscow: Pedagogika, 1970.

30. Ernst Kretschmer, *Hysteria*. New York: NMDP, 1926.

31. Lev Vygotsky, *Diagnostika Razvitiya i Pedologicheskaya Klinika (The Diagnosis of Development and the Pedological Clinic)*. Collected Papers, vol. 5, p. 277 (original paper written in 1931).

32. Ibid, p. 279.

33. Sigmund Freud, *The Unconscious. Standard Edition*, vol. 14, p. 199 (original paper published in 1915). See also Peter Knapp, "Image, symbol and person". *Archives of General Psychiatry*, vol. 21, 1969, pp. 392–406.

34. Lev Vygotsky, *Thought and Language*. Cambridge, MA: MIT Press, 1986, p. 247.

35. Piaget in his earlier works had been considerably influenced by psychoanalytic ideas. See Jean Piaget, *The Language and Thought of the Child*. London: Routledge and Kegan Paul, 1959 (original work published in 1923).
36. Ibid, p. 43.
37. Vygotsky, *Thought and Language*, pp. 20–2.
38. Eugen Bleuler, "Autistic thinking". In D. Rapaport, ed., *Organization and Pathology of Thought*. New York: Columbia University Press, 1951, p. 427 (original work published in 1912).
39. Ibid, p. 427; see also Rapaport's note on the same page.
40. Jean Piaget, Comments, in L. Vygotsky, *Thought and Language*, p. 263.
41. Lev Vygotsky, *Collected Papers*, vol. 6, p. 16.
42. Lev Vygotsky, *O Psikhologicheskih Sistemah* (*On Psychological Systems*). *Collected Papers*, vol. 1, p. 110 (original paper written in 1930).
43. Alexander Luria, *The Role of Speech in Regulation of Normal and Abnormal Behavior*. New York: Pergamon, 1960.
44. The precise developmental sequence, however, was disputed by Robert Wozniak, "Verbal regulations of motor behavior". *Human Development*, vol. 15, 1972, pp. 13–57.
45. Luria, *Mozg Cheloveka*, pp. 105–10.
46. Alexander Luria, *The Working Brain*. New York: Basic Books, 1973, p. 202.
47. Alfred Storch, *The Primitive Archaic Forms of Inner Experience and Thought in Schizophrenia*. New York: NMDP, 1924.
48. On the history of the recapitulation doctrine, see Stephen Jay Gould, *Ontogeny and Phylogeny*. Cambridge, MA: Harvard University Press, 1977.
49. The idea of historical recapitulation has been recently revived by Kieran Egan, *Primary Understanding*. New York: Routledge, 1988.
50. See John Hughlings Jackson, *Selected Writings*. New York: Basic Books, 1958 (original papers written in the 1880s–1890s).
51. Freud, *The Interpretation of Dreams. Standard Edition*, vol. 5, pp. 548–9.
52. Sigmund Freud, *Group Psychology and the Analysis of the Ego. Standard Edition*, vol. 18, p. 117 (original paper published in 1921).
53. See Silvano Arieti, *The Interpretation of Schizophrenia*. New York: Basic Books, 1974.
54. Norman Cameron, "A study of thinking in senile deterioration and schizophrenic disorganization". *American Journal of Psychology*, vol. 51, 1938, pp. 650–64.

55. Heinz Werner, *Comparative Psychology of Mental Development.* New York: International Universities Press, 1948, p. 17.
56. Ibid, pp. 26 and 34.
57. See Sylvia Scribner, "Vygotsky's uses of history". In J. Wertsch, ed., *Culture, Communication, and Cognition.* London: Cambridge University Press, 1985.
58. Alexander Luria, *Cognitive Development.* Cambridge, MA: Harvard University Press, 1976.
59. Vygotsky, *Collected Papers*, vol. 3, pp. 30–1.
60. Lev Vygotsky, "Thought in schizophrenia". *Archives of Neurology and Psychiatry*, vol. 31, 1934, p. 1067.
61. Lev Vygotsky, *Problema Soznaniya (The Problem of Consciousness).* *Collected Papers*, vol. 1, p. 161 (the lecture was given in 1933).
62. Lev Vygotsky, "Thought in schizophrenia". *Archives of Neurology and Psychiatry*, vol. 31, 1934, p. 1067.
63. Ibid, p. 1068.
64. Eugenia Hanfmann and Jacob Kasanin, *Conceptual Thinking in Schizophrenia.* New York: NMDP, 1942.
65. For details of method see Vygotsky, *Thought and Language*, p. 103; Hanfmann and Kasanin, *Conceptual Thinking in Schizophrenia*, pp. 103–8.
66. Hanfmann and Kasanin, *op. cit.*, p. 16.
67. Ibid, p. 24.
68. Vygotsky, "Thought in schizophrenia"; see also John Benjamin, "A method of distinguishing and evaluating formal thinking disorders in schizophrenia". In J. Kasanin, ed., *Language and Thought in Schizophrenia.* New York: Norton, 1964.
69. See Jacob Kasanin, ed., *Language and Thought in Schizophrenia.* New York: Norton, 1964 (original volume published in 1944).
70. See Kurt Goldstein, "A methodological approach to the study of schizophrenic thought disorder". In Kasanin, *Language and Thought in Schizophrenia.*
71. E. von Domarus, "The specific laws of logic in schizophrenia". In Kasanin, *Language and Thought in Schizophrenia.*
72. Heinz Werner and Bernard Kaplan, *Symbol Formation.* New York: Wiley, 1963.
73. Vygotsky, "Thought in schizophrenia", p. 1076.
74. For a review of recent approaches to schizophrenic language, see Ann Hotchkiss and Philip Harvey, "Linguistic analysis of speech disorder in psychosis". *Clinical Psychology Review*, vol. 6, 1986, pp. 155–75.
75. D. R. Rutter, "Language in schizophrenia: The structure of

monologues and conversations". *British Journal of Psychiatry*, vol. 145, 1985, pp. 399–404.

76. Vygotsky, "Thought in schizophrenia", p. 1072.
77. For example, Arieti, *Interpretation of Schizophrenia*.
78. David Olson and J. Astington, "Talking about texts". Paper presented at the Boston Conference on Language Development, October 19–21, 1986.
79. Ernst Kris, *Psychoanalytic Explorations in Art*. New York: International Universities Press, 1965.
80. Ibid, p. 312.
81. Vygotsky, *Thought and Language*, p. 246.
82. Philip Holzman, "Theoretical models and the treatment of schizophrenics". In M. Gill and P. Holzman, eds, *Psychology vs. Metapsychology*. New York: International Universities Press, 1976, p. 135.

CHAPTER SEVEN

The Life of Ideas

T HE RESEARCH conducted by Vygotsky's group, described in the last two chapters, did not take place in a social vacuum. Political storms raged not only beyond the walls, but also within the halls of academic institutions. One episode described by Luria recreates the atmosphere of those days.[1] Luria had been searching for a situation in which an acute emotional response in an individual could be studied. He found such a situation at Moscow University, at which purges were regularly taking place. During these purges a special commission evaluated each student's academic performance and, more important, his or her social-political inclinations, including the social background of their parents. The commission was empowered to purge a student from the university immediately if he or she was found to have an undesirable social profile.

During the 1920s those psychologists who were not entirely opposed to Marxism could still pursue their research projects, but the situation deteriorated as the 1930s drew closer.[2] On the one hand, Stalin, who had pronounced 1929 as "the year of great breakthrough", was tightening Party control over the previously "soft" fringes of science and culture; on the other, Soviet psychologists themselves displayed a remarkable eagerness to denounce each other as "renegades". Each of the rival groups claimed that its methodology was the most scientific, and its ideology the most purely Marxist. Pavlovians claimed that only their brand of behavioral science was genuinely materialistic, Konstantin Kornilov and his "Marxist psychologists" in turn accused Pavlovians of physiological reductionism, and both groups were considered renegades by some of Bekhterev's students who promoted their own reflexological doctrine. For a time, psychologists could defend their positions by claiming that in the absence of a commonly accepted Marxist methodology for behavioral and social sciences, individual psychologists were doing their best to define such principles themselves. This line of defense collapsèd when, as the result of a number of "philosophical discussions", the founding fathers of Marxism-Leninism were pronounced the chief authorities in all fields of knowledge: "The real founders of Soviet psychology as a dialectical-materialistic discipline are neither schools nor trends in psychology, but the founders of Marxism-Leninism". All those who attempted to form psychological theory on the basis of Western studies were condemned because they were now expected to derive their theories from "the philosophical heritage of Marx, Engels, and Lenin, Bolshevik experience, and the works of Stalin".[3]

A group of young Party members at the Moscow Institute of Psychology hastened to denounce Kornilov's leadership of the Institute, accusing him and his colleagues of all sorts of "ideological deviations". Neither Luria nor Vygotsky escaped criticism. Their cultural-historical theory was branded as leading to an anti-materialistic revision of psychology, and their appreciation of the French sociological school and Gestalt psychology was considered to be a reflection of their "bourgeois" inclinations.[4] Moreover, Luria's cross-cultural study of cognitive functions was condemned as allegedly denigrating national minorities. As a consequence, the study was denied publication, and the issue of cross-cultural analysis became taboo for the next forty years.

There is very little documentary evidence that might allow us to understand the behavior of Vygotsky's group under the mounting ideological pressure. The only published "confession" is Luria's renunciation of his earlier interest in psychoanalysis. But even that was rather ambivalent, because simultaneously with the publication of his renunciation in Russian, Luria author-ized the translation of his psychodynamically inspired study of human conflicts into English.[5] According to Leontiev's recollec-tions, a critical "discussion" was scheduled to take place some-time in 1933 or 1934 with Vygotskian theory as a major target. Leontiev also claimed that some of the notes published for the first time in the 1980s reflect Vygotsky's preparation for this discussion. If so, then Vygotsky apparently had no intention of recanting any of his views, since the notes in question reflect an unflinching belief in the principles of cultural-historical theory.[6]

One may only guess about Vygotsky's feelings in the last years of his life. He had an attack of tuberculosis, but continued working to the very end, dictating his papers. Only in the 1980s did one of the last survivors of that era, Bluma Zeigarnik, finally address the issue of Vygotsky's anguish over being misunder-stood by his contemporaries. "Since we talk about Vygotsky", related Zeigarnik, "I must say that he had a very hard time. He was accused of not being a Marxist, while he was a real Marxist. He suffered a lot from the lack of understanding. And actually he killed himself, or, more precisely, he did everything to shorten his life".[7] Even this comment is cryptic in many respects; it is not clear whether Vygotsky was bitter only about the ideological campaign against his theory, or whether he also suffered from being misunderstood by some of his own stu-dents.[8] The reference to Vygotsky's desire to die is also not entirely clear. Was it the result of his disappointment with what *had* happened (with his ideas, school, etc.) or that of the fear of what *could* happen in the future (arrest, show trial, imprison-ment)? On June 11, 1934 Vygotsky died in a suburban Moscow sanatorium. His last words, as reported by his friends, under-scored the profound ambiguity of human verbal expression, for they were: "Ia gotov . . .", which could mean "I am ready . . .", but also "I am finished".[9]

THE PSYCHOLOGY OF ACTIVITY

Vygotsky's relationship to Marxism and his being misunderstood by his contemporaries continue to be the subject of considerable debate and disagreement among scholars half a century after his death.[10] Let us start with Marxism, although the term itself is unfortunate, because it is liable to multiple interpretations ranging from a particular critique of nineteenth-century capitalism to an all-embracing ideology of the Stalinist state. As has already been argued in Chapter Three, Vygotsky completely rejected Marxist ideology in its role as a yardstick for scientific research. Probably his contemporaries would have been less puzzled had he dispensed with Marx altogether, but he did not. Vygotsky took Marx seriously, not as an icon, but as a real thinker belonging to the European cultural tradition. Vygotsky's Marx became one of the voices of the European thought on a par with Dilthey, Durkheim, neo-Kantians, and others. This placement of Marx in the context of European thought could not but be puzzling for Vygotsky's colleagues who became accustomed to the division of culture into "bourgeois" and "socialist", and for whom Marxism signified a break with the European tradition rather than its fulfillment.

Equally sincere, but in the final analysis also ambivalent, was Vygotsky's commitment to the tasks set up by the socialist government. He enthusiastically worked on the projects related to the new system of education and social welfare, but his intellectual reflection upon these projects was carried out in a form that seemed alien to his contemporaries. People around Vygotsky were the engineers of the social utopia, one major prerequisite of which was a decisive break with the past. New goals presupposed new methods. Vygotsky was also seeking a new psychology in a new society, but he saw it as a fulfillment of the European tradition rather than its negation. The tension caused by the acceptance of social tasks which in Vygotsky's hands immediately became stripped of their socialist appearance, pointed to a paradigmatic creative conflict between the thinker and the society. One may wonder whether the entire Russian cultural explosion of the 1920s—in literature, the arts, and the theater—was not the result of similar creative tensions.

Certainly Vygotsky was misunderstood by his contemporaries at least in part because of the sophistication of his arguments, but there seems to have been another reason. Vygotsky's position was not easy to pigeonhole. Many of his contemporaries had become accustomed to the system of intellectual identification through group allegiances. Instead of inquiring about a person's ideas, they asked to which group or clique the person belonged. In this respect Vygotsky broke all the rules. His pre-Revolutionary record was clean, and his acceptance of Marxism seemed sincere, so he was expected to join the ruling clique. Instead, he seemed to respect the wisdom of the disgraced poet Mandelstam much more than all the volumes of his Marxist contemporaries. To resolve this "cognitive dissonance", Vygotsky's contemporaries had either to expose Vygotsky as pseudo-Marxist, or to persuade him to stick to the common truth and abandon his dangerous deviations.

Despite all the criticisms and misunderstanding, however, some of Vygotsky's works were published posthumously in 1934 and 1935.[11] The final blow came only in 1936 when the Central Committee of the Communist Party issued a decree, "On Pedological Distortions",[12] which abolished all forms of mental testing and psychological evaluation of students. It redirected most of the learning disabled children from special classes to ordinary ones, and ordered the removal of all pedological textbooks from libraries. There was no provision for any discussion of this decree; in a telling detail it *ordered* "the books published to date on the theory of contemporary pedology to be criticized in the press".[13] Pedology, being a catchword to designate all those works in educational psychology which transcended traditional pedagogy, covered much of what Vygotsky had studied in the 1920s. The decree deemed his manuscripts unpublishable and the published works banned.

The members of Vygotsky's group started to experience problems several years before the death of their teacher. As an official biography put it, "In 1930, circumstances forced Alexei N. Leontiev to leave both the Academy of Communist Education and the Institute of Cinematography".[14] Luria, although he was already a recognized psychologist, decided to return to medical school as a student, possibly in an attempt to shift to a less ideologically charged sphere of clinical neuropsychology. Finally, in 1931–32 a group of Vygotsky's students, including Alexei Leontiev, Lidia Bozhovich and Alexander Zaporozhets, left Moscow and established a new research center in the Ukrainian city of Kharkov, where they were joined by the local psychologists Peter Galperin and Peter Zinchenko. The work of the Kharkov school of developmental psychology was foundational for the future development of Soviet psychology. Many of the ideas and the concepts formulated in Kharkov became characteristic features of Soviet developmental theory in the 1960s. Yet at that time the school was almost invisible; very little was published, and then only in obscure institutional proceedings in the Ukrainian language. For example, in 1935 a volume was prepared, dedicated to the problem of "scientific" concepts and learning, but it was never published.[15]

Taking into account an ambivalent attitude of the Kharkov group toward Vygotsky's theory, it is important to emphasize that the Kharkovites remained the "Vygotskian school" even when they rejected the ideas of their teacher. To understand this one should remember that the phenomenon of scientific school presupposes the existence of a corpus of texts and ideas that could be challenged, but which would remain the standard point of reference. The Kharkovites could disagree with Vygotsky and deviate from his research program, but even in disagreement they were tied to *his* and no other theory.

In his first independent paper, Leontiev apparently continued where Vygotsky left off with the issue of the concept formation in children. In this important theoretical paper written in 1935, Leontiev sketched the route taken by the child's concept from a primitive everyday life representation to a systematic "scientific" concept.[16] The central question Leontiev posed concerned the forces behind the process of transformation of a primitive representation into an advanced concept. These forces could be found at play in a dialectical contradiction between representational meaning as it exists in the child's consciousness and the "same" meaning as defined in the child's practical activity. In one experiment, for example, this contradiction revealed itself in the gradual assimilation of the "scientific" concept of the "stepchild", which was unknown to a primary school student at the beginning of the study. The notion of a stepchild first appeared in the context of a fairytale about a poor girl and a wicked stepmother. Thus the student first identified the stepchild simply as a "girl". Later, in the course of specially designed play activity the student encountered a contradiction between this early definition and the fact that a boy could also be a stepchild. The existence of the contradiction was revealed in the student's readiness to deform reality to fit the representation: pointing to a picture of a boy he claimed that "this is a girl" because according to the rules only a girl could be a stepchild. Only at the end of the learning process did the student acquire the notion of a stepchild based on the concept of familial relations.

From experiments and observations such as these, Leontiev concluded that "the development of [word] meaning cannot be explained from the fact of verbal communication alone; behind the development of meaning always stands the development of the child's activity as related to objective reality. . . . The change in the child's consciousness occurs as a result of the changes in his intellectual activity understood as a system of psychological operations, which in their turn, are determined by the actual relationship between a child and reality".[17]

This insistence on the actual relationship with reality mediated by operations of a practical, rather than a semiotic, character became a major point of departure of the Kharkovites from classical Vygotskian theory. For Vygotsky consciousness had a radical transformatory power: "Of course life defines consciousness. [Consciousness] is only one of its moments. But once it has emerged, consciousness itself [starts] to define life; or more precisely, conscious life defines itself though consciousness".[18] The primary instruments of consciousness are verbal "meanings" and "senses", and their development depends primarily on interpersonal semiotic interaction. Without denying the importance of such an interaction, Leontiev shifted the emphasis to the practical interaction of a child with the objective world of things.

What in Leontiev's paper appeared as one of the possible readings of the Vygotskian program, in a few years became a full-scale critique of Vygotsky's theory as such. Zinchenko, who joined Leontiev's group in Kharkov, expressed his opposition to this theory thus:

Indeed, one of the most basic of all problems, the conceptualization of the nature of the mind, was incorrectly resolved. The central characteristic of the human mind was thought to be *mastery* of the natural or biological mind through the use of auxiliary psychological means. Vygotsky's fundamental error is contained in this thesis, in which he misconstrued the Marxist conception of the historical and social determination of the human mind.

Vygotsky understood the Marxist perspective idealistically. The conditioning of the human mind by social and historical factors was reduced to the influence of human culture on the individual. The source of mental development was thought to be the interaction of the subject's mind with cultural, ideal reality rather than his actual relationship to reality.[19]

This general disagreement regarding the role of culture as a mediator was translated into the alternative strategy of studying psychological functions. The emphasis on psychological tools was replaced by that of so-called leading activity. In a series of simple but ingenious experiments, Zinchenko challenged the Vygotskian idea that the sign-mediator is decisive in the transformation of natural *mneme* into the cultural mnemotechnique. He argued that an ontogentically primordial form of memory is *involuntary* memorization, or accidental learning. Such memorization occurs within the activity of different, non-mnemonic nature and it develops following the changes in this other, leading activity. From Zinchenko's point of view it is not a sign-mediator that transforms the original, impressionistic memorization into a higher form of memory, but rather a goal-directed activity that absorbs the elements of accidental learning and, by turning them into the means for this activity, creates the structures of involuntary memory. On the other hand, voluntary or purposeful memorization is a goal-directed activity on its own and should be mastered by a child as a specific form of activity before it can become an effective mnemonic function.[20]

Leading activity was seen by Zinchenko as fulfilling the requirement of placing the practical interaction between the individual and the world to the forefront: "We cannot reduce the development of the human mind, the development of memory in particular to the development of the relationship between 'external' or 'internal' means to the object of activity. . . . The development of theoretical or 'ideal' mediation must be considered in the context of the subject's real, practical relationship with reality".[21]

Although Zinchenko's overall attack of Vygotsky's theory was hardly justified, his comments did reveal important lacunae in this theory. Vygotsky's notion of mediation allowed for three large classes of mediators: signs and symbols, individual activities, and interpersonal relations. The relationships between these three classes of mediators, however, had not been properly explored. While Vygotsky (and Leontiev in his earlier works) focused on the mediational role of signs and symbols, the Kharkovites devoted their entire attention to activities, thus bringing them closer to the Piagetian program with its emphasis on the internalization of sensory-motor schemas (this rather obvious affinity, however, was played down by the Kharkovites). As a result the notion of symbolic psychological tools, and the role of culture embodied in them, became underrepresented in Soviet psychology starting in the mid-1930s. The issue of the mediating effect of interpersonal relations was taken up only in the 1960s.[22]

In the works of the Kharkovites the concept of leading activity was amplified to include the formation of the intellectual function in children as a by-product of practical or playful activity. It was argued that each age has its own form of leading activity within which specific intellectual skills can be developed. Three major avenues of research have been defined: (1) the study and design of age-specific leading activities, such as play, practical activity, social group activity, etc., which would generate, as their by-products, cognitive functions; (2) the study of particular goal-directed classroom activities, such as reading, writing and logical reasoning directly aimed at the formation of higher mental processes; and (3) investigation of the stages and conditions of the internalization of both types of activity.

To give some idea of what form the activity research took at the later stages of its development in the 1970s, I will now focus on one study that seems quite representative.[23] The authors of this study applied the activity approach to the phenomenon of individual understanding and coping with texts that contain contradictory statements. Their major claim was that a human mind does not possess the spontaneous impulse to search for contradictions, and that only through a particular activity aimed at detecting the contradictions could an individual spot them in a text. To prove this point the authors composed a text resembling a two-paragraph excerpt from an adventure book describing a white-water river trip. The text was plausible as prose, but it contained statements contradicting simple laws of physics. These statements referred to the river "ascending" and "conquering the mountain peak". In the experimental sessions the subjects (university students and high-school teachers) were asked to read the text; in the first session looking for grammatical errors, in the second session memorizing the text, and in the third session searching for contradictions. As predicted by the authors, only the *relevant* activity of searching for contradictions yielded a significant number of discoveries, while under the condition of irrelevant activities such as looking for grammatical errors and memorization, the discovery of contradictions was infrequent.

The conclusion reached by the authors was that in order to detect a problematic statement an individual must actively search for it, spontaneous discovery being a matter of sheer chance. They also claimed that memorization cannot play the role of a leading activity with respect to the discovery of contradictions because the correctness of a statement does not effect memorization. This conclusion carried an implicit educational message, namely, that one cannot expect a student to discover incorrect statements unless he or she is trained to do this as a special form of activity.

This study, which in many respects was typical of activity research, has left a number of questions open. First, the lack of spontaneous search for contradictions might reflect not so much the nature of the cognitive processes involved, but the social constraints (such as the authoritarian atmosphere and the subjects' obedience) specific to the Soviet sample. Second, if one accepts that memorization is irrelevant for the discovery of contradictions, then the question remains as to what kind of activity is relevant and would generate accidental discovery as its by-product. And finally, it seems important to investigate whether the introduction of some pictorial or verbal tool-mediators would change the outcome of the experiment.

To answer these questions I replicated this contradictions study with certain modifications.[24] My subjects were American students and young professionals who were examined by their peers, rather than an authority figure such as a faculty member. This eliminated the authoritarian atmosphere which I suspected was responsible for the lack of spontaneity in the Soviet subjects. In addition, beyond such "irrelevant" activity as the search for typos, the subjects were offered two other forms of mediation: a multiple-choice list and a picture kit. The multiple choice was intended to provide a relevant activity. The subjects were presented with a list of questions related to the story, with multiple-choice answers, and were asked first to check the answers and then to retell the story. Finally the subjects were presented with a picture kit including a picture of a mountain landscape, strips of blue paper to represent the river, and a toy boat. They were asked to re-enact the story using the picture kit and to retell it once again. One of the experimental tricks was that the blue "river" strips could be placed either to indicate a continuous flow of the river from the mountains down to the valley, or to indicate a downhill flow changing into an uphill ascent of the river. The introduction of the picture kit was intended to test the role of psychological tools in the detection of contradictions.

Some of the results of the study I had predicted, but others were unexpected and because of that they were particularly interesting. As predicted, many more American subjects than Soviets discovered contradictions spontaneously in the course of looking for typos (28 versus 3.8 percent). The unexpected result was that neither the presumed relevant activity of answering questions from the multiple-choice list, nor the use of such mediating tools as the picture kit had a significant effect on the discovery of contradictions. Only 12 percent of the subjects benefited from these mediators, while 60 percent did not. This result is theoretically important, because one of the questions in the multiple-choice list referred directly to a contradictory statement. From the point of view of the activity paradigm, answering such a question should have directly facilitated the discovery of contradictions, yet only three subjects seemed to benefit from this activity. Moreover, some subjects checked the "river goes uphill" answer, but did not mention this as a contradictory statement. The importance of these negative data goes beyond the question of the universality of the relevant activity paradigm. It indicates that the correct selection in a multiple-choice test does not guarantee the fully conscious comprehension of the information involved.

Even more surprising was the total ineffectuality of a mediator such as the picture kit. One should remember that the psychological tools paradigm relies, without exception, on the facilitating influence of sign-mediators on psychological processes. I had expected the picture kit to serve as a powerful tool for the discovery of contradictions; to provide a dynamic, almost cinematic medium for the recreation of a story that included contradictory statements. Contrary to these expectations, however, the picture kit was used by some subjects to *suppress* or *alter* the contradictory information. From the subjects' narratives and their manipulations with the kit it became clear that they seized the opportunity offered by the kit and turned it into an instrument for rendering the contradictory statements uncontradictory. Using the elements of the kit the subjects alleged the existence in the story of such elements as "intersection" or "waterfall", or even turned the whole picture at a right angle to change the direction of river.

The replication of the contradiction study shed some light on both the activity and the psychological tools paradigms. With regard to the activity approach it became clear that a subject's performance of the "relevant" activity did not guarantee his or her conscious control over the dependent cognitive proesses. It was also clear that the degree of spontaneous critical reflection of an individual was underestimated by the activity school. At the same time, the psychological tools paradigm was deficient in that it failed to contemplate the repressive role of sign-mediators, which proved to be capable of altering cognitively dissonant information.

From the limitations of the activity research, let us turn now to the theory of psychological activity as formulated by Leontiev. Although the Kharkovites insisted on the social determination of human behavior and mind, the focus of their studies was on concrete forms of the internalization of individual actions. In order to present those actions as socially meaningful a general theory of psychological activity had to be elaborated. This task was taken up by Leontiev in a series of books starting with *Essays on the Development of Mind* (1947) and concluding with *Activity, Consciousness, and Personality* (1978).[25] Leontiev suggested that human activities differ depending on their object, which serves as a particular activity's true motive. Since all activities belong to the realm of social existence their motives should be understood in terms of the Marxist analysis of production and appropriation. For example, food as a motive for human activity presupposes a complex structure of the division of labor in human society. The activity of aquiring food, therefore, reflects social rather than natural relationships between the individual and the world: "For satisfying the need for food [one] must carry out actions that are not aimed directly at getting food. For example, the purpose of a given individual may be preparing equipment for fishing".[26]

In its relation to a number of specific goals an activity is subdivided into actions. So, what in terms of motives appears as an activity, in terms of specific goals is defined as a chain of actions. The activity has no constituent parts other than actions, and yet it is not an additive phenomenon: the activity is realized in actions, but its overall social meaning cannot be deduced from individual actions. On a yet lower level one can discern operations that reflect specific conditions under which a give action is taking place.

What was problematic in this apparently neat schema are two different conceptual languages: one used on the level of activity and the other on the level of actions and operations. In discussing human activities Leontiev employed the categories of Marxist social philosophy such as production, appropriation, objectivation and disobjectivation. The subject presumed by the use of these categories was the social-historical, and therefore psychologically rather abstractive subject. At the same time actions and operations were studied within the psychological paradigm, which was not very different from Piaget's paradigm of the internalization of overt actions in the form of mental schemas, and which had no immediate linkage to the higher-order social categories. This gap in Leontiev's theoretical model was noticed by his major opponent Sergei Rubinshtein, who claimed that Leontiev had incorrectly identified the processes belonging to the social essence of Man as the mastery of concrete actions and operations.[27] One may suggest that what was missing from Leontiev's model was precisely the stratum of culture—emphasized by Vygotsky, and neglected by his followers—that could provide a link between individual action and the social systems from which it derives its meaning.

By rejecting semiotic mediation and by insisting on the dominant role of practical actions Leontiev forced himself to elaborate the connection between the Marxist categories of production and objectivation, and the psychological category of action. This task was not an easy one by any standards. Even the most sophisticated of Western Marxists succeeded in doing this only with regard to the critique of the alienation of human action.[28] The Marxists were remarkably unsuccessful in depicting the positive, creative aspects of human action as conditioned by a social system. This lack of success had been explained as a reflection of the true condition prevalent in capitalist society, the condition of alienation. Unalienated, free action was reserved for future socialist life. But Leontiev could not use this line of defense because he was studying people in what was called a "state of accomplished socialism". He chose to avoid the psychological discussion of these issues, delivering instead the standard ideological verbiage about the alienation of the human mind under capitalism versus its free development under socialism.[29] In the context of current self-criticism by Soviet Marxists prompted by *glasnost*, Leontiev's "sermon" looks truly pathetic.

It is also instructive that when Leontiev made an attempt to outline the forms of human consciousness corresponding to activity, he opted for the category of "meaning" and "sense" rather than that of internalized operations. Thus an interplay between personal sense and socially codified meaning—and not that of an actual relationship with reality—became important when the problem of human consciousness came to the forefront. This inconsistency in Leontiev's position also did not escape the eyes of his critics. They correctly observed that although Leontiev had declared that human psychology should be understood in terms of practical activity, he actually identified it as a system of social meanings. But, in Marxist parlance, social meanings belong to the sphere of *social consciousness*, rather than that of *social practice* on which Leontiev promised to base his theory.[30]

All these inconsistencies notwithstanding, Leontiev's activity theory prospered from the late 1950s through the late 1970s. In 1963 his *Problems of the Development of Mind* won the highest government award for scientific research—the Lenin Prize. At that time he already held the prestigious Chair of General Psychology at Moscow University, and other former Kharkovites held senior professorial positions in Moscow. In addition, in the late 1950s the ban was lifted from Vygotsky's works: some of his papers were reprinted and some published for the first time.[31] Once again it became fashionable to be considered his disciple.

Given the circumstances it was not difficult for Leontiev to gain the status of official interpreter of Vygotsky's views, and his interpretations—at least for a time—enjoyed wider circulation than had the original texts. In his 1956 foreword to Vygotsky's *Selected Psychological Investigations*, Leontiev suggested that the emphasis on semiotic mediation was transitory for Vygotsky and that the activity theory furthered the development of what was authentic in the cultural-historical school.

In the late 1970s, however, Leontiev's theory began to be scrutinized more critically. One trigger for this scrutiny was Vygotsky's *Historical Meaning of the Crisis in Psychology*, underground copies of which had been in circulation among the Moscow psychological community some years prior to its official publication in 1982. Leontiev's theory of activity, being elevated to the level of an all-embracing psychological doctrine, ran into the trouble Vygotsky had warned about in his early work. The notion of activity was used at the same time as an explanatory principle and as the subject of concrete psychological investigations. The phenomena of human activity were "explained" by reference to the principle of activity.

The necessary distinction between activity as an explanatory principle and activity as a subject of scientific inquiry was made in a philosophically elaborated form by Eric Yudin.[32] First, Yudin restored the connection between the notion of activity and its original meaning developed in the philosophy of Hegel and Marx. That was important because in the heat of discussion psychlogists often neglected the philosophical roots of the very concepts they defended or attacked. Yudin emphasized that activity as the universal explanatory principle was introduced by Hegel as an alternative to the individualistic model of human conduct advocated by the British empiricists. In Hegel's philosophy, the individual becomes an "organ" of activity. Human activity, as an explanatory principle, cannot be reduced to the manifestations of individual consciousness; on the contrary, these manifestations presuppose activity as their true source.

Human activity could also become a subject of concrete scientific investigation. But in this case—and this was Yudin's crucial statement—the structural elements elaborated for activity as the explanatory principle become irrelevant. Activity as a subject of psychological investigation should have its own system of structural elements and its own explanatory principles. One and the same notion of activity cannot serve these two functions simultaneously, but this is precisely what happened in Leontiev's theory in the course of its development. The structural elements (activity–action–operation and motive–goal–condition) were first suggested as an elaboration of the explanatory principle, but were later used in the context of activity as a subject of study.

The decisive point in the re-evaluation of the relationship between Leontiev's activity theory and classical Vygotskian ideas was reached in 1979. Addressing a symposium on Vygotsky's theoretical legacy, Moscow philosopher and psychologist G. P. Schedrovitsky resolutely challenged the myth of succession and suggested that the activity theory substantially deviated from Vygotsky's original program. Schedrovitsky emphasized that the principle of semiotic mediation is the cornerstone of cultural-historical theory, representing its primary focus.[33]

To give some idea of how Vygotsky's theoretical legacy was developed in the 1970s and 1980s I will concentrate on three directions. The first direction included a constructive critique of Vygotsky's notion of "scientific" concepts and the development of a new program for the study of theoretical concept formation in schoolchildren. The second direction of research was associated with the revival of the fundamental epistemological critique of psychology based on the natural-scientific model and proposals for the new humanistic psychology and psychotherapy. The third direction explored the philosophical importance of Vygotsky's work together with the work of Bakhtin. The problem of the dialogical nature of human consciousness came to the forefront, and proposals were made for a new logic based on a dialogue between different "cultures of thinking."

THEORETICAL LEARNING

The revived interest in "scientific" concepts, and in the ways of providing students with the skills of *theoretical* learning is firmly associated with the Moscow psychologist Vasili Davydov.[34] Davydov's relationship to the Vygotskian school was originally conditioned by the fact that he was a student of Daniel Elkonin who had studied under Vygotsky in his youth. Elkonin and Davydov's inquiry into the problems of theoretical as opposed to empirical learning, apart from its purely intellectual sources, had an immediate social context. In the late 1950s American society had experienced a much-publicized "Sputnik shock" and made some resolute steps to improve its systems of science teaching. At the same time, a no less severe, but hardly noticed crisis was also brewing in Soviet schools. To a superficial observer the curriculum developed by Soviet educators could have been the envy of American critics of progressive education. The curriculum was clearly and uniformly structured, its emphasis was on science and mathematics, and elective courses in less academic subjects were practically nonexistent. And yet Soviet educators and psychologists had to acknowledge that this curriculum and the authoritarian methods of instruction associated with it had led to stifling the creativity of students and to a lack of correspondence between the science taught in school and the new science of the hi-tech revolution.[35]

A bold proposal to remedy this situation was made by Davydov and his research team, and was based on drawing a sharp distinction between empirical and theoretical learning. Davydov's argument ran roughly as follows. Traditional methods of instruction are based on the empiricist theory of knowledge. For this theory the starting point in any learning process is an immediate, observable property of an object. By abstracting some common features observed in a number of objects the empiricist arrives at a generalization which then can be verbally labeled and thus turned into a concept. A technique of generalization such as this can rarely transcend the principles of simple classification and formal logic. In the process of empirical learning an essential distinction between everyday generalizations and scientific concepts is obliterated and the student fails to appreciate the distinctive logic of scientific inquiry. As a result the hours spent in science and math classes are wasted because students remain unprepared to face nonstandard problems and phenomena.[36]

The conceptual source of the failure of the traditional curriculum was seen by Davydov in its blind adherence to the empiricist logic exemplified by the epistemology of John Locke. The innovative interpretations, formulated beginning with Hegel, of logical thought in general and the problem of generalization in particular, were somehow overlooked by psychologists and educators alike. Combining Hegel's dialectical insights with Marxist social analysis, Davydov suggested considering generalizations embodied in concepts as products of collective human activity. Concepts are those universal semiotic models that serve as hypothesized formulas of collective experience. The task of psychology is to investigate the process of *appropriation* of these models by an individual. The task of the educator is to elaborate activities relevant to the task of developing in a student the skills of theoretical generalization.

In pursuing this program Davydov found it necessary to undertake a constructive critique of both Vygotsky's and Leontiev's concepts of learning. While accepting the major premises of Vygotsky's developmental theory, Davydov pointed out that the important distinction between "scientific" and everyday concepts had not been properly elaborated. The distinction, as it was presented by Vygotsky, rested on the difference in the sources of acquisition of concepts—an asystematic individual experience in the first case, and systematic classroom instruction in the second. Such a basis for discrimination seemed to be inadequate, first because spontaneous concepts can display a certain degree of systematicity, while much of what is traditionally taught at the primary school level does not go beyond "nonscientific", empirical generalizations. According to Davydov the central discriminating factor between "scientific" and spontaneous concepts should be their content, which is theoretical for the first group, and empirical for the second. Such a dichotomy, however, cannot be formulated within psychological theory, and requires an appropriate epistemological study, which, according to Davydov, was neglected by Vygotsky as well as other specialists in learning processes.[37]

Davydov accepted Leontiev's theory as an authentic development of Vygotsky's ideas. He subscribed to Leontiev's notion of leading activity as the principal source of psychological development and accepted the periodization of child development based on this notion. Thus the period from three to six years was believed to be dominated by *play* activity, which facilitates the development of imagination and symbolic functions, the generalization of experience, and orientation into the world of human relations and actions. The next period (six to ten years) is dominated by *learning* activity, which engenders theoretical reasoning, analysis, conscious planning of actions, and mental reflection. The period from ten to fifteen years is characterized by the pre-eminence of *socially useful activity* (such as study, work, sport, public activity). In the process the ability to participate in any kind of collective effort is formed, together with the appreciation of social roles and the corresponding development of self-reflection and self-consciousness. The role of *professional-learning* activity becomes central during the final years of schooling (fifteen to eighteen years). On the basis of activity aimed at preparing for productive work, features of mental life such as professional interests, career planning, and the civic position of the personality are developed.

The above schema has been challenged a number of times, but Davydov has continued to support it, claiming that it corresponds to the characteristics of the development of Soviet children under the conditions of education and upbringing prevalent in socialist society.[38] If we take Davydov's pronouncement at face value some interesting questions arise. First, the universality of such a developmental sequence rests on the uniform methods of upbringing allegedly prevalent in Soviet society. Taking into account the current critique (made possible by *glasnost*) of what once was called a "developed socialist society", the question arises as to whether this schema reflects the real conditions of upbringing, or their utopian ideal, which turned out to be so different from the actual state of affairs? Second, alternative developmental models are conspicuously absent from Davydov's analysis, while it seems quite natural to inquire into the possible outcome of psychological development based on alternative sequences of leading activities implemented in educational practice.

While accepting the developmental sequence and its relations to activity, Davydov was critical of Leontiev's handling of the problem of the "translation" of a leading activity into the acquisition of, for example, "scientific" concepts: "Basic to the *scientific concept* is the *discursive activity* of the child, allowing him 'to possess the concept in its verbal expression'. But how does one go about constructing this activity? Leontiev notes that the general condition for this is a change in the relationship of the child to reality. But, he does not supply the concrete traits of this process".[39]

Davydov's own interests focused specifically on the elaboration of those activities that generate theoretical, conceptual reasoning, and in defining the essential difference between the resultant form of reasoning and the empirical one. It should be mentioned in passing that while emphasizing the role of theoretical generalization, Davydov paid no attention to preconceptual and archaic forms of reasoning, which feature so prominently in everyday thinking and ideological consciousness. At times it seems that for him all nontheoretical forms of reasoning appeared to be essentially similar.

The method of empirical generalization rests on the procedures of identification of similar features in a group of concrete objects or observable phenomena, and then labeling this feature with a verbal notion. For example, the notion of circle is traditionally introduced in primary school by pointing to a number of round objects, such as a wheel, the sun, a pancake, etc., and then explaining that all of these objects have one common feature, roundness, which, as a geometric form, is called a circle. The concepts introduced in such a way differ little from those achieved with the help of simple isolating abstraction which, as Vygotsky mentioned, can be developed by habit formation.

The method of theoretical generalization has an essentially different nature. It enables a student to reproduce the essence of an object in the mental plane. To understand an object or a process theoretically means to construct its ideal form and to be able to experiment with it. The method of theoretical learning takes as its prototype the method of mental experiments that have featured so prominently in the development of classical science since Galileo. For example, the theoretical definition of a circle (suggested by Spinoza) defines it as a figure produced by the rotation of a line with one free and one fixed end. Such a definition is "genetic" because it provides a procedure for engendering circles, it is universal because all possible circles can be generated in such a way, and it is theoretical because it requires no previous knowledge of round objects.

One may argue that there is little difference in introducing the notion of a circle to a child through the comparison of a number of round objects, or through the manipulation of a rotating line; in both cases the child would most probably understand what a circle means. The difference, however, is significant because in the first case the child would only learn how to distinguish circles, while in the second case he or she would acquire the skill of theoretical comprehension. Such a comprehension requires a multitude of mental techniques far beyond the simple operations of comparison, abstraction and classification. A child who relies on the method of "genetic" reproduction of the essence of an object thus liberates him or her from the domination of the empirically given. A child starts to learn that the essential characteristics of objects do not necessarily lie on the surface, but should be uncovered. To achieve this an object should be placed in a special theoretical space where its former as well as its possible future appearance are juxtaposed, and its relations to other empirically dissimilar objects are revealed. In the process the student receives an important lesson in that the lack of coincidence between the empirical appearance and the theoretical essence is the norm, and not a deviation.

Acquisition of the theoretical mode of reasoning is possible even by the age of six or seven if the child is engaged in an appropriate learning activity. The task of educators and psychologists is to design special scenarios of learning activity that can lead to theoretical reasoning. Such an activity should guide students from the abstract to the concrete, that is, from the most general relationship characteristic of the given educational subject to its concrete, empirical manifestations. Once the central relationship is identified it acquires a symbolic form, becoming a *contentful abstraction*. After exploring the links between the contentful abstraction and various empirical manifestations of the object or phenomenon in question, students must turn toward establishing links between the original abstraction and abstractions of the second order. Gradually the original abstraction becomes a true concept that will help students to orientate themselves with respect to any empirical problem pertaining to the given educational subject.

To give some idea of how these principles can be translated into concrete educational practice let us examine an experimental program in teaching math to first-graders. The major task at this initial stage of mathematical education is to provide children with the theoretical notion of a *number*. This is done in an indirect way by introducing the notion of *value* and teaching the children relations like $a > b$, $a = b$, $a + c > b$, etc. This can be achieved first with the help of material models (sticks, strips of paper, etc.) and then in a symbolic, algebraic form. Next the children are confronted with a problem in which two objects cannot be compared immediately. They are thus compelled to seek a mediator ("measure") that will enable them to establish the relationship between the values of the two objects involved. By using a concrete measure c, a short stick which can be placed a certain number of times along the length of the original sticks A and B, children learn the relation of multiplicity A/c and B/c. This relation is first objectivized as a simple marking (////), then verbally ("one, two, three, four"), and finally in algebraic form $A/c = 4$. Thus the notion of a number is introduced as an objectivation of the relation of multiplicity. This is a "genetic" definition because it provides a method for generating numbers, and it is universal because any whole number can be generated in this way. At the next stage of learning activity, the children explore what happens when the value of the measure c is changed while the value of A remains the same; for example, $A/c = k$ and $b < c$, then $A/b > K$. Then they learn what happens with the value of an object when different measures are applied. Children understand that the value of the object can be represented by different concrete numbers depending on the measure selected. Thus the essential properties of numbers are learned prior to their concrete, arithmetic use.[40]

A similar approach has been used in the design of learning activities for the acquisition of Russian orthography. The traditional learning of orthography was replaced by an experimental program based on the principle of the phonematic analysis of words. The unit of analysis and study became the phoneme taken in the different oppositions which alone define its value in actual words. If the mental experiments of famous physicists and mathematicians helped to design a program for math and science, in a study of language the classical works of structural phonology served as a prototype.

Davydov's program did not confine itself to basics such as math and language, but also ventured into the complex and controversial fields of history and art. The acceptance of this program was neither immediate, nor was it universal. During the 1970s Davydov's group amassed an impressive amount of evidence in favor of the theoretical learning program. At the same time it became clear that the existing cadre of Soviet teachers could not be trusted with the implementation of this program, which they did not and probably could not understand being themselves educated along the lines of empiricist thinking. In addition, there was an implicit contradiction between the free creative spirit of theoretical learning and the social conditions of its implementation. Soviet school education of the 1970s remained a highly centralized and authoritarian institutional system. School curricula and methods of instruction could not be chosen by individual school districts but were always selected by the Ministry of Education, so the only possibility for the program of theoretical learning to reach beyond the stage of experimentation was in gaining support from the educational bureaucrats. If they became attracted by a program they would then implement it statewide. The rigidity of the educational policy thus contained a threat for the program of theoretical learning even in the unlikely event of winning the approval of the establishment. In defending his program of theoretical learning, Davydov skillfully demonstrated its strong intellectual points and its relevance to the problems of the contemporary scientific and technological revolution. What he could not do— taking into account the sociopolitical climate of that period— was to project the proposed program into the reality of Soviet life and Soviet schools. To put it bluntly, if a student in the 1970s were to take a strictly conceptual-theoretical attitude toward the study of Soviet history, he or she would most probably be purged from the school as a dissident and if old enough could end up in Siberian exile. But even beyond these obvious political limitations, Davydov's program provided very few clues regarding the society he had in mind when he suggested the primacy of theoretical learning. He would hardly have objected to the view that politics, ideology and practical decision making do not obey the laws of conceptual reasoning, and yet his writings leave the impression that all Soviet schoolchildren are destined to become either scientist-theoreticians or rational critics of the false consciousness produced by different ideologies.[41]

The program, however, did not get a chance to prove itself

on a large scale. In the early 1980s Davydov's group found itself under fire from critics and Davydov lost his position as director of the Moscow Institute of Psychology. The recent atmosphere of *glasnost*, however, seems to be giving Davydov and his program a second chance, and Davydov has been promoted to the position of vice-president of the Academy of Pedagogical Sciences. This same *glasnost* has revealed problems in Soviet schools serious enough to render the dispute between empiricists and theoreticians almost frivolous. The educational system of the "advanced socialist society" is now beset with such mundane problems as a lack of proper school buildings, absence of transportation in rural areas, a high crime rate, drug abuse, teenage pregnancy, nationalist bigotry, and so on. Taking this into account one may feel that a simple advocacy of the intellectually attractive program of theoretical learning is not feasible. Davydov and his followers would probably be compelled to engage in a social critique of a society and schooling system that does not correspond to their ideal of education. At the same time Davydov's program could be profitably used, on a limited basis, by those Western educators who have the privilege of working in a relatively affluent educational environment and whose students are seeking an intellectually rewarding course of study.

TOWARD A HUMANISTIC PSYCHOLOGY

Even at the darkest moments in its history, Soviet psychology was relatively open to the fundamental question of what constitutes the subject matter and method of psychological inquiry. Unlike their more pragmatic colleagues in the United States and United Kingdom, Soviet psychologists have always felt obliged to confront these questions. Without answering them the everyday research routines seemed to be lacking foundation. Such issues became even more urgent after the dominant theoretical systems—first Pavlovian reflexology and later Leontiev's activity theory—began to crumble. One of the latest attempts of this kind is based on a fresh reading of Vygotsky's ideas regarding different *practices* as underlying different forms of mental life.[42] The immediate impulse toward this new attempt came from the observation that psychology, and particularly cognitive psychology, devoted most of its attention to the executive side of mental activity, leaving the issue of creative thinking with only a marginal scientific status. This research bias corresponds to the dominant position of natural-scientific methodology (and its approximations) in modern psychology. Natural-scientific methodology should be recognized as a special kind of cognitive and physical practice that allows one to create some artificial conditions under which the plane of theoretical representations can be put into correspondence with the plane of physical (or psychological) manipulation with the objects of inquiry. This practice is organized in such a way that the discovered characteristics of the object under study are independent of the procedures involved. Moreover, the laws of the behavior of the object are deemed to be truly natural and objective only if they are not affected by either the methods of experimentation, or by the fact of experimentation itself.

It has been argued more than once that even the most rigorous of psychological experiments cannot comply with the requirements of this natural-scientific model because of the essentially interactive nature of any psychological encounter.[43] Moreover, much of what constitutes the subject matter of psychology depends on the process of irreversible change in the mental operations of an individual. The program of theoretical learning, for example, took the "formative experiment" as its major methodological tool. In the course of such an experiment some learning capacities are generated in a child which were absent before and, more importantly, which would not emerge unless the child is engaged in the appropriate activity. In a broader sense, any study of creative cognition changes the mode of the mind's operation in such a way that it cannot return to its original state. By the same token, any psychotherapeutic encounter is an experimental situation during which the conditions of the client's mind can be studied only in so far as they are irreversibly changed.

Vygotsky's theory, which aimed at what is uniquely human in human behavior, presupposed a new understanding of psychological practice, and this understanding required a methodology that went beyond the models borrowed from the natural sciences. In its most general and abstract form, this new methodology was already contained in the notion of psychological tools. A psychological tool is a kind of symbolic agent that causes a fundamental change in the relationships between human mental functions. Vygotsky explored only the most primitive of these tools, but the paradigm itself allowed for almost unlimited experimentation with different symbolic systems and the conditions of their involvement in human life.

In *The Psychology of Experiencing*, which was probably the first original Soviet contribution to psychodynamic theory in fifty years, Fyodor Vasilyuk advanced a new model of critical situations based, in part, on Vygotsky's methodology.[44] At the heart of Vasilyuk's proposal lies the notion of experiencing or, more precisely, "living through" a crisis. Such a living through is defined as a special activity or inner work by means of which an individual succeeds in reintegrating his or her self damaged by the psychological crisis. This work is truly creative because the problem facing the individual at the critical point is not in "recognizing the meaning of the situation, not in elucidating a hidden but existent meaning, but in creating a meaning, in bringing meaning into existence or constructing it".[45] The work of living through a crisis is complicated by the fact that the meaning should not only be generated, but also realized in human existence. The work is, therefore, "toward achieving correspondence of meaning between consciousness and existence—providing meaning for the latter, and inducing the former to accept the meaning for existence".[46] To cope with such a crisis in the life-world, which is internally complex and externally difficult, requires psychological work whose prototype is creative activity. As, for example, a work of art or literature is simultaneously present and not-yet-present in the mind of its creator at the moment of its conception, in the same way the life restored, the unity of the self, is present and not-yet-present for a person living through a crisis.

Vasilyuk's reference to the artistic or literary prototype of human mental life is significant because it allows us to talk about the revitalized humanistic tradition in Russian psychology. Vygotsky and Bakhtin should then be recognized as the founding fathers of this tradition and Vasilyuk as their contemporary follower. Within this tradition human behavior is comprehended not through its reduction to the behavior of an animal, a computer, or even an ideal social individual suggested by Marxism, but through an analysis of the creative, transformatory manifestations of the human mind, objectivized in works of art and literature. Instead of providing clinical vignettes to substantiate his model, Vasilyuk suggested the reconstruction of the living through the crisis of a fictional character—Dostoevsky's Raskolnikov. By doing this Vasilyuk further amplified, but also compounded, the literary model of the human mind.

Raskolnikov's original crisis can be defined as a contradiction between his abhorrence of being "with people" and his failure to stay away from them. Out of this conflict a pathological solution does emerge—to be above people. Raskolnikov, however, does not succeed in consciously reconciling this theory with his inner feelings, and he commits his crime in a state of paralyzed will and confused consciousness.

After the murder it becomes clear that Raskolnikov's theory of superiority has failed dismally in its role as a defense mechanism. He is unable to integrate the crime into his life because his very nature, unlike his purely cerebral speculations, refuses to accept the theory of superiority as a feasible defense. As a result of the collision with the actuality of the crime his nature, that is, Raskolnikov's personality, is about to disintegrate. The first attempt at reintegration takes the form of defensive actions aimed at lowering the level of tension between the actuality of the crime and the reproaches of his conscience. Since nothing can be done about the crime already committed, and Raskolnikov's own conscience can not bear the guilt, he projects this guilt onto his mother and sister, whom he begins to hate. But such a projective defense fails because its method clashes with Raskolnikov's love for his family. Raskolnikov "escapes" this contradiction by distancing himself from his loved ones. By doing this he returns to the original conflict of being attracted by people and at the same time being unable to be with them. This time, however, the original conflict is amplified by the terrible guilt.

I will skip all the intermediate stages of the attempted reintegration of Raskolnikov's personality and focus only on the last and ultimately successful one. The success of the reintegration depends on Raskolnikov's newly discovered ability to move through the experiential stages of guilt, repentance and redemption. To be able to move through these stages the individual must shed his or her alienation and "plug into" a sociocultural schema, as Vasilyuk called it. Such a schema provides the individual with culturally organized psychological tools and systems of meanings that can help in the reintegration of personality. In the case of Raskolnikov the role of such tools is played by the system of religious beliefs and rituals. But the task of plugging into the sociocultural schema is not easy even without a crisis such as the one in which Raskolnikov found himself. To restructure one's own personality the individual must go beyond him or herself, to find support and mediation in a significant other. For Raskolnikov such a significant other was Sonya who represents the new system of meanings and who connects Raskolnikov to the religious schema. Thus the sociocultural schema, the tool of personal reintegration, becomes accessible only through a human mediator. In a dialogue with this other Raskolnikov achieves repentance, that is, a re-evaluation of his crime and his guilt from the point of view of the new (religious) system of values. Raskolnikov's individual crime is now seen in the timeless perspective of a fight between good and evil. The crime itself becomes meaningful as a minute surrender to arrogance [gordynya]. Only by acquiring this new meaning can the crime, however painfully, become a part of Raskolnikov's life. The beginning of redemption starts for Raskolnikov with ritual acts aimed at condemning arrogance: kissing the feet of Sonya, of his mother, kissing the earth, and publicly declaring his guilt.

Vasilyuk's analysis of Raskolnikov's living through his crisis reveals the ultimate type of critical experience—that of overcoming. Unlike defense mechanisms, which locally and temporarily help to alleviate the problem, overcoming, when successful, leads to the complete restructuring of the inner world of the individual. The prototype here is not a neurotic or dreaming person, but an artist or thinker, and overcoming is conceived of by analogy with the act of "authoring". Overcoming is thus simultaneously both more and less stereotypical than defense mechanisms. It is more stereotypical in the sense that the individual lives through the crisis only by plugging into the sociocultural schemas that are supra-individual; at the same time plugging into the sociocultural schemas does not lift the requirement of authoring but rather emphasizes it. Like poetry, which is based on the supro-individual foundation of the entire development of language and literature but remains uniquely individual, overcoming is impossible without sociocultural schemas but can be accomplished only in a highly individual way.

In Vasilyuk's work the idea of psychological tools was thus extended to include the sociocultural schemas of religious character, and the important issue of mediation through the significant other has been raised. The technique of overcoming, demonstrated with the help of Raskolnikov's case, outlines one version of psychological methodology that is based on the humanistic rather than scientific prototype.

The final offshoot of Vygotsky's influence to be discussed here reaches far beyond the sphere of psychology and into the area of the philosophical comprehension of human thought. The starting point here is the realization on the part of some contemporary philosophers that Vygotsky's analysis of inner speech is suggestive not only in a psychological, but also in a philosophical respect. The relationship between thought and language as revealed in the phenomenon of inner speech was recognized as relevant to one of the central problems of modern philosophy— that of the "grounding" of human thought in what is not yet intelligible.

Let us recapitulate the major points of Vygotsky's analysis of inner speech. In inner speech the most intimate and important psychological process is taking place—the generation of thought in the form of word meanings. At this stage of its inner development thought is not yet associated with definite words, while language is not yet infused with definite meaning. Inner speech thus reveals a fundamental gap between thought and word, indentifying at the same time their potential forms of existence. The primordial thought is still devoid of a rationality that will later become its primary definition. For example, the past and the future of the thought are collapsed together in inner speech. The structure of premises and conclusion characteristic of discursive logic is not yet formed. In inner speech we are thus observing a theoretically important phenomenon of thought becoming itself out of what is not yet thought.

The process of thought formation is reflected in the dichotomy between "meaning" and "sense". In the meaning the core of the object's already established characteristics is preserved. These characteristics, however, are not necessarily adequate for a particular situation in which the given object becomes involved in individual thinking. It is in the sense that the new contextual definitions of the object are captured. In the sense the object is becoming defined by its contextual meanings, but it does not yet exist as an entity in its own right apart from its context. In the act of thinking the object is constantly assimilated by thought, only to require a moment later an accommodation on its part. This dialectic of thought/object relations is observable in inner speech as occurring within the process of thought formation. Moreover, the dichotomy between sense and meaning indicates the original dichotomy within the thinking subject him or herself. On the one hand, inner speech is the product of the internalization of overt speech; this is how stable meanings find their way into it. On the other hand, the same sphere of inner speech is a generator of the idiosyncratic sense, which is unique for a given subject and in given circumstances. The interaction between sense and meaning constitutes the inner *dialogue* between two different subjects of one thought. One subject accommodates his or her thought to the pre-existing system of meanings, while the other immediately turns them into idiosyncratic sense, which later will be transformed again into intelligible words. The subject of thought is therefore simultaneously engaged in two conversations, one outbound, the other inbound. The outbound thought and speech are orientated toward real or imaginary interlocutors, while the inbound thought brings the meanings of others back to the subject. The coexistence of these inbound and outbound processes ensures the dialogical nature of human thought. In this sense inner speech provides a psychological definition of the individual as a subject, that is, as a source of thinking.

Vygotsky's analysis of inner speech has recently been invoked by Vladimir Bibler as an avenue toward the philosophical comprehension of the inherent paradox and dialogical nature of human thought.[47] Inner speech suggests a psychological analogue to the fundamental cultural process of generating new knowledge or new understanding. Such a new understanding emerges in a dialogue between already established cultural forms and just created literary or scientific "utterances" which still lack a definite cultural meaning. What psychologically appears as a process of thought and speech formation, in the objectivized, cultural dimension reveals itself as an inner dialogue of the text. This is particularly true of poetic and philosophical texts. Poetic speech is thoroughly cultural belonging to the culturally formed medium of literary language, yet at the same time it is also pre-cultural, expressing the individual idiom. In poetic speech the process of culture formation is suspended: idiosyncratic sense literally becomes a new poetic meaning in front of us. The same is true of the philosophical thought which is conceptual by definition, but also concept-generative and in this capacity not-yet-conceptual: "Poetic and philosophical speech are important for psychology as culturally expressed, objectively embodied analogues of inner speech".[48]

This remark of Bibler's draws our attention to the relationships between psychology and those disciplines that study already objectivized forms of human activity. Linguistics, poetics and logic form the outer perimeter of psychology proper. Psychology becomes aware of its own subject matter only in so far as it trespasses across these boundaries, identifying the moment at which written speech becomes a poem, and an act of reasoning a theorem. Thus only by realizing that a product of psychological activity has a cultural meaning can the psychological moment itself be defined as distinct from its objectivation.

According to Bibler the culturally expressed analogues of inner speech constitute the pivots of the modern re-evaluation of the centuries-old problem of the relationship between human thought and its object. Such a re-evaluation depends on the recognition of the paradox inherent in any intellectual or logical system:

> The principles of logical movement cannot be grounded in the forms of logical inference and proof that themselves proceed from these principles and rest on them. This would be a vicious circle. To ground the principles of a logic, it is necessary to go beyond (a) *this* [and] (b) *logic*. But to go beyond the limits of *this* logic, in order to logically ground it, is possible only in another logic, and since logic is universal, in another universe. But going beyond the bounds of this logic means to go beyond the bounds of logic as such, beyond the bounds of thought, to exit into the

non-logical as a foundation for the logical. [This means] to exit into the sphere of the *possibility* of logic, the possibility of thought, i.e. into the sphere of the "logic of being".[49]

This paradox has long been appreciated by philosophers, but its solutions either presupposed the "absorption" of the logic of being by the logic of thought (as in Hegel's absolute Spirit), or an exit into the sphere of nonintelligible, mystical phenomena. What is remarkable, however, is the relative neglect of the elaboration of the nation of *activity* as a possible generative source of thinking. In Hegelian philosophy the principle of activity is very powerful; in the final account it becomes absorbed by the encompassing Idea, that is, logic. This does not mean, however, that the philosophical principle of activity cannot be reinstated as a viable approach to the paradox of the grounding of logic. To do this one should find a form of activity that is not reducible to the activity of cognizing reason as presented in Hegelian or any other form of rationalism.

Bibler's solution to this paradox is based on the elaboration of one special type of activity—the dialogue between different systems of logic. From his point of view the exit into the "logic of being" is possible only through the representation of the object in different systems of thought. The dialogue of these systems would reveal the object as "encircled" by different forms of cognitive representation, no one of which is either final or encompassing. Such a dialogue, however, is impossible as long as the scientific inquiry is taken as a prototype of the logic of human thought. Scientific epistemology, as it was formulated in the seventeenth through the nineteenth centuries, presupposes a continuous progression of thought and the sublation of the achievements of the past into new, higher forms of theorizing. Such a prototype would not allow for a truly dialogical relationship between different systems, because one of them should necessarily appear as a special case of the more developed one. There is, however, an alternative area of human activity in which dialogue is the norm rather than the exception. This is a sphere of literature and art "in which every new cultural event, every new image of culture, even merely every new reader, entering into co-existence with the 'past' world of art—with Hamlet, for example—does not 'sublate' it, even in the most refined Hegelian understanding of sublation, but enters into a dialogue with it, actualizing new meanings in the figure of Hamlet, Hamlet's tragic conflict, and endlessly develops its own 'meaning', its own sense".[50]

This dialogical understanding, which for centuries belonged exclusively to the sphere of art and literature, in the face of the recognized paradox of human thinking, now becomes the essential feature of any system of conscious representation. This applies first of all to the changing attitudes toward non-Western systems of thought, but also to the alternative understanding of past systems of Western thought itself. The intellectual and spiritual systems of antiquity, the Middle Ages, the Renaissance, etc., should no longer be viewed as mere steps toward modern scientific rationalism, but rather as self-sufficient cognitive styles that are irreducible to the later, more "advanced" forms of thinking. The task of the philosopher of culture is to identify the relationships between these different styles and to outline the possible logic of the unfolding of their dialogues. The object of human inquiry will then appear to be gradually clarified through its reflection in these mutually irreducible and at the same time complementary systems.

While Vygotsky's study of inner speech suggested to Bibler the psychological model of the process of thought formation, Bakhtin's analysis of the novel armed him with the philosophy of culture based on the idea of dialogue.[51] For Bakhtin, dialogue is the fundamental characteristic of any literary and humanistic text. What is meant by Bakhtin is not an explicit, overt dialogue in which two voices are engaged, but an inner dialogic quality of a text, every element of which is incorporating the overtones of other texts. This sometimes hidden dialogic nature of a text is a reflection of the essentially dialogical nature of human consciousness. At this moment it seems relevant to recall Vygotsky's distinction between consciousness and intellect. Intellect, and its objectivized form, scientific reasoning, are monologous and object-oriented, while consciousness, which is organized by the system of "senses", is necessarily dialogical. That is why language, according to Vygotsky, is a microcosm of the human consciousness rather than of the intellect.

Starting with an analysis of the poetics of Dosteovsky's novels, Bakhtin demonstrated how these "polyphonic" novels reveal the previously overlooked inner dialogic quality of human thought and language. The literary analysis undertaken by Bakhtin thus becomes a prototype for humanistic methodology in general. Just as individual consciousness matures only in dialogue with the consciousnesses of others, so the objectivized, cultural cognition of a given epoch becomes possible only as a construction erected at the crossroads of the new reading of the past and the cultural projection into the future. Twentieth-century thought is particularly sensitive to such dialogism, because it is in this century that awareness of the existence of other cultural universes has reached its high point, while the embeddedness of thought in the routines of contemporary life have became severely disrupted. The cultural past thus becomes a real contemporary of our consciousness and our cultural standing essentially depends on our dialogue with it. At this point Bakhtin's idea of culture merges with that of philosophical hermeneutics: "Reading and understanding means that the information is led back to its original authenticity. . . . However, this 'information' is not what the speaker or writer originally said, but what he wanted to say indeed even more: what he would have wanted to say to me if I had been his original interlocutor".[52]

The logic of the dialogue proposed by Bibler provides a method for interpreting any culturally significant text, including a psychological one. Bibler thus not only got some of his leads from Vygotsky, but handsomely repaid this "debt" by supplying us with a dialogical approach to Vygotsky's own work. This work, from the dialogical point of view, is not a *step* toward our contemporary understanding of the human mind (although it certainly may have this meaning as well) but a self-sufficient cultural universe to which one can return again and again in the same fashion as we "return" to the music of Mozart or plays of Shakespeare without exhausting or sublating them.

NOTES

1. Alexander Luria, *The Nature of Human Conflicts*. New York: Liveright, 1932, pp. 47–9.

2. Alex Kozulin, *Psychology in Utopia*. Cambridge, MA: MIT Press, 1984.

3. Boris Ananiev, "O nekotoryh voprosah Marxistsko-Leninskoi rekonstrukcii psikhologii" ("Some problems of the Marxist-Leninist reconstruction in psychology"). *Psikhologiya*, No. 3–4, 1931, p. 332.

4. See Michael Cole, "A portrait of Luria". In A. Luria, *The Making of Mind*. Cambridge, MA: Harvard University Press, 1979. See also David Joravsky, "Vygotsky: The muffled deity of Soviet psychology". In M. Ach and W. Woodward, eds, *Psychology in Twentieth-Century Thought and Society*. Cambridge: Cambridge University Press, 1987.

5. Alexander Luria, "Krisis burzhauznoi psikhologii" ("The crisis of bourgeois psychology"). *Psikhologiya*, No. 1–2, 1932, pp. 63–88; see also Luria, *The Nature of Human Conflicts*.

6. See Alexei N. Leontiev, Kommentarii (Comments). In L. Vygotsky, *Collected Papers*, vol. 1. Moscow: Pedagogika, 1982, pp. 466–7. Vygotsky, "Problema Soznaniya" ("The problem of consciousness"). In *Collected Papers*, vol. 1, pp. 156–67.

7. Bluma Zeigarnik, quoted in Mikhail Yaroshevsky, "V shkole Kurta Lewina" ("In the school of Kurt Lewin: Conversation with B. Zeigarnik"), *Voprosy Psikhologii*, No. 3, 1988, p. 179.

8. A student of the history of the Vygotskian school, Andrei Puzyrei refers to a "split between Leontiev and Vygotsky which occurred a short time before the death of the latter. Vygotsky, according to some of his students, suffered a lot because of this" (unpublished manuscript on the cultural-historical theory, Moscow, 1987).

9. Semion Dobkin, "Ages and days". In K. Levitin, *One is not Born a Personality*. Moscow: Progress, 1982, p. 38.

10. Differing opinions can be found in Kozulin, *Psychology in Utopia*, pp. 102–20; James Wertsch, *Vygotsky and the Social Formation of Mind*. Cambridge, MA: Harvard University Press, 1985, pp. 61–7; Joravsky, "Vygotsky: The muffled deity", pp. 199–207. The official Soviet position is presented by Mikhail Yaroshevsky, *Lev Vygotsky*. Moscow: Progress, 1989.

11. Notably, *Thought and Language* in 1934, but also the edited volumes *Umstvennoe Razvitie Detei v Processe Obucheniya* (*Child Mental Development in the Course of Instruction*). Moscow: Uchpedgiz, 1935, and *Umstvenno Otstalyi Rebenok* (*The Mentally Retarded Child*). Moscow: Uchpedgiz, 1935.

12. The text of the decree is given in the Appendix to Joseph Wortis, *Soviet Psychiatry*. Baltimore, MD: Williams and Wilkins, 1950, pp. 242–5.

13. Ibid, p. 245.
14. A. A. Leontiev, "The productive career of A. N. Leontiev". *Soviet Psychology*, vol. 23, 1984, p. 14.
15. See Alexei N. Leontiev's comments in his *Izbrannye Psikhologicheskie Proizvedeniya (Selected Psychological Works)*, vol. 1. Moscow: Pedagogika, 1983, pp. 389–90. Some works of the Kharkovites were translated in a special issue fo *Soviet Psychology*, vol. 18, 1980, No. 2.
16. Alexei N. Leontiev, "Ovladenie uchaschimisia nauchnymi ponyatiyami kak problema pedagogicheskoi psikhologii" ("The acquisition of scientific concepts by students as a problem of educational psychology"). In *Izbrannye*, vol. 1, pp. 324–47.
17. Ibid, pp. 345 and 347.
18. Lev Vygotsky, *Problema Umstvennoi Otstalosti (The Problem of Mental Retardation). Collected Papers*, vol. 5, p. 252.
19. Peter Zinchenko, "The problem of involuntary memory". *Soviet Psychology*, vol. 22(2), 1983, pp. 66–7 (original paper published in 1939).
20. Ibid, pp. 78–111. See also Peter Zinchenko, "Involuntary memory and the goal directed nature of activity". In J. Wertsch, ed., *The Concept of Activity in Soviet Psychology*. New York: Sharpe, 1979 (original paper published in 1962).
21. Zinchenko, "The problem of involuntary memory", p. 70.
22. Maya Lisina , *Child–Adults–Peers*. Moscow: Progress, 1985.
23. Oleg Tikhomirov and V. E. Klochko, "The detection of contradiction as the initial stage of problem formation". In J. Wertsch, ed., *The Concept of Activity in Soviet Psychology*. New York: Sharpe, 1981.
24. Alex Kozulin, "Psychological activity, psychological tools and the discovery of contradictions". Paper presented at the Symposium on Human Activity Psychology, First European Psychological Congress, Amsterdam, July 1989.
25. Alexei N. Leontiev, *Ocherk Razvitiya Psikhiki (Essay on the Development of Mind)*. Moscow: Military Institute, 1947; Alexei N. Leontiev, *Activity, Consciousness, and Personality*. Englewood Cliffs, NJ: Prentice Hall, 1978.
26. Leontiev, *Activity, Consciousness, and Personality*, p. 63.
27. Sergei Rubinshtein, "Problemy sposobnostei i voprosy psikhologicheskoi teorii" ("The problem of abilities and the questions of psychological theory"). *Voprosy Psikhologii*, No. 3, 1960, p. 7. See also Alex Kozulin, "The concept of activity in Soviet psychology". *American Psychologist*, vol. 41, 1986, pp. 264–74.
28. See Erich Fromm, *Escape from Freedom*. New York: Avon Books,

1965; Lucien Seve, *Man in Marxist Theory and the Psychology of Personality*. Atlantic Heights, NJ: Harvester Press, 1978.

29. Alexei N. Leontiev, *Problemy Razvitiya Psikhiki* (*Problems of the Development of Mind*). Moscow: Moscow State University, 1981, pp. 318–49 (original paper published in 1959).

30. Ksenia Abulkhanova, *O sub'ekte psikhicheskoi deyatelnosti* (*The Subject of Psychological Activity*). Moscow: Nauka, 1973, p. 157.

31. Lev Vygotsky, *Izbrannye Psikhologicheskie Issledovaniya* (*Selected Psychological Investigations*). Moscow: Academy of Pedagogical Sciences, 1956; Lev Vygotsky, *Razvitie Vysshikh Psikhicheskikh Funktsii* (*The Development of Higher Mental Functions*). Moscow: Academy of Pedagogical Sciences, 1960; Lev Vygotsky, *Psikhologiya Iskusstva* (*The Psychology of Art*). Moscow: Iskusstvo, 1968.

32. Eric Yudin, "Deyatelnost' kak obyasnitelnyi printisyp i kak predmet nauchnogo issledivaniya" ("Activity as an explanatory principle and as a subject of scientific study"). *Voprosy Filosofii*, No. 5, 1976, pp. 65–78.

33. Schedrovitsky's views are reviewed in Karl Levitin, *One is not Born a Personality*. Moscow: Progress, 1982.

34. The major works of Vasili Davydov are as follows: *Vidy Obobscheniya v Obichenii* (*The Forms of Generalization in Learning*). Moscow: Pedagogika, 1972; *Problemy Razvivayuschego Obucheniya* (*The Problems of Development-Generating Learning*). Moscow: Pedagogika, 1986; V. Davydov and A. Markova, "A concept of educational activity for schoolchildren." *Soviet Psychology*, vol. 21, 1983, pp. 50–76; "The concept of theoretical generalization", *Studies in Soviet Thought*, vol. 36, 1988, pp. 169–202.

35. See Kozulin, *Psychology in Utopia*, pp. 138–46.

36. Davydov, *Vidy Obobscheniya*, p. 95.

37. V. Davydov. "The problem of generalization in the works of L. S. Vygotsky". *Soviet Psychology*, vol. 3, 1969.

38. Davydov, *Problemy Razvivayuschego*, p. 61.

39. Davydov, "The concept of theoretical generalization", p. 181.

40. Davydov, *Problemy Razvivayuschego*, pp. 158–60.

41. Kozulin, *Psychology in Utopia*, pp. 152–4.

42. Andrei Puzyrei, *Kulturno-istoricheskaya Teoriya Vygotskogo i Sovremennaya Psikhologiya* (*Cultural-historical Theory of Vygotsky and Modern Psychology*). Moscow: MGU, 1986.

43. See Neil Friedman, *The Social Nature of Psychological Research*. New York: Basic Books, 1967; see also Sigmund Koch, "The nature and limits of psychological knowledge". *American Psychologist*, vol. 36, 1981, pp. 257–69.

44. Fyodor Vasilyuk, *The Psychology of Experiencing*. Moscow: Progress, 1988.
45. Ibid, pp. 30–1.
46. Ibid, p. 34.
47. Vladimir Bibler, "Vnutrennyaya rech v ponimanii Vygotskogo" ("Vygotsky's understanding of inner speech"). In *Nauchnoe Trorchestvo Vygotskogo i Sovremennaya Psikhologiya (Vygotsky's Scholarship and Modern Psychology)*. Moscow: Institute of Psychology, 1981.
48. Ibid, p. 19.
49. Vladimir Bibler, "On the philosophical logic of paradox". *Soviet Studies in Philosophy*, vol. 28, 1989, p. 11.
50. Ibid, p. 25–6.
51. Vladimir Bibler, *M. M. Bakhtin and the Foundations of Humanistic Thinking*. Moscow, 1986 (unpublished manuscript).
52. H.-G. Gadamer, "Text and interpretation". In B. Waterhouser, ed., *Hermeneutics and Modern Philosophy*. Albany, NY: SUNY Press, 1986, p. 393.

Epilogue

THIS BOOK distinguishes three different planes of Vygotsky's theory. The first plane corresponds to the understanding of his theory by his contemporaries in the 1920s and the 1930s. The second plane emerges from the gradual discovery of Vygotsky by the West in the 1960s. The third plane is just becoming visible and is dependent on the projection of the ideas of cultural psychology onto the future of psychological theory.

For Vygotsky's contemporaries, his theory was firmly connected to the overall task of creating a new psychology for a new society. Within this perspective the idea of *cultural* mediation of human behavior has easily acquired the form of a theory of *social* mediation. The new structures of social life—including the industrialization of work activity, compulsory schooling and collective forms of everyday life—became seen as determinants of the nascent forms of behavior and cognition of a "new man". The theoretical thesis "from action to thought" was understood in this context as corresponding to the project of changing people's behavior through their engagement in the new, socialist forms of activity. Although, with the wisdom of hindsight, this plane of Vygotsky's work appears too abstract and ideological, this does not mean that it is not genuine. There is no denying that Vygotsky's own understanding of his theory often coincided with that of his contemporaries. This coincidence, however, was not only incomplete, but Vygotsky as the author was not necessarily always in accord with Vygotsky as interpreter of his own ideas. This essential discrepancy allows us to seek other planes of his theory of cultural psychology.

The discovery of Vygotsky's ideas in the West has had its own particular pattern. First, these ideas were discovered at a very special historical-psychological moment: on the wave of the growing popularity of Piaget's theory and the revival of cognitive psychology in the United States. In this context, Vygotsky's work was first seen as a necessary corrective to Piaget's quasi-naturalistic stage theory, and second as an interesting attempt to reconcile behavioral and cognitive perspectives on the basis of the socially informed notion of human activity. As a growing number of his studies were translated, Vygotsky has become recognized as an important precursor of psychological trends that quite independently became fashionable in the 1970s and 1980s. His works thus began to serve as a source of outside validation for such studies as cross-cultural analyses of cognition, sociocultural studies of child learning, literacy research, and so on.

The third plane of Vygotsky's theory, the contours of which are only just emerging, presupposes both the re-evaluation of its origins and its projection onto the future of psychology. What in the 1920s appeared to be a rather straightforward thesis of social mediation, and in the 1960s as a necessary correction to the overly individualistic approaches of Western psychology, nowadays appears as a new problem emerging from the realization that social and cultural mediatory mechanisms do not coincide. Vygotsky's analysis of the crisis in psychology, earlier perceived as a critique of psychology's past, is now recognized as an inquiry into the fundamental mechanism of psychology's divergent development. The origins and context of Vygotsky's theory are now being seen in a new light; in the place of comparisons to Pavlov, the Gestaltists and Piaget comes the context of philosophical hermeneutics and the theory of communicative action. In an even broader sense, what once looked like Vygotsky's contribution *to* psychology appears now as leading *beyond* psychology or at least beyond traditional psychology and into the sphere of human studies based on the humanistic, rather than the scientific model.

Index

281

CPSIA information can be obtained at www.ICGtesting.com
Printed in the USA
BVOW04s1229170414

350946BV00015B/423/P

9 780674 943667